Pro Perl Debugging

From Professional to Expert

RICHARD FOLEY WITH ANDY LESTER

Apress®

Pro Perl Debugging: From Professional to Expert

Copyright © 2005 by Richard Foley with Andy Lester

Lead Editor: Jason Gilmore
Technical Reviewer: Andy Lester
Editorial Board: Steve Anglin, Dan Appleman, Ewan Buckingham, Gary Cornell, Tony Davis, Jason Gilmore, Jonathan Hassell, Chris Mills, Dominic Shakeshaft, Jim Sumser
Associate Publisher: Grace Wong
Project Manager: Emily K. Wolman
Copy Edit Manager: Nicole LeClerc
Copy Editor: Julie Smith
Production Manager: Kari Brooks-Copony
Production Editor: Linda Marousek
Compositor and Artist: Kinetic Publishing Services, LLC
Proofreader: Sue Boshers
Indexer: Rebecca Plunkett
Cover Designer: Kurt Krames
Manufacturing Manager: Tom Debolski

Library of Congress Cataloging-in-Publication Data

Foley, Richard.
　　Pro Perl debugging : from professional to expert / Richard Foley with
　　　Andy Lester.
　　　　p. cm.
　　Includes bibliographical references and index.
　　ISBN 1-59059-454-1 (alk. paper)
　　1. Perl (Computer program language)　　2. Debugging in computer science.
　　I. Lester, Andy.　　II. Title.

　　QA76.73.P22F62　　2005
　　005.13′3—dc22

                                                        2005016006

ISBN: 1-59059-454-1

Printed and bound in the United States of America 9 8 7 6 5 4 3 2 1

Distributed to the book trade in the United States by Springer-Verlag New York, Inc., 233 Spring Street, 6th Floor, New York, NY 10013, and outside the United States by Springer-Verlag GmbH & Co. KG, Tiergartenstr. 17, 69112 Heidelberg, Germany.

In the United States: phone 1-800-SPRINGER, fax 201-348-4505, e-mail orders@springer-ny.com, or visit http://www.springer-ny.com. Outside the United States: fax +49 6221 345229, e-mail orders@springer.de, or visit http://www.springer.de.

For information on translations, please contact Apress directly at 2560 Ninth Street, Suite 219, Berkeley, CA 94710. Phone 510-549-5930, fax 510-549-5939, e-mail info@apress.com, or visit http://www.apress.com.

The information in this book is distributed on an "as is" basis, without warranty. Although every precaution has been taken in the preparation of this work, neither the author(s) nor Apress shall have any liability to any person or entity with respect to any loss or damage caused or alleged to be caused directly or indirectly by the information contained in this work.

The source code for this book is available to readers at http://www.apress.com in the Downloads section. You will need to answer questions pertaining to this book in order to successfully download the code.

I'd like to dedicate this book to my wife, Joy, and to my daughters, Catherine and Jennifer. Without them it would all seem rather pointless—even if they do call me an angeber (show-off) while pointing to daddy's name as the actual author of a programming book. And to Spot, for being a friend for 15 years.

—Richard

For Amy and Quinn, the two girls who make me laugh the most.

—Andy

Contents at a Glance

Contents

About the Authors

RICHARD FOLEY (http://www.rfi.net) is a professional contract Perl and Oracle developer working out of Munich, Germany, and enjoys hiking in the Alps and skiing in his copious spare time. His work has involved online military aircraft and satellite documentation projects, airline booking system testing, investment bank feed and database processing, code analysis, and optimization.

Richard has worked with the Perl community for a number of years. Alongside submitting patches to the Perl source distribution, and being a CPAN module author, he is a member of the YAPC::Europe committee.

ANDY LESTER (http://petdance.com) has been a professional programmer for nineteen years and a Perl evangelist for a decade. As one of the core Perl developers, Andy's interests are focused on quality assurance—he maintains eight testing modules on the CPAN, as well as the Perl QA website (http://qa.perl.org).

Andy is a frequent speaker at the O'Reilly Open Source Convention, YAPC, and at Perl Monger meetings around the country. He's spoken around the United States on a variety of programming topics including automated testing, Perl security, web agent automation, project management, and effective job searching for programmers.

Andy has written or edited for a dozen books. Three of the articles on his popular WWW::Mechanize module are included in O'Reilly's "Spidering Hacks." Andy has also written articles for every single Perl magazine published in the United States (both of them).

By day, Andy manages a crack squad of web programmers for Follett Library Resources (http://www.titlewave.com) in McHenry, Illinois. He lives with his wife, Amy; daughter, Quinn; and Baxter, the world's neediest dog.

Acknowledgments

First, I'd like to thank Larry Wall for the Perl programming language—it's just so much fun to use. Also, thanks are due to the many people who took his original debugger and made it into the complex and functional beast that it is now. I'd particularly like to thank Gabor Szabo for his part in getting this project off the ground, and Joe McMahon for his advice and support during the writing phase. Many thanks to Andy Lester for agreeing to help get the book finished when time was of the essence, and for at least doubling his work load in one fell swoop. Thanks to Emily Wolman for retaining belief in the book through a long and protracted cat-herding exercise. Many thanks to Jason Gilmore for being the third and most stalwart of editors, his many suggestions and lively presence keeping the book on track as well as helping to form its content into a coherent whole. Thanks also to the many unseen people in the actual production phase who are essential to the process of creating the final book you are now holding, including our erstwhile copy editor Julie Smith, and Linda Marousek, who was responsible for its production. Finally, if there remain any errors or omissions, these are of course my sole responsibility.

—Richard

Introduction

Ever since computers were invented, and every day since then, bugs have been found in program code. Although the use of the term "bug" to refer to a problem predates computers, it was defined in our context when Lady Lovelace squashed a moth that was interfering with the clean operation of a valve in the early computer she was developing. From big bugs that crash the operating system of a single PC, to little bugs that send a space probe millions of miles past its intended destination, these things will always be with us. Because programmers will always be human we must learn how to recognize a bug in the first place, to identify the location of the bug, and finally to safely remove it from the code

The ability to efficiently debug code is a necessary part of any competent programmer's skill set. The code may belong to a body of work produced by the programmer herself, or adopted in a maintainance role from a predecessor. Whatever the case, debugging succesfully appears at times to be a black art. Some people can do it very well indeed, and others just never really get to grips with it at all. While a methodical approach is required to identify the precise location of any bug, using sensible tools can make the task much easier, and much faster, to complete. When programming using Perl, the tool of choice will be the Perl debugger, supplied with every Perl distribution since the first one.

This book is an in-depth tutorial and reference for the Perl debugger, perhaps the most powerful debugging tool available for Perl programs today. It was written with two groups in mind. The first is the large number of Perl programmers who don't know that a debugger for Perl even exists. The second group is the Perl programmers out there who shy away from using the debugger because it's a new, and apparently complex, animal.

Our aim is to demonstrate the debugger in the many real-world environments the professional programmer will actually work with. We cover everything from the inspection and modification of Perl code on-the-fly at run time and compile time without changing the source on disk; to tracing and breaking program execution selectively. You'll learn to debug multiple library object-oriented modules, including both in-house code and code written by a third party, to step through both a standard CGI program and a mod_perl-enabled apache handler from within the web server (but at the Perl level), and to debug multi-tasking Perl programs using both fork and threads.

By the time you finish this book, you will be able to make informed decisions for when to use the humble print statement or the powerful Perl debugger to help you in your quest to search and destroy those troublesome, ever-present gremlins of the programming world. You will know how to use the debugger as a Perl shell to experiment with different code constructs, in advance of typing them into a system file for later execution. You will no longer be constrained by the unsteady feeling of not knowing, or repelled by the fear of the unfamiliar. By the final chapter you will be able to revel in the ability to use a powerful investigative and exploratory tool, should you wish to use it, which is always at your fingertips. Above all, you will have a choice.

CHAPTER 1

■■■

Introduction

Mars attacks!

Mention the Perl debugger to the average Perl programmer, and you often receive a strange contorted grimace in response, and a spluttered, "I always use the print statement!," as they retreat down the corridor, waving incense in the air, looking as if they're being chased by aliens. In fact, similar behavior seems to apply to nearly all programmers when they're approached with a matter known to elicit debate in the programming community. After all, most would acknowledge that programmers can often be divided into many factions—for instance, those who use object-oriented methods or procedural functions (but not both), those who always use modules and those who never do, those who prefer vi and those who worship emacs. In the same fashion, it seems as though we can also classify two other species of programmers on the planet, those who use a debugger and those who are unable to.

We hope that by the end of this book, the truth will emerge . . . that there are in fact many Perl programmers on this planet; all of whom use the print statement, all of whom can also use the debugger, if they so choose, and that the world will be a better place for having the choice.

What Is It?

The Perl debugger is an extremely useful tool for troubleshooting your Perl applications. It can help you locate, identify, and then fix the problems in your code, whether you've written it yourself or have inherited it in some manner.

This book won't be the panacea to all of your programming problems, but it will give you the capability to use a tool which can help you bugfix your applications, quickly and with confidence. After reading this book, you will be able to find all those elusive bugs, and be able to do so with absolute precision.

You could, of course, follow the lead of many lost programmers we've seen, and just cruise about aimlessly looking at various bits of code, scattering ever more desperate print statements around, in the often forlorn hope that one might fall over the problem, more or less accidentally. This is the kind of approach that could also be described as the programming equivalent of trench warfare, where the damage inflicted on our side is presumed to be an unavoidable side effect of the main aim or purpose.

When you change the source code of a program in pursuit of the bug, you should know that you have other options. Changing code is often regarded as inevitable by people without the knowledge to do otherwise. Do not make the simple mistake of confusing *finding the bug* with *fixing the bug*. Otherwise you are just as likely to unwittingly create a new one.

1

Perhaps the most important benefit of using the Perl debugger is the capability to use it to pinpoint a problem quickly, and most importantly, without touching or altering the source code in any way. The entire behavior of the running Perl program, both at compiletime and at runtime, can be inspected, paused, restarted, and entirely modified, at will, **without changing one single bit of code**. In the greater scheme of things, this simple and critical fact is usually overlooked.

Down the Rabbit Hole

Using the debugger efficiently requires that you have a thorough knowledge of what it can do for you and how you can leverage that functionality to best advantage. The debugger is vastly underused, even by Perl afficionados—probably due in part to having a slightly different and sometimes (at least at first sight) obtuse command set.

Breakpoints, Call Stacks, Tracing, and More

Also, there are many Perl programmers who have never attended a computer science course at university or technical college, and are thus unfamiliar with the very concept of setting a breakpoint or of displaying the call stack.

■**Note** For those who do not know, a *breakpoint* is a point in the program code where the debugger will stop execution during runtime, thus enabling the programmer to inspect or change the value of variables, objects or code. The call stack is the sequence of subroutines which have been called from the outermost, or main(), context to the current innermost subroutine. When tracing a program, the information given with the call stack may be expanded to include subroutine arguments.

It might seem daft at first sight, especially to traditionally trained programmers, that a programmer would not know this information. But partly because Perl is such a good and intuitive language to learn, there are, in fact, many experienced Perl programmers working today who do not know how to use a debugger, and are missing out on the power that has always been at their fingertips. Indeed, the debugger has been available in every release of Perl since version 1.

I hope and expect that as you work through this book, you'll meet many familiar friends and concepts, and you'll see that the rabbit hole really isn't that strange after all.

Why Should You Use the Perl Debugger?

Given the control over the content and execution of a program that the debugger provides, the range of excuses for *not* using this tool is extraordinary. These excuses demonstrate the wildest imaginations of the creative programmer including, among many others, the following gems (see Table 1-1) that are particularly worth listing.

Table 1-1. *Common Debugger Myths*

Argument	Answer
It is unreliable.	Actually, it is very reliable. In all my dealings with the debugger, a segmentation fault or core dump has usually been the problem of the program itself rather than the debugger.
It is too slow.	It is inevitable that the debugger will be slower than a raw program, because it does so much extra work on your behalf. This is exactly the same reason that the profiling tools described in Chapter 13 are slower too. Besides, if it were any faster, you wouldn't be able to keep up.
It is too complicated.	Once certain basic operations are grasped, the debugger is intuitive and very easy to use. The actual implementation is overdue for a rewrite and that is on the cards as we speak, but the user interface will remain the same or similar.
The commands are obtuse.	Actually the commands are remarkably intuitive, just as you would expect from Perl. For instance, the command p denotes print, b denotes breakpoint, and so on. Some of these commands might seem a bit strange at first sight, but by the time you have read this book, they will seem like old friends.
It doesn't do *abc* or *xyz*.	It performs most of the tasks required for debugging both simple and complex applications. In fact there are probably even commands capable of performing *abc* and *xyz*, you just haven't learned about them yet. And if the command really doesn't exist, feel free to submit a patch!
It cannot debug web/ CGI applications.	The debugger will debug any Perl program, CGI or otherwise. However, certain situations may need clarification. Where mod_perl programs, for example, are running as part of an Apache process, these need to be debugged using the Apache::DB module (described in Chapter 9).
It cannot debug forked programs.	The debugger will support any forkable Perl program, and you can see examples in this book in Chapter 9. There are caveats though—where the operating system or environment doesn't support forking, it plainly can't be done, for example.
It doesn't support threads.	Actually, it does, though you must use a version newer than 5.8.5 to have a threads-enabled debugger.

In the final analysis, the real reasons for not using the debugger are perhaps a lot less numerous and may be reasonably reduced to the following short list:

- The programmer has not used it before.

- The debugger has an unfamiliar syntax.

While these comments are perfectly reasonable, and are in fact related to one another, we hope this book will resolve both these cases, and enable you to use the debugger for what it's best at: helping you to find and squash bugs. This is not to say that using the Perl debugger, or indeed any debugger, is necessarily easy or simple. Like using any good tool, it takes time and effort to become technically proficient and useful with it.

This will be time well spent.

Using the Debugger

Although we'll really dive into this topic in the next chapter, let's take a quick moment to get our feet wet with using the debugger by considering a simple example. Also, any programming book worth its salt starts with the traditional *Hello World* program, therefore we thought we'd get it out of the way as soon as practically possible.

For starters, let's launch the debugger, print a short message, and simply quit.

```
> perl -d -e 0
Loading DB routines from perl5db.pl version 1.27 Editor support available.
Enter h or 'h h' for help, or 'man perldebug' for more help.
main::(-e:1): 0
  DB<1> print "Hello World\n"
Hello World
  DB<2> q
>
```

In all cases throughout the book, you are encouraged to try the examples offered. You cannot damage your program from within the debugger, as it is within a runtime context. As a certain well-known advert once said, "Let your fingers do the walking!"

Book Layout

This book consists of 16 chapters, and is intended to foster a progressive learning experience, with many of the chapters building on material appearing earlier in the book. In this section we'll summarize the chapter content.

Section 1

The first section introduces the Perl debugger to the programmer who has not used the debugger before. Here, we discuss what the debugger is, what to call it, and the basic commands available. Programmers who already use other debuggers on a regular basis, may wish to skim this section.

- **Chapter 1** offers a general introduction to the debugger as a topic, and shows you how to invoke the debugger, execute a command, and exit.

- **Chapter 2** introduces many of the debugger's most commonly used commands, enabling you to navigate around the interface, and to retrieve the help and manpages.

- **Chapter 3** takes you through the most essential commands for competent debugging: including setting breakpoints, enabling variable watches, setting action commands, and inspecting variables.

- **Chapter 4** walks you through the actual debugging of a short command line program, and gives you a feel for how this all works on a real-life problem.

Section 2

The second and central section takes up the bulk of the book, and shows you how to use the debugger in a number of both common and unusual situations. This section deals with all the commands of the standard Perl debugger and, as your skill level increases, how to customize it to build your own version of the debugger.

- **Chapter 5** explores tracing program execution, and functionality that is settable per line, per block, per file, globally, or *on-the-fly* by command.

- **Chapter 6** demonstrates debugging a program that uses several libraries or modules, and certain special breakpoint commands which are designed specifically with this in mind.

- **Chapter 7** focuses on debugging object-oriented Perl.

- **Chapter 8** looks at the debugger as a Perl shell, and is a place to experiment with Perl programming constructs.

- **Chapter 9** offers several approaches to debugging a program running as part of a web server on a remote machine, and both as a plain *CGI* program and the special case of running under mod_perl.

- **Chapter 10** shows how the debugger supports working with forked and multi-threaded Perl programs, and how it is possible to follow the multiple *STDIN, STDOUT, STDERR* and debugger filehandles in those processes.

- **Chapter 11** shows detailed *regular expression* debugging, an existing support which is especially overlooked.

- **Chapter 12** covers customizing the debugger, and how to change its behavior to suit your particular environment or requirements.

Section 3

The third and final section is essentially a reference section including advanced optimization suggestions, such as a list of every debugger command, variable, option, book, perldoc, and book reference.

- **Chapter 13** offers optimization as well as performance hints and tips for working with Perl. It includes examples from some of the many development-oriented modules that are available either via the CPAN or that come with the standard distribution.

- **Chapter 14** compares the standard command line debugger and the various GUI alternatives available from different sources, some *open source*, some *proprietary*.

- **Chapter 15** is a comprehensive command reference for all the available commands and options available in the standard debugger.

- **Chapter 16** is a list of useful perldoc, book, and URL references. Here, you can get more information on both the Perl debugger, and the general topic of debugging itself.

Technical Notes

For all the examples in this book we use the 1.27 version of the debugger, distributed with the current, stable version of Perl v5.8.5. We mostly use the command line debugger, which comes with Perl and should work on all systems as long as Perl is installed. There are also a number of GUI (Graphical User Interface) options, which are explored in Chapter 14.

The environment in which we demonstrate our command line examples is the bash shell on Linux. While all examples should run equally well on all variants of Unix, there may be some lack of support for Windows and Macintosh users in certain cases. Generally speaking the debugger behaves equally well in all cases, but the system calls and file commands are distinctly operating system specific. For example, when executing a one-line Perl program via the -e command, you may use single quotes on Linux, like this:

```
perl -e 'print $0'
```

Whereas on Windows, you may be forced to use double quotes, like this:

```
perl -e "print $0"
```

Read the documentation specific to your OS—it came with your Perl installation and you can access it with the 'perldoc perlport' command—for more information on this and other compatibllity issues.

■**Note** In the examples throughout this book we use perl to call the Perl interpreter, even when it may have been installed under your system under a different name or a different path.

Development

Perl has seen continual development since version 1. Indeed every version of Perl has had a debugger as part of the toolkit, and it can only be expected that the debugger would also develop. In this book therefore, we track the major differences between debugger versions since Perl v5.0053, (see Chapter 15), to make it as useful for as many people as possible. Many people have contributed large and small patches, and in particular the following people (see Table 1-2) deserve special mention for their contributions to debugger development to date.

Table 1-2. *A Tribute to Debugger Contributors*

Contributor	Description
Tom Christiansen	Security checks and many shell-centric enhancements.
Richard Foley	Rationalized command set, implemented threads support and other fixes.
Joe McMahon	Extensive internals documentation.
Larry Wall	For giving us both Perl and the debugger in the first place.
Ilya Zakharevich	Multiple TTY contributions and a high-level API.
Many Others	There have been many contributors over the years, to the beast that is the Perl debugger. To all of them, although we all appreciate that the debugger would benefit from a ground-up rewrite, we extend a heartfelt thanks, for giving us such a powerful tool in the first place.

Summary

By the conclusion of this introductory chapter, you should have a good overview of the Perl debugger itself, and of how this book will approach the subject of debugging Perl programs. You should be able to start the debugger, execute some Perl code or a debugger command, and quit the debugger and return to your operating system environment.

The next chapter will discuss the most commonly used commands for inspecting the environment of your program, and how to list the code and inspect the runtime variables within it. We also find out how to use the built-in help facility to get more information for a particular command from both the debugger and the system itself.

CHAPTER 2

■■■

Inspecting Variables and Getting Help

I suspect nobody, and I suspect everybody!

—Inspector Clousseau in *The Return of the Pink Panther*

In this chapter you'll familiarize yourself with the basic command line debugger interface, learn how to inspect the data of your running program, and explore your environment. Instead of using your infallible intuition, like Clousseau, you will use the tools at your disposal to determine what variables are available to you at any given moment throughout a programs execution.

You'll also learn how to examine code in a file loaded elsewhere in Perl space, for example an entry in the %INC hash, which is the list of loaded modules, as well as how to retrieve a list of subroutines or methods available for a particular class or object. Not content to stop there, you'll also learn how to find the help and manual pages, and take advantage of the command history mechanism.

Note that you won't do any actual debugging in this chapter—we are solely concerned with helping you to become familiar with the debugging environment and to determine what information the debugger makes available to you.

A Gentle Introduction to the Debugger

To start the debugger we supply the -d runtime switch to Perl, assuming we have a program named 'progname' and possibly optional arguments, like this:

```
%> perl -d progname [args]
```

However, to enter the debugger just to get a feel for how it works, or to experiment with a code construct, for example, you'll also need to include the -e runtime switch, which tells the debugger to expect a Perl expression on the command line. The expression doesn't need to be complicated—in our first example a simple zero will suffice:

```
%> perl -d -e 0
Loading DB routines from perl5db.pl version 1.27
Editor support available.
```

```
Enter h or 'h h' for help, or 'man perldebug' for more help.
main::(-e:1):    0
  DB<1>
```

You might find the introduction text varies slightly on your system. For example, the version number may well be different, and you may have man perldebug or perldoc perldebug. These are minor differences depending on your Perl installation, the options set under the debugger, and which version of the debugger you are actively running.

The debugger prompt indicates the number of the command it is waiting for. The command prompt actually offers more information as program execution continues, but we'll get to that in a later chapter. At this point we are in Perl space, or a Perl shell if you like, and can explore our environment with familiar commands.

Let's continue our initial investigation of the debugger, by executing a simple Perl command, print $^O. This is the Perl dollar-caret-zero variable, which displays the operating system identifier:

```
DB<1> print $^O
 linux
DB<2>
```

Next let's calculate the result of a simple expression:

```
DB<2> print 1 / 42
 0.0238095238095238
DB<3>
```

Moving forward, let's review the library paths searched by Perl for modules:

```
DB<3> print join("\n", @INC)
 /usr/local/lib/perl5/5.8.2/i686-linux
 /usr/local/lib/perl5/5.8.2
 /usr/local/lib/perl5/site_perl/5.8.2/i686-linux
 /usr/local/lib/perl5/site_perl/5.8.2
 /usr/local/lib/perl5/site_perl/5.8.0/i686-linux
 /usr/local/lib/perl5/site_perl/5.8.0
 /usr/local/lib/perl5/site_perl
 .
DB<3>
```

Reviewing the Debugger Help Page

Of course the debugger is much more than just a Perl shell, and to really see what the debugger is capable of, we should read the documentation. There is a helpful single-window sized help page, which was alluded to when the debugger was started, and which should be our first port of call. You can retrieve the help page by typing h at the prompt, like so:

```
DB<3> h
```

This will return a long listing of commands and corresponding instructions available to you via the debugger. Because this listing isn't in a format that's convenient for display in a book, we'll summarize these commands in Tables 2-1 through 2-4. Remember also that while this is a summarized overview, Chapter 15 is a complete and definitive debugger command reference.

Table 2-1. *Listing and Searching Source Code*

Command	Description
l [ln|sub]	List source code for line or subroutine
- or .	List previous/current line
v [line]	View code around line
f filename	View source code in file
/pattern/	Search forward
?pattern?	Search backward
M	Show module versions

Table 2-2. *Controlling Program Execution*

Command	Description
T	Stack trace
s [expr]	Single step [in expr]
n [expr]	Next - step over subs [in expr]
<CR/Enter>	Repeat last n or s (carriage return)
r	Return from subroutine
c [ln|sub]	Continue until position
L	List break/watch/actions
t [expr]	Toggle trace [trace expr]
b [ln|event|sub] [cnd]	Set breakpoint
B ln|*	Delete a particular breakpoint by line number, or all, breakpoints
a [ln] cmd	Do cmd before line
A ln|*	Delete a particular action by line number, or all, actions
w expr	Add a watch expression
W expr|*	Delete a particular watch expression, or all watch expressions
![!] syscmd	Run cmd in a subprocess
R	Attempt a restart

Table 2-3. *Debugger Options and History Management*

Command	Description
o [...]	Set debugger options
<[<]|{[{]|>[>] [cmd]	Do pre/post-prompt
! [N|pat]	Redo a previous command
H [-num]	Display last num commands
= [a val]	Define/list an alias
h [db_cmd]	Get help on command
h h	Complete help page
|[|]db_cmd	Send output to pager
q or ^D	Quit

Table 2-4. *Data and Variables Examination*

Command	Description
e	Display current thread id (if running under -dt).
expr	Execute Perl code.
i class|object	Display inheritance tree for class.
x|m expr	Evals expr in list context, dumps the result or lists method.
p expr	Print expression (uses script's current package).
S [[!]pat]	List subroutine names [not] matching pattern.
V [Pk [Vars]]	List variables in Package. Vars can be ~pattern or !pattern.
X [Vars]	Same as V current_package [Vars].
y [n [Vars]]	List lexicals in higher scope <n>. Variables same as V.

At first sight, it may look as though there are too many commands to work out what they all do, and certainly for a single session, trying to use all of them usefully would be no small task. Don't let this put you off. Just as with Perl itself, in normal usage one might expect to use a comparatively small subset of the available commands.

Learning More About a Command

To learn more about a particular command, pass its name as an argument to the help command:

```
DB<4> h a
 a [line] command
 Set an action to be done before the line is executed;
 line defaults to the current execution line.
 Sequence is: check for breakpoint/watchpoint, print line
 if necessary, do action, prompt user if necessary,
 execute line.
 a               Does nothing
DB<4>
```

To retrieve the full explanation for all available commands use the special h h command. This is most often used in combination with the pager command | to present the long listing one page at a time.

```
DB<4> | h h
Help is currently only available for the new 5.8 command set.
No help is available for the old command set.
We assume you know what you're doing if you switch to it.
T               Stack trace.
s [expr]        Single step [in expr].
n [expr]        Next, steps over subroutine calls [in expr].
<CR>            Repeat last n or s command.
r               Return from current subroutine.
c [line|sub]    Continue; optionally inserts a one-time-only breakpoint
                at the specified position.
l min+incr      List incr+1 lines starting at min.
l min-max       List lines min through max.
l line          List single line.
```

```
l subname       List first window of lines from subroutine.
l $var          List first window of lines from subroutine referenced by $var.
l               List next window of lines.
-               List previous window of lines.
v [line]        View window around line.
.               Return to the executed line.
<...multiple lines snipped here...>
During startup options are initialized from $ENV{PERLDB_OPTS}.
You can put additional initialization options TTY, noTTY,
ReadLine, NonStop, and RemotePort there (or use
'R' after you set them).
q or ^D         Quit. Set $DB::finished = 0 to debug global destruction.
h               Summary of debugger commands.
h [db_command]  Get help [on a specific debugger command], enter |h to page.
h h             Long help for debugger commands
man manpage     Runs the external doc viewer man command on the
 named Perl manpage, or on man itself if omitted.
 Set $DB::doccmd to change viewer.
Type '|h h' for a paged display if this was too hard to read.
DB<5>
```

There are various shortcuts for this facility, and you can use any of the following interchangeably: man, perldoc, or doc.

```
DB<5> doc FileHandle
 Reformatting FileHandle(3), please wait...
FileHandle(3)     Perl Programmers Reference Guide    FileHandle(3)
NAME
    FileHandle - supply object methods for filehandles
SYNOPSIS
    use FileHandle;
$fh = new FileHandle;
if ($fh->open("< file")) {
    print <$fh>;
    $fh->close;
}
<...multiple lines snipped here...>

SEE ALSO
    The IO extension, perlfunc, "I/O Operators" in perlop.
perl v5.8.2            2003-09-30            FileHandle(3)
Manual page FileHandle(3) line 77/128 (END)
DB<6>
```

Going Beyond Help

Having seen how to get help, we should try out a couple of the more interesting debugger commands referred to previously, but before we do, it is worth taking a moment to consider their form. Because the debugger has been designed to be an efficient aid to problem solving, most commands are very short, usually consisting of a single letter. They are all designed to be quick and easy to use, intuitive, and at your fingertips, instead of being long, explicit, and slow. This can take a short while to get used to, as a new bunch of commands need to be learned, but once you understand them the convenience greatly outweighs any perceived issues.

If you don't like the default commands, you can use the alias command to remap all the commands to something more suitable for your way of working. The Perl motto, TMTOWTDI (There's More Than One Way To Do It), comes to mind. We will see how to use the alias command in Chapter 12.

Most commands have some form of mnemonic relation to their function. For example instead of typing the five characters of print, you can use the simple p in its place. Similarly h for help, l for list, t for trace, and so on. Of course there are a limited number of single letters to use, although the debugger makes judicious use of upper/lower case and the occasional punctuation mark to good effect.

Keep in mind that when faced with all this new information, new commands, and contexts (debuggers tend not to be the most beginner-friendly places in even a technical environment), the best thing to do is to not get stressed by it, but rather to explore and to extend your boundaries at your own speed as suits your experience.

The Print Command: p

Let's take a look at p. First we will need to declare a simple variable with which to work:

```
DB<9> @x = qw(first second third fourth fifth)
DB<10>
```

Now we can use p to display the second element of the array:

```
DB<10> p $x[1]
 second
DB<11>
```

And of course p can also be used to print the entire array:

```
DB<11> p @x
 firstsecondthirdfourthfifth
DB<12>
```

In this case, that isn't particularly useful however, as all the elements have been by default printed out one after the other, with no visible separation, making it hard to see the individual contents of the variable. We can further resolve this by using a simple Perl join() expression:

```
DB<12> p join(' ', @x)
 first second third fourth fifth
DB<13>
```

All well and good, but a better way to see what is going on inside our variable might be to use the x command, introduced next.

The Dump-Value Command: x

To dump the entire expression thoroughly, use the x command, which will dump the given value completely:

```
DB<13> x @x
 0  'first'
 1  'second'
 2  'third'
 3  'fourth'
 4  'fifth'
DB<14>
```

That's better, but it's still a bit clunky. x is better used by giving it a reference to the variable, forcing it to be dumped out with the proper indentation and offering much more clarity:

```
DB<14> x \@x
 0  ARRAY(0x83560d0)
 0  'first'
 1  'second'
 2  'third'
 3  'fourth'
 4  'fifth'
DB<15>
```

Of course, the same thing can be done with multi-level data structures or objects. It's when you can really see what an otherwise complex variable consists of that the indentation really becomes useful. First we need to create our variable, and to do this, we're going to take advantage of the fact that the debugger will accept a multi-line command, if you backslash the newline at the end of each line. This will simply make the example easier to read, as well as to type:

```
DB<15> %x = (\
cont: 'this' => 'that',\
cont: 'chars'=> { 'vowels' => qw(a e i o u), 'others' => qw(s q w r k) },\
cont: 'obj'  => bless({'_member' => 'variable', '_context' => 'init'}, 'Class'),\
cont: )
DB<16>
```

We'll include a self-referential reference too, to see what happens when the debugger attempts to dump out an infinite loop:

```
DB<16> $x{'self ref'} = \%x
DB<17>
```

Now when we dump this out, everything becomes much more obvious. Note the REUSED_ADDRESS memory reference indicated by the hexadecimal number: 0x83ca658. This is the memory address where the reference to the variable is actually stored, and you can see the same value both at the head of the hash dump, and at the self ref location for confirmation:

```
DB<17> x \%x
 0  HASH(0x83a50f0)
 'chars' => HASH(0x83ca658)
   'e' => 'i'
   'o' => 'u'
 'others' => 's'
   'q' => 'w'
```

```
 'r' => 'k'
  'vowels' => 'a'
 'obj' => Class=HASH(0x83ca838)
   '_context' => 'init'
   '_member' => 'variable'
 'self ref' => HASH(0x83a50f0)
   -> REUSED_ADDRESS
 'this' => 'that'
DB<18>
```

Although this variable dump looks a lot like that produced by the standard Perl module used for dumping complex structures: Data::Dumper, in fact it is produced by a core library called dumpvar.pl, which Data::Dumper largely supercedes.

If you like, you can take a look at this library by loading it for viewing via the f command, introduced next.

The File View Command: f

Continuing with the previous example, we can view the file by using the f command, which accepts a regex against which to match a filename from within the values of %INC:

```
DB<18> f dumpvar
 Choosing /usr/local/lib/perl5/5.8.2/dumpvar.pl matching 'dumpvar':
 1       2       3
 4       # Needed for PrettyPrinter only:
 5
 6       # require 5.001;  # Well, it coredumps anyway undef DB in 5.000 (not now)
 7
 8       # translate control chars to ^X - Randal Schwartz
 9       # Modifications to print types by Peter Gordon v1.0
 10
DB<19>
```

And to continue listing code and look further down the file, we can use the l (lowercase letter *ell* for listing code) command.

```
DB<19> l
 11      # Ilya Zakharevich -- patches after 5.001 (and some before ;-)
 12
 13      # Won't dump symbol tables and contents of debugged files by default
 14
 15:     $winsize = 80 unless defined $winsize;
 16
 17
 18      # Defaults
 19
 20      # $globPrint = 1;
DB<19>
```

If you want to see the code below the chunk that has just been displayed, you can use another l command, which will continue to list the code from our current position. There are multiple ways to list code in the debugger via the l command. Use the h l help command to get a complete listing of the possibilities.

```
DB<19> l
 21:      $printUndef = 1 unless defined $printUndef;
 22:      $tick = "auto" unless defined $tick;
 23:      $unctrl = 'quote' unless defined $unctrl;
 24:      $subdump = 1;
 25:      $dumpReused = 0 unless defined $dumpReused;
 26:      $bareStringify = 1 unless defined $bareStringify;
 27
 28       sub main::dumpValue {
 29:        local %address;
 30:        local $^W-0;
DB<19>
```

It is important to realize that this is purely a viewing mechanism, and that we are not executing code at this point in the viewed file. Rather, we are able to inspect any of the files loaded into the %INC array via this mechanism. This can, to the uninitiated, lead to some confusion, because it is very easy to forget exactly where one is in the runtime process. Therefore we have a reset display command, with which we can remind ourselves.

The Reset Display Command: .

We can return to viewing the code at our present position by using the . command:

```
DB<19> .
 main::(-e:1):   0
DB<19>
```

In this case, the code is simply the integer 0 which we gave on the command line, and the program name is -e. Later on, when we use a real program, and we can see the program name and a line of informational code, this may make more sense. The point being made here is that while the debugger display context was in the other file (dumpvar.pl earlier), it became necessary to visually return to our current context via the . command.

The Subroutine Display Command: S

Another useful command enables us to see all the subroutines available to us in our current context. To use it just type **S**:

```
DB<19> S
 Carp::BEGIN
 Carp::caller_info
 Carp::carp
 Carp::cluck
 Carp::confess
<...multiple lines snipped here...>
```

```
warnings::register::import
warnings::register::mkMask
warnings::unimport
warnings::warn
warnings::warnif
  DB<19>
```

Because the resulting list tends to be so long, you would normally pipe the output through a pager, with the | command, exactly as we did previously for the | h command. Alternatively we can reduce the result set altogether by using the S command and giving it a regular expression, or regex, as an argument. Note that whatever string follows the S command is the actual regex, that is, the forward slashes (/) you may be used to surrounding a regex with, will be included in the regex if given. Here the command displays all subroutines that include BEGIN in the name:

```
DB<19> S BEGIN
 Carp::BEGIN
 IO::BEGIN
 IO::Handle::BEGIN
 SelectSaver::BEGIN
 Symbol::BEGIN
 Term::Cap::BEGIN
 Term::ReadLine::BEGIN
 main::BEGIN
 vars::BEGIN
 warnings::BEGIN
DB<20>
```

Of course anywhere you can use a regex, you can negate one too, by using the exclamation mark. In this case the command displays all subroutine names which do not include an a, or an e, or a u character in their name.

```
DB<20> S ![aeu]
 IO::BEGIN
 IO::import
 Symbol::BEGIN
 strict::bits
 strict::import
DB<21>
```

In a similar manner the debugger provides a way to inspect the available variables in a given namespace. As in the preceding example, this also takes a regex as an optional argument to make finding the appropriate variable's easier.

The Display Variables Command: V

The V command takes the optional argument of a package name, followed by the (also optional) argument of a variable name. Note that the variable should have no type-specifier, or prefix, in front of it, and that the variable argument is a regex. In this example we're looking for any variables in the main package that have the letter x in their name:

```
DB<21> V main x
@x = (
0   'first'
1   'second'
2   'third'
3   'fourth'
4   'fifth'
)
%x = (
'chars' => HASH(0x836a0ec)
   'e' => 'i'
   'o' => 'u'
   'others' => 's'
   'q' => 'w'
   'r' => 'k'
   'vowels' => 'a'
'obj' => Class=HASH(0x83c31c0)
   '_context' => 'init'
   '_member' => 'variable'
'this' => 'that'
)
DB<22>
```

The Display Current Package Variables Command: X

The X command is particularly useful as this is equivalent to using V currentpackage [vars] without having to define the current package.

The Inheritance Tree Command: i

The inheritance tree command will not only show the class of an object, but it will also list the classes from which it inherits its characteristics. You can use either an object or a plain class. For the purposes of this demonstration, let's take a look at the FileHandle, because that inherits from various other modules. We have to use it first to load it, as it is not loaded by default:

```
DB<22> use FileHandle
DB<23>
```

Now we can take a look at the FileHandle class inheritance tree by giving the name of the class as the argument to the i command:

```
DB23> i FileHandle
FileHandle 2.01, IO::File 1.10, IO::Handle 1.24, IO::Seekable 1.09, Exporter 5.58
DB<24>
```

We can see from the listing that any FileHandle object will also inherit from IO::File, IO::Handle, IO::Seekable, and Exporter. This can be useful, when you're not sure which object has access to which methods, via which classes.

Tracking Command History: H

The Perl debugger supports a raw command history mechanism. You can see the history list by using the uppercase H:

```
DB<24> H
 21: V main x
 20: S ![aeu]
 19: S BEGIN
 18: f dumpvar
 17: x \%x
 16: $x{'self ref'} = \%x
 15: %x = (
 'this' => 'that',
 'chars'=> { 'vowels' => qw(a e i o u), 'others' => qw(s q w r k) },
 'obj'  => bless({'_member' => 'variable', '_context' => 'init'}, 'Class'),
 )
 14: x @x
 13: x \@x
 12: p join(' ', @x)
 11: p @x
 10: p $x[1]
 9:  @x = qw(first second third fourth fifth)
 8: doc FileHandle
 7: | h h
 6: print "still running...\n"
 5: h a
 4: print 1 / 0
 3: print join("\n", @INC)
 2: print 1 / 42
 1: print $^O
DB<24>
```

Unfortunately, the standard history mechanism discards every command that is only a single character, or less, in length. Presumably this is an unfortunate optimization of some kind, but therefore you may sometimes wonder where a particular command sequence has disappeared to. Rest assured that if you use the save, source, and rerun commands, they will honor the real history list, but it's something to be aware of.

The Redo Command: !

Using this history mechanism, any command you have typed in the current session may be recalled by using the ! n command, where n is a valid history integer:

```
DB<24> !6
 print "still running...\n"
 still running...
DB<25>
```

The most recent command may be replayed by using !!, and previous commands may also be referred to by the number'th-to-last command or by a regex, which is of course a little more risky.

Note that to use the *arrow* keys to work with the command history it is necessary to have the Term::ReadKey module installed. Although this doesn't offer *vi*-like command line editing, it is still very useful to have available, and worth the minimal trouble of installing.

Installing this module via the CPAN could be done with a command like this:

```
%> perl -MCPAN -e 'install Term::ReadKey'
```

The Quit Command: q

Finally, we need to know how to quit the debugger. Referring to the help menu, we can see that typing a q will do the trick:

```
DB<25> q
%>
```

Note that CTRL-D will also work as an alternative for q.

Supplying a Program Name

To run the debugger on an actual program, Perl requires the name of a program to debug as an argument, followed by any program arguments, as shown in the example at the head of this chapter, like this:

```
%> perl -d progname arg1 arg2 etc.
```

To supply further runtime arguments to Perl, to add an extra library path (-I...) or a module name (-M...) for example, simply include them *after* the Perl binary name and *before* the program to debug name. The sequential order of these commands is otherwise largely irrelevant. To read more about Perl runtime switches, see perldoc perlrun.

```
%> perl –I/home/perltut/perllibs –d –MMyModule progname arg1 arg2 etc.
```

We cover this more completely in the next and following chapters.

Summary

In this chapter we have shown several of the most common commands available to list both your code and the libraries it uses. You now know how to inspect any of the variables in your package or in any other package, at runtime.

You can now find out which methods and subroutines are available at any place in the program, either to a particular object or to a class. You can repeat recent commands or one which was run much earlier in the program and you know it would be laborious to have to type in all over again—now you can simply use the command history mechanism.

Finally, you know how to query the debugger help and the system manpages, to find an explanation of any available command or system call, while your program is running and while you retain control over it.

While this chapter has been primarily concerned with *observing* the runtime execution of your program, the next chapter discusses how to *control* it.

CHAPTER 3

■ ■ ■

Controlling Program Execution

Veni Vidi Vici.

—Julius Caesar in Rome, celebrating his triumph over King Pharnaces of Pontus

Caesar did not conquer Gaul, consolidate the Roman Empire, and subjugate all his enemies by allowing them to do whatever they wished. Whatever we may think of his methods, he certainly took control of his environment and made it behave according to his intentions, much as we try to do as programmers every day—we control the programs we write. In the same manner, we can use Perl debugger commands to extend control of the runtime execution of our Perl program to regions that either need the control but don't know it, or that have slipped by unnoticed. We'll show you how to conquer those bugs.

In this chapter, we demonstrate how to control the execution of your program. You'll learn how to set a breakpoint on a variable or a line, interrupt code execution under certain conditions, make the program do something at a particular point when a variable changes value, and how to move to different points in your code, (or in someone else's code), via a used library or module.

Note that in this chapter we are not trying to fix any code—the sole purpose here is to learn how to control the execution of your Perl code at runtime.

A Sample Program: charcount

For the purposes of this chapter we need to have a program available to debug, and in this case we will use a program titled charcount (see Listing 3-1).

charcount is a short program which you will use throughout this book. It simply prints out the number of consonants, vowels, and special characters found on each line of a file given to it as an argument. In the output, hard refers to consonants found, soft refers to vowels found, and special refers to more or less every other character the program finds on each line. This moderately arbitrary processing is designed simply to give us something to work with—something to inspect, change, and control. This is quite a short program, and the source for it can be copied from the following text, or if you prefer, you can download it from the Apress web site, along with the other examples. Note that the numbers located to the left are purely to reference the code in the text and are not part of the code itself.

■**Note** You are always encouraged to experiment by either executing the commands as given or trying your own variations. This will help you learn how to move about the debugger with confidence. There's no point in *reading* how to use it, unless you actually *do* use it.

Listing 3-1. *A Sample Perl Program,* charcount

```
01 #!/usr/bin/perl
02 #
03 # prints the line number and the number of consonants, vowels and special
04 # characters found on each line of the filename given as an argument.
05
06 use strict;
07 use FileHandle;
08
09 my $file = $ARGV[0] || '';
10 my $verbose = $ARGV[1] || 0;
11
12 unless (-f $file) {
13 die("Usage: $0 filename [-v]");
14 }
15 my $FH = FileHandle->new("< $file") or die("unable to open file($file): $!");
16
17 my $i_cnt  = 0;
18 my $i_cons = 0;
19 my $i_vows = 0;
20 my $i_spec = 0;
21
22 # parse the file
23 while (<$FH>) {
24   my $line = $_;
25   $i_cons += my $cons = &parse($line, '[bcdfghjklmnpqrstvwxyz]');
26   $i_vows += my $vows = &parse($line, '[aeiou]');
27   $i_spec += my $spec = &parse($line, '[^a-z0-9\s]');
28   print sprintf('%6d', $i_cnt).':'.
29     ' hard'.('.'x(8-length($cons))).$cons.
30     ' soft'.('.'x(8-length($vows))).$vows.
31     ' spec'.('.'x(8-length($spec))).$spec;
32   print $verbose ? "  $line" : "\n";
33   $i_cnt++;
34 }
35
36 print ' total:'.
37   ' hard'.(' 'x(8-length($i_cons))).$i_cons.
38   ' soft'.(' 'x(8-length($i_vows))).$i_vows.
39   ' spec'.(' 'x(8-length($i_spec))).$i_spec.
```

```
40 "\n";
41
42 sub parse {
43   my $str = shift;
44   my $reg = shift;
45   my $cnt = my @cnt = ($str  =~ /($reg)/gi);
46   return $cnt;
47 }
48
49 exit 0;
```

Running charcount

Running Listing 3-1 without any arguments generates the following error and simple usage information:

```
%> perl ./charcount
Usage: ./charcount filename [-v] at ./charcount line 14.
%>
```

Now we'd like to correct the call to include a filename argument. In this case, we use the walrus file as the input and then generate the typical output from the program to get a feel for what is expected when you run this program. The walrus file may be downloaded from the Apress web site along with the rest of the code. We've included part of the file listing here for reference. We picked it because it's such an entertaining read—how many books on debugging make you smile?

```
The Walrus and the Carpenter by Lewis Carroll
The sun was shining on the sea,
Shining with all his might:
He did his very best to make
The billows smooth and bright
And this was odd, because it was
The middle of the night.

The moon was shining sulkily,
Because she thought the sun
Had got no business to be there
After the day was done
"It's very rude of him," she said,
"To come and spoil the fun!"

The sea was wet as wet could be,
The sands were dry as dry.
You could not see a cloud, because
No cloud was in the sky:
No birds were flying overhead
There were no birds to fly.
```

Running charcount with Arguments

The output for the first line, for example, simply says that the program found 15 hard (consonant) characters, 7 soft (vowel) characters and 10 special (non-alphanumeric) characters. The terminology is somewhat arbitrary, but for the purpose of this demonstration it should suffice.

Note that passing the -v (verbose) switch to charcount will tell the program to print out the incoming line from the input file for your reference. This might be useful to get a feel for how each line is treated by the program.

```
%> perl ./charcount walrus

     0:  hard......20  soft......12  spec.......1
     1:  hard.......0  soft.......0  spec.......0
     2:  hard......14  soft.......9  spec.......1
     3:  hard......15  soft.......6  spec.......1
     4:  hard......13  soft.......8  spec.......0
     5:  hard......17  soft.......7  spec.......0
     6:  hard......15  soft.......9  spec.......1
     7:  hard......12  soft.......6  spec.......1

<...multiple lines snipped...>

   123:  hard......15  soft......10  spec.......2
   124:  hard......12  soft.......9  spec.......0
   125:  hard......18  soft.......9  spec.......1
   126:  hard.......9  soft.......8  spec.......2
   127:  hard.......0  soft.......0  spec.......0
 total:  hard    1454  soft     893  spec     171
%>
```

Although this is hardly rocket science, there is enough mileage in this short program to comfortably demonstrate simple usage of the debugger and to prepare you for the rest of the book. Now you're going to run the Perl debugger on this program to see how you can use the motion commands to both alter and control its execution.

Debugging a Perl Program

As we saw in Chapter 2, you can start the debugger with a piece of Perl code as an argument by including the -e switch on the command line. To debug a particular program instead, we substitute the program name to be debugged, along with any required arguments. So let's dive into our current program with the debugger:

```
%> perl -d ./charcount inputdata
Loading DB routines from perl5db.pl version 1.27
Editor support available.
Enter h or 'h h' for help, or 'man perldebug' for more help.
main::(./charcount:9):  my $file = $ARGV[0] || '';
  DB<1>
```

Here we have stopped on the first runtime executable line of the code, which, from the information line given, is confirmed as line 9 of our file. The first thing to notice when you run the debugger is that it always stops at what it considers to be the first executable line of your code. It will run through all your BEGIN blocks, all your use statements, and any consequential code first. Only *then* will it stop and wait for your instructions. This is not entirely true—you can actually get it to stop in a library or module that you are about to load, but we cover that sort of advanced technique later on.

Reviewing Executed Code

It's often useful to review code that has already been executed, as well as the code to come. In particular, this is useful for double-checking exactly where you are in the algorithm, and for reinforcing the awareness of your current environment. In this section, we'll show you how to do so using the debugger.

Looking Backward

We can review code that has already been executed by using the - (list *previous* code) command:

```
DB<1> -
01        # $Id: 03.pod,v 1.6 2004/03/15 20:23:19 perltut Exp $
02        #
03        # prints the line number and the number of consonants, vowels and special
04        # characters found on each line of the filename given as an argument.
05
06:       use strict;
07:       use FileHandle;
08
09==>  my $file = $ARGV[0] || '';
10:     my $verbose = $ARGV[1] || 0;
DB<1>
```

Looking Forward

By using the l command introduced in the last chapter, we can see the code we will shortly be executing.

```
DB<1> l
11
12:     unless (-f $file) {
13:             die("Usage: $0 filename [-v]");
14       }
15:     my $FH = FileHandle->new("< $file")
        or die("unable to open file($file): $!");
16
17:     my $i_cnt  = 0;
18:     my $i_cons = 0;
19:     my $i_vows = 0;
20:     my $i_spec = 0;
DB<1>
```

Looking Sideways

You are not restricted to looking at the next n lines of code, and in fact, you can choose any code that is currently compiled. To help make this intuitive, Perl makes the l command (lowercase letter L) very versatile. This command takes a number of different arguments, which can be looked up by using the h command on it:

```
DB<1> h l
 l min+incr      List incr+1 lines starting at min.
 l min-max       List lines min through max.
 l line          List single line.
 l subname       List first window of lines from subroutine.
 l $var          List first window of lines from subroutine referenced by $var.
 l               List next window of lines.
DB<2>
```

For example, let's use the l command to look at lines 18 through 33:

```
DB<2> l 18-33
 18:     my $i_cons = 0;
 19:     my $i_vows = 0;
 20:     my $i_spec = 0;
 21
 22:     while (<$FH>) {
 23:             my $line = $_;
 24:             $i_cons += my $cons = &parse($line, '[bcdfghjklmnpqrstvwxyz]');
 25:             $i_vows += my $vows = &parse($line, '[aeiou]');
 26:             $i_spec += my $spec = &parse($line, '[^a-z0-9\s]');
 27:             print sprintf('%6d', $i_cnt).':'.
 28                     ' hard'.('.'x(8-length($cons))).$cons.
 29                     ' soft'.('.'x(8-length($vows))).$vows.
 30                     ' spec'.('.'x(8-length($spec))).$spec;
 31:             print $verbose ? "  $line" : "\n";
 32:             $i_cnt++;
 33     }
DB<3>
```

Although we're now looking down to line 33, we haven't actually moved anywhere yet. We can see that we are actually still way up on line 9 after resetting our display pointer using the . command:

```
DB<3> .
 main::(./charcount:9):  my $file = $ARGV[0] || '';
DB<3>
```

Continuing Execution Command: c

After looking through the receding code listings, you'll note that line 15 looks interesting. This is, perhaps, the first place in the code where we might like to run to and inspect our environment. To continue execution directly to line 15 we use c for continue, with 15 as an argument. You can think of this as setting a temporary breakpoint on that line, which is more or less what actually happens internally:

```
DB<3> c 15
 main::(./charcount:15): my $FH = FileHandle->new("< $file")
 or die("unable to open file($file): $!");
DB<4>
```

As noted earlier, the debugger is now showing you the line of code *about to be executed*. We can display the value of the $FH and $file variables for curiosity's sake by using the p (for print) command and giving it a simple string within which we interpolate our two variables: Very often you see programmers simply printing a variable with no surrounding characters. This can be ok if you know the value contains all visible characters, for instance, but, particularly while debugging, it can be very illuminating to see *exactly* what the value of the variable is, end to end. The reason we use FH(...) is to wrap the variable in a specific string which we can then use to absolutely identify the value held by the variable itself:

```
DB<4> p "FH($FH) file($file)"
 FH() file(./inputdata)
DB<5>
```

To actually execute this code we could use the c command again to continue past it, but because we have no breakpoints anywhere yet, this would take us off the end of the program— and we don't wish to do that at this stage.

Instead, because we wish to step to the *next* executable statement, we will use the aptly named n command to do so. Note that this will step *over* any subroutine calls in the statement— see s for stepping *into* them:

```
DB<5> n
 main::(./charcount:17): my $i_cnt  = 0;
DB<5>
```

You'll probably also have noticed that we hopped from line 15 to line 17. This is because the debugger cannot stop or place a breakpoint on any line that consists of empty space. It needs code on which to work its magic.

Working with History Management

In the previous listing we didn't appear to have been stopped cold with an error message, so let's have a look at that FileHandle variable. In fact, because we've already done this earlier, this is an ideal time to try out our history command (H). To see where our print command is in the history listing, and which history number we can use to refer to it, use the H (history listing) command:

```
DB<5> H
 4: p "FH($FH) file($file)"
 3: c 15
 2: l 18-33
 1: h l
DB<5>
```

The debugger, by default, uses the ! character to recall a previous command by referring to it by history number(we can look at changing this later by using the alias command). The command to recall the correct history in this case, is !4:

```
DB<5> !4
 p "FH($FH) file($file)"
 FH(FileHandle=GLOB(0x83d75a4)) file(./inputdata)
DB<6>
```

The debugger gets the appropriate command from the history listing, prints it to inform the user which command is being run, and then executes it. The $FH variable looks good at this point, so we can continue. Before we do, let's just quickly remember where we are with a current code listing:

```
DB<6> l
 17==>    my $i_cnt  = 0;
 18:      my $i_cons = 0;
 19:      my $i_vows = 0;
 20:      my $i_spec = 0;
 21
 22 # parse the file
 23:      while (<$FH>) {
 24:              my $line = $_;
 25:              $i_cons += my $cons = &parse($line, '[bcdfghjklmnpqrstvwxyz]');
 26:              $i_vows += my $vows = &parse($line, '[aeiou]');
 27:              $i_spec += my $spec = &parse($line, '[^a-z0-9\s]');
DB<6>
```

Now we're about to hit the meat of this program down in the while loop where we will parse each line of the input file. This might be a good place to stop and decide if we want to place a breakpoint somewhere that could stop the program in an interesting location.

Setting a Breakpoint

A breakpoint is a command to the debugger to stop execution of the program at a particular line. Breakpoints become particularly useful when they are associated with a given condition.

Although the most common sort of breakpoint is simply bound to a particular line number, breakpoints may also be set against the calling or compiling, for example, of a particular subroutine or file. That said, the breakpoint will still be set, unless a line number is given, against the first executable line of a subroutine or block of code. We'll address all of these points in this book, particularly in Chapter 6, which covers setting breakpoints to take effect both at runtime and at compiletime, to help with debugging use'd libraries and modules.

Returning to our program, let's tell the debugger that we'd like to stop on line 22 of the input data with the b (for breakpoint) command:

```
DB<6> b 22
 Line 22 not breakable.
DB<7>
```

That's strange—the debugger appears not to like line 22. We had better have a look at it with a code listing around line 22. Use the l command to specify to the debugger which line to display:

```
DB<7> l 22
 22 # parse the file
DB<8>
```

As you can see, the debugger doesn't like lines which are commented out entirely, or empty lines. As we pointed out in the preceding text, it needs a line with some code on it. Let's try again with line 25:

```
DB<8> b 25
DB<9>
```

Unfortunately, although setting the breakpoint was successful, we don't get much feedback. You can see if the breakpoint has been set, by using the L b (for List breakpoints) command:

```
DB<9> L b
 ./charcount:
  15:    my $FH = FileHandle->new("< $file") or die("unable to open file($file): $!");
  25:         $i_cons += my $cons = &parse($line, '[bcdfghjklmnpqrstvwxyz]');
 break if (1)
DB<9>
```

The output tells us that in the file ./charcount, we have a breakpoint on both line 15 and line 25, and that the lines of code are also shown. We also see that this breakpoint will be used if, and only if, the condition (shown in the brackets) is true. Because we didn't specify a condition, this condition defaults to the simple expression 1, which is another way of saying always true, meaning the program will stop when it gets to line 25, whatever the circumstances.

Continuing Program Execution After a Break

So, lets use the c command to simply continue execution of our program. This will now run straight down to the newly set breakpoint at line 25, because we do not hit any other breakpoints enroute:

```
DB<9> c
 main::(./charcount:25): $i_cons += my $cons =
                         &parse($line, '[bcdfghjklmnpqrstvwxyz]');
DB<9>
```

Now we can see that the debugger has stopped at the next breakpoint it came to (line 25). At this point we can check a couple things, but first let's use the abbreviated print command to have a look at the line count:

```
DB<9> p $i_cnt
 0
DB<10>
```

Secondly, we can check the contents of the first line located in the $line variable:

```
DB<10> p $line
The Walrus and The Carpenter by Lewis Carroll.
DB<11>
```

Using the c command again a couple of times, we can check the contents of $line as we move through the file:

```
DB<11> c
  0:  hard......20  soft.......12  spec......1
main::(./charcount:25): $i_cons += my $cons =
&parse($line, '[bcdfghjklmnpqrstvwxyz]');
DB<11>
```

Back at line 25 again, print out $line again:

```
DB<11> p $line

DB<12>
```

Note that in the previous output, the line beginning with the 0: hard... is the output of the previous parse(), and is the standard output of the program.

Now we can use the c command again:

```
DB<12> c
  1:  hard.......0  soft.......0  spec.......0
main::(./charcount:25): $i_cons += my $cons =
&parse($line, '[bcdfghjklmnpqrstvwxyz]');
DB<12> p $line
The sun was shining on the sea,
DB<13>
```

It can be clearly seen that, although this can be very useful, in this particular case, this isn't a very intelligent use of the breakpoint functionality. If this was a large file, then we would stop here on every line, and our fingers would get very tired of even the minimal work of typing c and p $line continually.

Executing a Command Before Each Debugger Prompt

The first thing we could do about that would be to print out the incoming line each time we pass it. For this we can use the < (pre-prompt Perl) command.

```
B<13> < print "line($i_cnt): $line"
DB<14>
```

Again, we don't get much feedback on this, but we can check the contents of our pre-prompt Perl commands by entering the command followed by a question mark:

```
DB<14> <?
 pre-perl commands:
 < -- print "line($i_cnt): $line"
DB<15>
```

Now when we simply use the c command, we get the incoming line helpfully printed for us just before our debugger prompt:

```
DB<15> c
  2:  hard......14  soft......4  spec.......1
main::(./charcount:25): $i_cons += my $cons =
&parse($line, '[bcdfghjklmnpqrstvwxyz]');
```

```
 line(3):  Shining with all his might: :
DB<15> c
  3:  hard......15  soft......6  spec.......1
main::(./charcount:25): $i_cons += my $cons =
&parse($line, '[bcdfghjklmnpqrstvwxyz]');
 line(4): He did his very best to make
DB<15> c
  4:  hard......13  soft......8  spec.......0
main::(./charcount:25): $i_cons += my $cons =
&parse($line, '[bcdfghjklmnpqrstvwxyz]');
 line(5): The billows smooth and bright
DB<15>
```

Not only is this less work for us, with more information than we had at the start, but it is also worth noting that we haven't changed the source code at all, even though we have changed the behavior of the program for this run.

Using Regular Expressions to Set Breakpoints

Another variation on setting a breakpoint is to use a conditional regular expression, (any Perl expression is in fact valid), to tell the debugger to stop on entry into a subroutine for example. The typical usage would be something like this:

```
b new $variable =~ m/this/i
```

Note that it is not important to use the if {...} syntax, it is only necessary to place the condition itself after the command, where it will be evaluated by the debugger.

Use h b to display the help and syntax for the many breakpoint-setting options, and also see the following examples.

Setting a Watch-Expression on a Variable

A *watch-expression* is an expression that the debugger will watch on your behalf. Each time the expression changes, the debugger will stop program execution, and then tell you what value the expression had and what value the expression has now.

An alternative way of stopping the program is to set a watch-expression on a variable. Each time that variable changes the old and new values of the variable will be printed, a one-time breakpoint is again set, the debugger will stop execution, and await further command input. This can be a very useful technique, particularly where a variable doesn't change value often, but is normally at a critical point in the program flow when it does.

Set a watch-expression on the $i_cnt variable so we can see the line counter value change each time it is incremented:

```
DB<15> w $i_cnt
DB<16>
```

List All Watch-Expressions

Again, just as when successfully setting a breakpoint, there is no feedback, but we can confirm our command with the L w (List watch-expressions) command:

```
DB<16> L w
 Watch-expressions:
  $i_cnt
DB<17>
```

Now use the c command again to see the result:

```
DB<17> c
  5:hard.......13  soft.......8  spec.......0
watchpoint 0:    $i_cnt changed:
old value:       '5'
new value:       '6'
main::(./charcount:24):        my $line = $_;
DB<17>
```

This time in addition to our normal program output, we get information that the $i_cnt variable has changed values, and that the debugger has stopped just as we are about to execute line 24. This is because it's the next executable line after our variable change.

Setting an Action

An *action* is an instruction to the debugger to execute a command on a particular line, each time that line is about to be executed. If no line number is given, the debugger will take the current line number and set the action to occur on this line.

In our case, we could print the total incrementing values each time we passed line 32, to give us an idea of our progress.

```
DB<17> a 32 print "line($i_cnt): i_cons($i_cons) i_vows($i_vows) i_spec($i_spec)"
DB<18>
```

List All Actions

Again we get no feedback but can check this with the L a (list actions) command:

```
DB<18> L a
 ./charcount:
   15:     my $FH = FileHandle->new("< $file")
           or die("unable to open file($file): $!");
   25:             $i_cons += my $cons = &parse($line, '[bcdfghjklmnpqrstvwxyz]');
   32:             print $verbose ? "  $line" : "\n";
 action:  print "line($i_cnt): i_cons($i_cons) i_vows($i_vows) i_spec($i_spec)"
DB<19>
```

Here you can see how the debugger regards actions and breakpoints as very similar, internally they are managed by the same data structure. Thus you can only have one breakpoint or action per line.

Using Debugger Hints in the Code Display

At this point it is also worth taking a look at the code between lines 24 and 33, to see how the debugger helps to identify lines of code which can be worked with. We can do this using the l 24-33 command.

In the resulting code listing, shown next, are several helpful hints to observe:

```
DB<19> l 24-33
 24==>          my $line = $_;
 25:b           $i_cons += my $cons = &parse($line, '[bcdfghjklmnpqrstvwxyz]');
 26:            $i_vows += my $vows = &parse($line, '[aeiou]');
 27:            $i_spec += my $spec = &parse($line, '[^a-z0-9\s]');
 28:            print sprintf('%6d', $i_cnt).':'.
 29                      '  hard'.('.'x(8-length($cons))).$cons.
 30                      '  soft'.('.'x(8-length($vows))).$vows.
 31                      '  spec'.('.'x(8-length($spec))).$spec;
 32:a           print $verbose ? "   $line" : "\n";
 33:            $i_cnt++;
DB<20>
```

The ==> marker indicates our current position at line 24. Additionally, any line with a colon (:) after the line number means it is possible to place a breakpoint or action there. In our example this includes every line between line 25 and 28, line 32 and line 33.

If a line has a breakpoint on it the colon has a letter b after it, like line 25. If a line has an action associated with it, the colon has a letter a after it, like line 32.

Stepping into a Subroutine or Method

There are two forms of moving by a single statement. The first is to step over function calls to each next statement (by using the command letter n which we've seen in the preceding examples). The second form is to step into function calls as they are executed, by using the command letter s.

Having looked at the code, it might be a good idea to step into the parse() subroutine on line 25. Let's do this now using the s command:

```
DB<20> s
main::parse(./charcount:43):            my $str = shift;
DB<20>
```

Although we could use a plain l to see the following code, in this case we'll use a variant that will show us the whole subroutine, because it might give us a better picture of our environment:

```
DB<20> l parse
 42      sub parse {
 43==>          my $str = shift;
 44:            my $reg = shift;
 45:            my $cnt = my @cnt = ($str  =~ /($reg)/gi);
 46:            return $cnt;
 47      }
DB<21>
```

Now that we're actually inside the subroutine call, we can inspect any of these variables, and we can alter them too should that be required. To demonstrate this, we first move down to line 47:

```
DB<21> c 47
main::parse(./charcount:47):            return $cnt;
DB<22>
```

At this point it may be worth pointing out that the direction of travel here is *one-way*, that is, it is not possible to go backwards. In this case, if you give the line number of a line that has already been passed, the debugger will continue until it falls off the end of the program. The debugger will follow the program faithfully, and of course subroutines and methods can be called anywhere in the code just as would be expected, but it's just not possible to actually *undo* a command. In this respect the debugger environment is just like real-life, but with more control.

Note that the version of the debugger distributed with Perl version 5.8.5 and higher has a rerun command which attempts to emulate a stepping backwards functionality.

Returning to our current debugging session, we should inspect our current variables to see what our input was and what was produced from it:

```
DB<22> p "str($str) reg($reg) -> cnt($cnt) \@cnt(@cnt)"
 str( The billows smooth and bright
 ) reg([bcdfghjklmnpqrstvwxyz]) -> cnt(17) @cnt(h b l l w s s m t h n d b r g h t)
DB<23>
```

Modifying a Variable

Although we're in the middle of the execution of this program, and both the source code and the input data has been read and is apparently fixed, we can still change it at will. Later we will tackle modifying the source code of your program while it is running, but for now, we will stick to changing only the data input.

We've seen the most recent line of input data (The billows smooth and bright). Now let's change this string ($str) with a simple assignment:

```
DB<23> $str = "xxx "
DB<24>
```

There's no more to it than that. A simple Perl assignment is all it takes to make our input data hold a different value from the one that was read from the original file. It would be prudent to print the variable just to make sure:

```
DB<24> p $str
 xxx
DB<25>
```

Now we can rerun the command on line 45 once more to generate our modified output:

```
DB<26> my $cnt = my @cnt = ($str =~ /($reg)/gi);
DB<27>
```

Of course there's no visible output from this, but again we can print out our variables to see what has happened using the same print command as before:

```
DB<27> p "str($str) reg($reg) -> cnt($cnt) \@cnt(@cnt)"
str(xxx) reg([bcdfghjklmnpqrstvwxyz]) -> cnt(3) @cnt(x x x)
DB<28>
```

In @cnt, we can see that we get different characters generated by the identical command on a different input string. Our final value for $cnt is 3 and this is what will be returned from the parse subroutine in this case.

Returning from a Subroutine

So far, we've been working in our subroutine, which has effectively been run twice, once by the execution of our program and once manually. Now we wish to continue, but instead of stopping at our next breakpoint, we'll just return from the subroutine to its calling context. A simple r (which stands for run this subroutine and return) will bring us back to our previous context:

```
DB<28> r
 scalar context return from main::parse: 3
 main::(./charcount:26):          $i_vows += my $vows = &parse($line, '[aeiou]');
 line(6):  xxx
DB<29>
```

A word on context here—the calling code sets the context to either scalar or list, and this context will affect the value returned. This is why when you say: print (1, 2, 3); Perl will print 123, but when you say: print ''.(1,2,3); Perl will print 3.

The r command returns from the current scope and uses a one-time-only breakpoint to stop the debugger. Because the PrintRet option was true (the default setting), the return value was also printed for us to see.

We can check it easily enough:

```
DB<30> p $cons
 11
DB<31>
```

Now we have quite a few breakpoints and actions set up, which are probably getting a bit unwieldy on such a small program. To fix this, let's remove a few of them. To remove a breakpoint, the command is B n where n is the line number, and to remove all breakpoints simply use an asterisk:

```
DB<31> B*
 Deleting all breakpoints...
DB<32>
```

The same applies to actions:

```
DB<32> A*
 Deleting all actions...
DB<33>
```

And to watch-expressions:

```
DB<33> W*
 Deleting all watch-expressions ...
DB<34>
```

The same command can be applied to pre- and post-prompt Perl commands:

```
DB<34> <*
 All < actions cleared.
DB<35>
```

If we now use the L command with no arguments all actions, breakpoints, and watches will be displayed, which in our case are none:

```
DB<35> L
DB<35>
```

Setting a Breakpoint Conditionally with an Expression

As indicated previously, another way to set a breakpoint, is to give an expression which must evaluate to a Boolean true value. The usual rules regarding scope and variable visibility only partly apply in the debugger environment. This means that although you may have a variable in a block that the rest of the program can't see, you can still refer to it in the debugger without affecting it by *autovivification*.

■**Note** Autovivication is the process by which a variable will be defined for you by Perl without having to declare it first. Use strict disallows autovivication of variable names, but you cannot have autovivication turned off for the internal keys of a hash, for instance, only for the name of the hash itself. This can be a problem, if your code is checking for whether a variable is defined or not, and you inspect the variable, thus creating it erroneously.

Referring to the preceding 'l parse' output, we can see that we can tell the debugger to stop in the parse() subroutine if the input $line or $str contains the word file and the regular expression to search for contains an a. In other words looking for a vowel:

```
DB<35> b 45 $str =~ /file/ && $reg =~ /a/
DB<36>
```

Setting a Pre-Prompt Debugger Command

The debugger supports the ability to set both pre- and post-prompt commands. These commands will be executed before each debugger prompt. You can think of this as an action unassociated with a line number. It is possible to set both pre- and post- types for a Perl command, although for a debugger command only a pre-prompt command is supported.

To demonstrate this, we will take a look at the $str variable before each prompt, along with the regex for reference:

```
DB<36> { p "str($str) reg($reg)"
DB<37>
```

Just as with breakpoints and actions, setting a pre-prompt command offers no feedback—unless it fails. Now we will continue to run the program and stop the next time $str and $reg satisfy the conditions from the preceding breakpoint command:

```
DB<37> c
  6:  hard......15  soft.......9  spec.......1
  7:  hard......12  soft.......6  spec.......1
main::parse(./charcount:45):          my $cnt = my @cnt = ($str  =~ /($reg)/gi);
 auto(-1)  DB<54> print "str($str) reg($reg)"
str(|The middle of the night.
 ) reg([aeiou])
DB<37>
```

The previous line, with the auto(-1) prefix to the debugger prompt, is the pre-prompt command being printed for reference. It can be seen in the resulting output of the string (The middle of the night.) and the regex ([aeiou]).

Once more:

```
DB<37> c
 main::parse(./charcount:45):         my $cnt = my @cnt = ($str  =~ /($reg)/gi);
 auto(-1)  DB<55> print "str($str) reg($reg)"
 str(The middle of the night.
 ) reg([^a-z0-9\s])
DB<37>
```

Once more still:

```
DB<37> c
  8:  hard.......0  soft.......0  spec.......0
  9:  hard......15  soft.......8  spec.......1
 10:  hard......13  soft.......9  spec.......0
 main::parse(./charcount:45):         my $cnt = my @cnt = ($str  =~ /($reg)/gi);
 auto(-1)  DB<56> print "str($str) reg($reg)"
 str(Because she thought the sun
 ) reg([aeiou])
DB<37>
```

On the last c, we went through three lines of the input file before coming to a halt, because our breakpoint conditions were not satisfied at the time. So, although we can see three lines of summary output from charcount, we only see the one line of output from the debugger pre-prompt command.

We've seen some of what the debugger can do, and how to control the execution of the running Perl program, so now we can clear up by deleting our breakpoints and actions before quitting the debugger:

```
DB<37> B*
 Deleting all breakpoints...
DB<38> {*
 All { actions cleared.
DB<39>
```

And run off the end of the program using a final c:

```
DB<39> c
 11:  hard......14  soft......10  spec.......0
 12:  hard......11  soft.......6  spec.......0
 13:  hard......14  soft.......8  spec.......5
 14:  hard......11  soft.......8  spec.......3
 15:  hard.......0  soft.......0  spec.......0
 16:  hard......13  soft......10  spec.......1

<...multiple lines snipped...>

 123:  hard......15  soft......10  spec.......2
 124:  hard......12  soft.......9  spec.......0
```

```
  125:  hard......18  soft.......9  spec.......1
  126:  hard.......9  soft.......8  spec.......2
  127:  hard.......0  soft.......0  spec.......0
total:  hard    1454  soft      893  spec      17
```

```
Debugged program terminated.  Use q to quit or R to restart,
use O inhibit_exit to avoid stopping after program termination,
h q, h R or h O to get additional info.
DB<39>
```

And finally a single q to quit:

```
DB<39> q
 %>
```

Summary

In this chapter you have learned how to work with the most commonly used debugger motion commands. You've learned to move around a piece of a real program code and control its execution by setting and deleting conditional breakpoints to stop your program under certain circumstances.

You've also learned how to set up an action that is triggered when the program passes a particular line of code, and how to watch the variables and stop the program when their values change. You now have the skills to step in and over both subroutines and method calls, and you know how to continue to either the next stopping position or end of the program. For a list of all available commands, and many other options, see the reference section at the end of the book.

The rest of this book takes the reader through various real-life debugging scenarios and introduces many techniques along the way. In particular, the next chapter looks at a real debugging session of a Perl program.

CHAPTER 4

■ ■ ■

Debugging a Simple Command Line Program

Your mission, should you choose to accept it . . .

—Mission Impossible

This chapter builds on the first introductory chapters and continues our mission—learning to debug a simple Perl program. Our mission is not impossible, although at times it may feel like that. Take heart when you're faced with a swath of code exhibiting strange or unexpected behavior, whether written by someone else or yourself long ago—we're here to help.

We hope to show you several techniques for approaching the problem, and specifically, teach you that the debugger can make it easier for you to find bugs. After you've located and fixed the bugs, we will also show you how to take a `diff` between the buggy code and the fixed code, and, finally, how to apply a `patch` to the original source, so as to provide a complete solution.

■**Note** `diff` is a program that shows the difference between two files, and the resulting output can be redirected into a difference file for later usage. `patch` is a program that takes a difference file as input and applies it to an original file to produce a patched version. These programs are exceptionally useful to programmers, though the use of these programs is not restricted by them.

---

findvars

For the purposes of this chapter we will use the slightly flawed program, `findvars`, described in Listing 4-1.

This program is designed to discover all of the variables in your modules. When run with a list of modules as arguments, it will simply print the lines of code it finds—which in Perl includes variables which have a sigil in front of their names, such as scalars ($), hashes (%), arrays (@), and globs (*).

Listing 4-1. findvars

```perl
01 #!/usr/bin/perl
02
03 %INC = ();
04
05 use FileHandle;
06
07 map { eval "require $_;" } @ARGV;
08
09 my $regex = $ENV{REGEX} || '[\$\@\%\*]]+';
10
11 map { $files{$_} = FileHandle->new("< $INC{$_}") } keys %INC;
12
13 &getdata(%files);
14 &report(%data);
15
16 exit 0;
17
18 sub wanted {
19     return ($_[0] =~ /$regex/ && $_[0] !~ /^\s*\*\#/ ? 1 : 0);
20 }
21
22 sub getdata {
23     my %files = @_;
24     foreach my $f (keys %files) {
25         $cnt = 0;
26         my $fh = $files{$f};
27         while (<$fh>) {
28             ++$cnt;
29             $data{$f}{$cnt} = $_ if &wanted;
30         }
31     }
32 }
33
34 sub report {
35     my %data = @_;
36     foreach my $k (sort keys %data) {
37         print "\n$k vars:\n";
38         foreach my $r (sort { $a <=> $b } keys %{$data{$k}}) {
39             print "\t[$r]\t$data{$k}{$r}";
40         }
41     }
42 }
43
44 __END__
45
46 =head1 NAME
```

```
47
48 findvars - display variables in loaded packages
49
50 =head1 SYNOPSIS
51
52     findvars [modulenames]+
53
54 =head1 DESCRIPTION
55
56 Given a list of module names, find and display all variables found.
57
58 =head1 REGEX
59
60 The regex to find variables is fairly: C<[$@%*]> by default.
61 To define another one, set the C<REGEX="xxx"> enviroment variable,
62 where C<xxx> is the regular expression to use.
63
64 =head1 NOTES
65
66 Note that although we ignore directly commented out lines,
67 we slurp up C<pod> indiscriminately.
68
69 =cut
70
```

An Example Run

We're going to cheat slightly by first digging out and executing a working version of findvars using three modules. Namely, we'll use the popular CGI module, a missing library called MissingModule, and finally the English module by passing them as parameters like this:

```
%> findvars CGI MissingModule English
```

which should ideally produce something like the following output:

```
CGI.pm vars:
    [21]    $CGI::revision = '$Id: 05.pod,v 1.10 2004/11/07 11:35:22 $';
    [22]    $CGI::VERSION=3.04;
    [36]     local $^W = 0;
    [37]      $TAINTED = substr("$0$^X",0,0);
    [40]    my @SAVED_SYMBOLS;
    <...snip...>
Carp.pm vars:
    [3]     our $VERSION = '1.02';
    [59]    packages explicitly marked as safe by inclusion in @CARP_NOT, or
    [60]    (if that array is empty) @ISA.  The ability to override what
    [61]    @ISA says is new in 5.8.
    [66]    trusts C, then A trusts C.  So if you do not override @ISA
    <...snip...>
```

```
English.pm vars:
    [3]     our $VERSION = '1.01';
    [6]     @ISA = (Exporter);
    [17]        if ($ERRNO =~ /denied/) { ... }
    [23]    which get triggered just by accessing them (like $0) will still
    [28]    the C<$/> variable can be referred to either $RS or
    <...snip...>
```

As you can see from the previous correct output, the program doesn't parse just the module itself, but also all the modules that are use'd or require'd by the modules themselves. We also get the line number of the file in each case.

The Problem

The problem is that when we run *our* program, using the same arguments, we get no output whatsoever:

```
%> perl ./findvars CGI MissingModule English
%>
```

The Mission

The mission, in this case, is to find out what's wrong and fix it.

Running findvars Under the Debugger

Our command for running our program under the debugger is similar to the one shown previously, and consists simply of giving the -d switch to Perl as a command line argument, like this:

```
%> perl -d findvars CGI MissingModule English
Loading DB routines from perl5db.pl version 1.27
Editor support available.
Enter h or 'h h' for help, or 'man perldebug' for more help.
main::(findvars:3):     %INC = ();
  DB<1>
```

The debugger has loaded our code, stopped at the first executable statement, and is now waiting for commands to execute on our behalf.

First, we list the code from our current position, to orient ourselves:

```
DB<1> l
    3==>    %INC = ();
    4
    5:      use FileHandle;
    6
    7:      map { eval "require $_;" } @ARGV;
    8
    9:      my $regex = $ENV{REGEX} || '[\$\@\%\*]&+';
    10
```

```
   11:     map { $files{$_} = FileHandle->new("< $INC{$_}") } keys %INC;
   12
DB<1>
```

You can see that the current location pointer (==>) is pointing from line number 3, to the %INC = (); code, confirming the line information we were given on startup. Then follows the next nine lines of code.

Checking the Input

One of the primary rules of debugging is to never assume anything. Therefore, we're going to start by checking the arguments the program received from the command line to make sure that we are working with the correct data. To do that, we simply dump the @ARGV array:

```
DB<1> x \@ARGV
   0   ARRAY(0x817e564)
 0  'CGI'
 1  'MissingModule'
 2  'English'
DB<2>
```

Note that the x (dump) command can be much clearer than the p (print) command when displaying arrays and hashes. Otherwise, all the elements of the array or hash get run together in one long string. Whenever you have a complex data structure to display, you should almost always use the x command instead of the p command.

Comparing Before and After

Lest anyone think, with a cursory look at the preceding code, that the %INC hash will always include the FileHandle module because the %INC = () statement comes first, remember that use is a compiletime directive. That is to say, the FileHandle module is already loaded, and when we empty the %INC hash, we don't actually remove FileHandle from Perl space. Instead, we literally just remove it from the %INC hash for the dubious purposes of our program.

Before

Let's take a quick look at our %INC hash before we do anything:

```
DB<2> x \%INC
   0   HASH(0x8171ea4)
 'Carp.pm' => '/opt/perl/lib/5.8.5/Carp.pm'
 'Carp/Heavy.pm' => '/opt/perl/lib/5.8.5/Carp/Heavy.pm'
 'Exporter.pm' => '/opt/perl/lib/5.8.5/Exporter.pm'
 'Exporter/Heavy.pm' => '/opt/perl/lib/5.8.5/Exporter/Heavy.pm'
 'Fcntl.pm' => '/opt/perl/lib/5.8.5/i686-linux/Fcntl.pm'
 'File/Glob.pm' => '/opt/perl/lib/5.8.5/i686-linux/File/Glob.pm'
 'File/Spec.pm' => '/opt/perl/lib/5.8.5/File/Spec.pm'
 'File/Spec/Unix.pm' => '/opt/perl/lib/5.8.5/File/Spec/Unix.pm'
 'FileHandle.pm' => '/opt/perl/lib/5.8.5/FileHandle.pm'
 'IO.pm' => '/opt/perl/lib/5.8.5/i686-linux/IO.pm'
```

```
 'IO/File.pm' => '/opt/perl/lib/5.8.5/i686-linux/IO/File.pm'
 'IO/Handle.pm' => '/opt/perl/lib/5.8.5/i686-linux/IO/Handle.pm'
 'IO/Seekable.pm' => '/opt/perl/lib/5.8.5/i686-linux/IO/Seekable.pm'
 'SelectSaver.pm' => '/opt/perl/lib/5.8.5/SelectSaver.pm'
 'Symbol.pm' => '/opt/perl/lib/5.8.5/Symbol.pm'
 'Term/Cap.pm' => '/opt/perl/lib/5.8.5/Term/Cap.pm'
 'Term/ReadLine.pm' => '/opt/perl/lib/5.8.5/Term/ReadLine.pm'
 'XSLoader.pm' => '/opt/perl/lib/5.8.5/i686-linux/XSLoader.pm'
 'attributes.pm' => '/opt/perl/lib/5.8.5/attributes.pm'
 'dumpvar.pl' => '/opt/perl/lib/5.8.5/dumpvar.pl'
 'perl5db.pl' => '/opt/perl/lib/5.8.5/perl5db.pl'
 'strict.pm' => '/opt/perl/lib/5.8.5/strict.pm'
 'vars.pm' => '/opt/perl/lib/5.8.5/vars.pm'
 'warnings.pm' => '/opt/perl/lib/5.8.5/warnings.pm'
 'warnings/register.pm' => '/opt/perl/lib/5.8.5/warnings/register.pm'
DB<2>
```

There are quite a lot of libraries already loaded, and they all come from either our use FileHandle statement, or the debugger itself. Having taken a look at the current state of affairs, next we can run down to line 9, which will ensure our program has run line line 7, which loads or reloads all the requested modules:

```
DB<2> c 9
    main::(findvars:9):      my $regex = $ENV{REGEX} || '[\$\@\%\*]]+';
DB<3>
```

After

Now let's have another look at our %INC hash:

```
DB<3> x \%INC
    0   HASH(0x8171ea4)
 'CGI.pm' => '/opt/perl/lib/5.8.5/CGI.pm'
 'CGI/Util.pm' => '/opt/perl/lib/5.8.5/CGI/Util.pm'
 'Carp.pm' => '/opt/perl/lib/5.8.5/Carp.pm'
 'English.pm' => '/opt/perl/lib/5.8.5/English.pm'
 'Exporter.pm' => '/opt/perl/lib/5.8.5/Exporter.pm'
 'constant.pm' => '/opt/perl/lib/5.8.5/constant.pm'
 'overload.pm' => '/opt/perl/lib/5.8.5/overload.pm'
 'strict.pm' => '/opt/perl/lib/5.8.5/strict.pm'
 'vars.pm' => '/opt/perl/lib/5.8.5/vars.pm'
 'warnings.pm' => '/opt/perl/lib/5.8.5/warnings.pm'
 'warnings/register.pm' => '/opt/perl/lib/5.8.5/warnings/register.pm'
DB<4>
```

You'll see that there's quite a difference from our original, with 11 libraries instead of 16 this time.

Let's just ensure that although FileHandle has been unfairly removed from the %INC hash, we still have access to all the code. We can do this by using the S command to ask the debugger to print us a list of all the subroutines that match the FileHandle pattern. We'll use a case-*in*sensitive search pattern because we're lazy:

```
DB<4> S (?i:filehan)
    CGI::to_filehandle
    FileHandle::BEGIN
    FileHandle::import
    FileHandle::pipe
 DB<5>
```

As you can see, the FileHandle library code is still accessible, which is just as well, because we're going to need this code later. This is because the Perl interpreter still knows all about the code that was originally loaded, but the %INC hash, which is effectively a utility provided by the Perl interpreter, doesn't. Think of it as an out-of-date report, rather than an on-the-fly query.

Examining Internal Variables

Coming back to our program, we can step over line 9, which sets our $regex variable, using n:

```
DB<5> n
    main::(findvars:11):    map { $files{$_} = FileHandle->new("< $INC{$_}") }
keys %INC;
DB<5>
```

Now we should print the $regex to check that it has either the value we set, (which we have not done explicitly in this case), or the default value set by the program itself:

```
DB<5> p $regex
    [\$\@\%\*]&+
DB<6>
```

Hmmm—that regex doesn't look particularly good. It looks as though the & has gotten itself stuck on the outside of the character set. We can check this briefly against what we want to actually match by simply running a couple of Perl commands. Remember, we're effectively in a Perl shell here, so we'll set up a command to print yup($1)\n if we match, and to print nope\n otherwise.

Should match:

```
DB<6> p ('this $string' =~ /($regex)/ ? "yup($1)\n" : "nope\n")
nope
```

Should not match:

```
DB<7> p ('this string' =~ /($regex)/ ? "yup($1)\n" : "nope\n")
nope
```

Should match:

```
DB<9> p ('this $&string' =~ /($regex)/ ? "yup($1)\n" : "nope\n")
yup($&)
```

Well, as suspected, that wasn't what we wanted. Let's change the regex, here and now, to something that looks more correct:

```
DB<10> $regex = '[\$\@\%\*\&]+'
DB<11>
```

Now we'll run those commands again, to see whether our regex has really been modified the way we wanted it to be. This time we'll take advantage of our history list to ensure we run exactly the same commands, and not some slight variation introduced by mistyping something. First we need to know the numbers of each command:

```
DB<11> H
    9: p ('this $&string' =~ /($regex)/ ? "yup($1)\n" : "nope\n")
    8: p ('this string' =~ /($regex)/ ? "yup($1)\n" : "nope\n")
    7: p ('this $string' =~ /($regex)/ ? "yup($1)\n" : "nope\n")
    6: p $regex
    5: S (?i:filehan)
    4: x \%INC
    3: c 9
    2: x \%INC
    1: x \@ARGV
DB<11>
```

Now we can run the commands themselves.
Should match:

```
DB<11> !7
p ('this $string' =~ /($regex)/ ? "yup($1)\n" : "nope\n")
yup($)
```

Should not match:

```
DB<12> !8
p ('this string' =~ /($regex)/ ? "yup($1)\n" : "nope\n")
nope
```

Should match:

```
DB<13> !9
p ('this $&string' =~ /($regex)/ ? "yup($1)\n" : "nope\n")
yup($&)
```

Good, that looks much better. We need to remember to make a note to change the regex to accurately reflect what we want to match against later. But, having fixed the problem in our current (runtime) code, for the moment we can continue.

Looping Through %INC

The next line is going to use map to loop through the keys from %INC and create a %files hash with module names for keys and opened filehandles for values. We can even take a look at the %INC keys first if we wish. We don't even have to be clever, and use a debugger command—instead we can simply ask Perl to print them out, joined by something to separate them easily:

```
DB<14> print join(', ', keys %INC)
    warnings/register.pm, English.pm, warnings.pm, CGI/Util.pm, Carp.pm, vars.pm,
    strict.pm, Exporter.pm, constant.pm, overload.pm, CGI.pm
  DB<14>
```

Now, although the mapping statement is a single line, it unrolls to a for loop, and because each loop is in fact a separate statement, this means we can step through it using the n command. This way, we can inspect the %files hash as it is built. To demonstrate this, let's take several steps at once:

```
DB<14> n
    main::(findvars:11):    map { $files{$_} =
            FileHandle->new("< $INC{$_}") } keys %INC;
DB<14> n
    main::(findvars:11):    map { $files{$_} =
            FileHandle->new("< $INC{$_}") } keys %INC;
DB<14> n
    main::(findvars:11):    map { $files{$_} =
            FileHandle->new("< $INC{$_}") } keys %INC;
DB<14>
```

Now we can take a look at our %files hash:

```
DB<14> x \%files
    0  HASH(0x839b4f0)
 'English.pm' => FileHandle=GLOB(0x853db90)
    -> *Symbol::GEN1
            FileHandle({*Symbol::GEN1}) => fileno(8)
 'warnings/register.pm' => FileHandle=GLOB(0x853dde8)
    -> *Symbol::GEN0
            FileHandle({*Symbol::GEN0}) => fileno(7)
DB<15>
```

This looks fairly promising, because the %INC keys are clearly setting the %files keys. Also, the appropriate %INC values (the location of the file itself) are being accepted by the read-only FileHandle-new statement and returning the appropriate (opened) filehandle, which in turn is setting the matching %files values. Note that if FileHandle fails to open the file for any reason, we would receive the undefined value instead.

Error Handling

Before we continue, let's just take a quick look at the piece of code in the middle of that harmless-looking eval command:

```
map { eval "require $_;" } @ARGV;
```

Although the eval seems to be working fine in our case, because of the lack of error-checking in our code, we won't actually know whether these modules are being opened for reading or not—until we receive a "failure to read a file" error message further downstream where it might be more awkward to catch.

This is exactly why there is never any feedback concerning our nonexistent MissingModule. The program just glides serenely past with no worries whatsoever—which may be what is wanted.

On the one hand, it may not be appropriate for this eval command to use the classic or die("unable to open $filename: $!") alternation. Indeed, in our case, we could reasonably argue that Perl has already opened these files via useing them, so perhaps the check is redundant. On the other hand, silently failing always tends to look suspiciously like sloppy programming.

Lest anyone think this is a silly example, let it be known that we've seen this in *production* code on multiple occasions, even when the operation is critical to further progress. Believe it or not, the responsible programmers never checked to make sure that the file open was successful—seriously!

It would be far better to give feedback of some sort, like

```
map { eval "require $_;"
    or print STDERR "Warning: unable to require $_: $@"
} @ARGV;
```

which would produce a message something along these lines:

```
Warning: unable to require MissingModule:
  Can't locate MissingModule.pm in @INC (@INC contains:
    /opt/perl/lib/5.8.5/i686-linux /opt/perl/lib/5.8.5
    /opt/perl/lib/site_perl/5.8.5/i686-linux .)
    at (eval 4) line 1.
```

Nevertheless, returning to the current program, we appear to be progressing nicely, so let's use the c command to trundle down to line 13, where we can take a look at our final %files hash:

```
DB<2> c 13
    main::(findvars:13):    &getdata(%files);
DB<4>
```

Checking Progress

Before we go any further, we can dump out our entire %files structure, and see whether we have all the expected filehandles stored away for future use:

```
DB<15> x \%files
    0  HASH(0x839b4f0)
 'CGI.pm' => FileHandle=GLOB(0x848888c)
    -> *Symbol::GEN10
          FileHandle({*Symbol::GEN10}) => fileno(18)
 'CGI/Util.pm' => FileHandle=GLOB(0x848e368)
    -> *Symbol::GEN3
          FileHandle({*Symbol::GEN3}) => fileno(11)
    <...snip...>
 'warnings.pm' => FileHandle=GLOB(0x848e524)
    -> *Symbol::GEN2
          FileHandle({*Symbol::GEN2}) => fileno(10)
 'warnings/register.pm' => FileHandle=GLOB(0x848e350)
    -> *Symbol::GEN0
          FileHandle({*Symbol::GEN0}) => fileno(8)
DB<15>
```

At this point, the dumped hash reference is moderately large, and you'll find that on a typical real-life program, the output may well scroll to fill several screens or more. Naturally, it would be nice if it was possible to control the throughput of data, and happily, the debugger lets you do this, too. In order to do this, you can simply use a pager. A pager is an external command that controls data throughput, for more convenient viewing.

If you want to check each value of the x \%files command, this is a good time to use the | pager command to pipe the output of the code dump through your pager, with a command like

```
| x \%files.
```
...

An alternative, if you are not interested in seeing the entire dumped structure, but perhaps just the first couple of elements for example, would be to restrict the dump to your numerical value of choice, by using the hashDepth option. Note that the debugger offers a number of options dealing with how variables may be dumped, including the following:

- arraydepth: This option shows you how deep to dump an array with the x command.

- compactdump: This option shows you how much whitespace to use when printing dumped data.

- dumpdepth: This option shows you how deep to dump a hash.

- dumpdfiles: This option shows you how to dump a debugger source file with X and V.

- dumpreused: This option shows you how to dump reused memory addresses. You need to be paranoid about self-referential (infinite recursion) memory loops.

- verycompact: This option allows you to use even less whitespace when printing.

To find out more about the options available, use the help command h o, read through the debug and debguts manpages, and take a look at Chapter 15.

In the current case, setting the hashDepth to a value of 2 would probably be appropriate, so the command should be

```
DB<15> o hashDepth=2
    hashDepth = '2'
DB<16>
```

Remember that we could have used hashdep as a unique short form for this option. But for the sake of setting a proper example, we should specify the entire case-sensitive option correctly. Now when we use the x command to dump a hash reference, we'll only go two keys deep:

```
DB<16> x \%files
   0  HASH(0x839b4f0)
 'CGI.pm' => FileHandle=GLOB(0x848888c)
    -> *Symbol::GEN10
          FileHandle({*Symbol::GEN10}) => fileno(18)
 'CGI/Util.pm' => FileHandle=GLOB(0x848e368)
    -> *Symbol::GEN3
          FileHandle({*Symbol::GEN3}) => fileno(11)
  ....
DB<17>
```

This ability to limit the hash depth can be useful in cases with very complex hash or object structures, especially if the objects have references to other objects.

Returning again to our %files hash, each of our modules has an associated filehandle, so at this stage, that looks fine. Now might be a good time to take a look at where we are by using the . reset pointer command:

```
DB<17> .
    main::(findvars:13):    &getdata(%files);
DB<17>
```

Remember that this never actually executes anything, and that you can safely use this command at any time, as we have just done, to establish your current position visually and to reorient yourself. Note that this will also reset your *debugger display context* to the executed line. We will see where this point is relevant shortly.

Now let's use s to step into the getdata subroutine:

```
DB<17> s
    main::getdata(findvars:23):              my %files = @_;
DB<17>
```

Followed by an l to list our code to see what we're about to execute:

```
DB<17> l
    23==>           my %files = @_;
    24:             foreach my $f (keys %files) {
    25:                     $cnt = 0;
    26:                     my $fh = $files{$f};
    27:                     while (<$fh>) {
    28:                             ++$cnt;
    29:                             $data{$f}{$cnt} = $_ if &wanted;
    30                      }
    31              }
    32      }
    33
DB<17>
```

Now we can see we've passed in our %files hash via the subroutine arguments, and the contents will get assigned to the lexical my %files at line 23.

Setting a Breakpoint

At this point, we place a breakpoint at line 27, which will stop our program before each file is processed. This way, we can process one file at a time, and see what happens to our %data hash each time.

```
DB<17> b 27
DB<18>
```

Using c we can run down to the breakpoint we just set:

```
DB<18> c
    main::getdata(findvars:27):                      while (<$fh>) {
DB<18>
```

Let's also print out the value of the filehandle we're using to verify that it contains a valid filehandle:

```
DB<19> x $fh
   0  FileHandle=GLOB(0x847dbf8)
 -> *Symbol::GEN0
      FileHandle({*Symbol::GEN0}) => fileno(8)
DB<19>
```

Our recently set breakpoint is inside the foreach my $f (keys %files) loop, so continuing until the next breakpoint will bring us back to our current position. (We have several files to process here, so we can afford to be a bit wasteful with our data.) Let's do that now to see what happens:

```
DB<20> c
   main::getdata(findvars:27):                          while (<$fh>) {
DB<20>
```

Now we can look at our %data hash, to see the data we have picked up:

```
DB<20> x \%data
   0  HASH(0x83b7a94)
   empty hash
DB<21>
```

Hmmm, nothing at all—that doesn't look good.

Let's run around our loop again, because we don't quite believe this, by using c once more:

```
DB<21> c
   main::getdata(findvars:27):                          while (<$fh>) {
DB<21>
```

And print out the %data structure once more.

```
DB<21> x \%data
   0  HASH(0x83b7a94)
   empty hash
DB<22>
```

Maybe we need to approach this with more of a plan, by looking at the source code in the file, before it is parsed.

Inspecting the Contents of a Loaded Library File

Before looking at the contents of a loaded file, let's see the name of the module we're going to look at next, by printing the contents of our $f variable:

```
DB<22> p $f
   English.pm
DB<23>
```

Because we are using loaded modules in this program, Perl already knows all about them and can actually help us to look at our input data. We can have a look at the contents of our input file, by using the f command, and giving the filename we wish to inspect as an argument:

```
DB<23> f English
    Choosing /opt/perl/lib/5.8.5/English.pm matching 'English':
    1         package English;
    2
    3:        our $VERSION = '1.01';
    4
    5:        require Exporter;
    6:        @ISA = (Exporter);
    7
    8         =head1 NAME
    9         10
DB<24>
```

Our file looks OK, and we know there are variables to be found as we loop through the next several lines of our code, so why does our subroutine appear unable to find any? It's possible that something could be wrong with the loop. How about printing out the line of code as we read it? That way we can see if our code actually has any data to work with.

Setting an Action

We can do this by setting an action for line 28:

```
DB<24> a 28 print "$f line: $_"
    Line 28() does not have an action?
DB<25>
```

Whoa there! The reason for this error is that we are in the English.pm module at the moment, and evidently it doesn't have a line 28 that we can set an action on. That is, line 28 in the English.pm module is not *breakable*. An action is related to a breakpoint in that the debugger inspects an internal data structure to check whether a particular line has an action or a breakpoint on it before it is executed. You can only have an action or breakpoint if there is code to set the breakpoint against, in other words, if the line is *breakable*.

What we should do first, is to reset our display pointer, and our context, by using the . command.

```
DB<25> .
```

Now we can try to set our action again:

```
DB<25> a 28 print "$f line: $_"
DB<26>
```

This time (although we get no feedback) the action has silently been registered. Remember that an action does not stop the debugger, but simply tells it to do something at a particular position.

Now we can use c to run round the file loop. Each time we pass line 28 the debugger will print out the line we are reading from the file. Then we'll stop at the first breakpoint we hit, which will be on our next file.

```
DB<26> c
    line: package English;
    line:
    line: our $VERSION = '1.01';
    line:
    line: require Exporter;
    line: @ISA = (Exporter);
    line:
    <...snip...>
    line:
    line: # *ARRAY_BASE                          = *[   ;
    line: # *OFMT                                = *#   ;
    line: # *MULTILINE_MATCHING                  = **   ;
    line: # *OLD_PERL_VERSION                    = *]   ;
    line:
    line: 1;
    main::getdata(findvars:27):                  while (<$fh>) {
DB<26>
```

It looks good; we can see that we are reading our file. Now we'll dump the %data structure, and we should now see all our filtered data stored ready for reporting on.

```
DB<26> x \%data
    0  HASII(0x83b7a94)
    empty hash
DB<27>
```

Still nothing!

Clearly the data is available, but our program still has a problem accessing it. Let's step back and remind ourselves of the contents of the getdata subroutine, so that we don't have to keep flipping back several pages to see what's going on.

```
DB<27> l getdata
    22      sub getdata {
    23:         my %files = @_;
    24:         foreach my $f (keys %files) {
    25:             $cnt = 0;
    26:             my $fh = $files{$f};
    27==>b         while (<$fh>) {
    28                 ++$cnt;
    29:a               $data{$f}{$cnt} = $_ if &wanted;
    30             }
    31         }
    32      }
DB<28>
```

We should also print out which file we will be looking at next:

```
DB<28> p $f
    constant.pm
DB<29>
```

Inspecting the Arguments to a Subroutine

We appear to be looking at the correct files, and we can even see each line of data as we read it from the clearly valid filehandle. We just seem to fail with the assignment if &wanted, so let's use l subname to take a proper look at the wanted subroutine.

```
DB<29> l wanted
    18        sub wanted {
    19:               return ($_[0] =~ /$regex/ && $_[0] !~ /^\s*\#/ ? 1 : 0);
    20        }
DB<30>
```

Hmmm, the subroutine appears to be using the arguments directly, without dereferencing them first. If you don't explicitly dereference subroutine arguments by placing them into a variable explicitly (usually, but not exclusively, using shift), these arguments are still accessible to the subroutine under a specially named array: @_. This means we can still take a look at the data in the subroutine parameters without going through the overhead of copying them into another variable. We'll set another action to inspect the inputs, so that we can see what is being sent (from line 28), and what is being received (at line 19).

```
DB<30> a 19 print "wanted(@_)\n"
DB<31>
```

Note the addition of the newline in our action, in contrast to our first action, where we were taking advantage of the fact that the input data had a newline already.

Having set our action on line 19, we don't have to run through the entire file. We can simply continue straight down there and take a look at the first set of parameters our subroutine is receiving. We've split the output over separate lines for easier reading.

```
DB<31> c 19
    line: package vars;
      wanted(
            Carp.pm FileHandle=GLOB(0x8478d74)
            warnings/register.pm FileHandle=GLOB(0x847da70)
            English.pm FileHandle=GLOB(0x84f6b40)
            Exporter.pm FileHandle=GLOB(0x84158c8)
            strict.pm FileHandle=GLOB(0x847d9b0)
            vars.pm FileHandle=GLOB(0x83026ec)
            constant.pm FileHandle=GLOB(0x84157a8)
            warnings.pm FileHandle=GLOB(0x847dc44)
            CGI/Util.pm FileHandle=GLOB(0x847da88)
            overload.pm FileHandle=GLOB(0x8476ef8)
            CGI.pm FileHandle=GLOB(0x8478d14)
      )
DB<32>
```

That looks like our problem. Even though the line read is correct (from the original file), the wanted input appears to be the modulename=filehandle keypairs from our %files hash! Clearly the arguments being passed are all wrong.

Let's have another look at the calling statement. We can do this just as easily from within the wanted subroutine, as we can from our calling context. We simply list the code using l with just the line number as an argument:

```
DB<32> l 29
    29:a            $data{$f}{$cnt} = $_ if &wanted;
DB<33>
```

Looking at this in the cold light of day, the call does look a bit suspicious in that there are no arguments explicitly passed. Perhaps the programmer thought that Perl's ubiquitous $_ would be passed as the default or implicit argument to the subroutine, if no explicit parameter was offered. It's time to RTFM: *Read The Fine Manual.*

Consulting the Documentation

We don't have to leave the debugger session to consult the documentation. We can just call the documentation up from our current session. If we don't know which manpage to look up, we could start with a command like perldoc perltoc, which would give us the perldoc TOC (Table Of Contents). See perldoc perltoc and Chapter 16 for more information on the vast repository of included documentation that comes with every Perl installation.

However, we like to live life on the edge here, and we're simply going to make a logical guess. If we want to look up information about subroutines in Perl, we know there might just be a manpage called perlsub. So the command we're going to try looks like this:

```
DB<33> doc perlsub
    Reformatting perlsub(1), please wait...
DB<34>
```

Sure enough, there is such a command (we checked), and it should bring up the requested documentation within the appropriate pager.

You can now either scroll through reading the whole thing, or you can search for a particular word or phrase using the facilities available within your particular pager. In our case, we're using less, and we can search by using a forward slash with our search term, just like in the debugger. If we happen to omit to specify any parameters, perhaps something unexpected might happen, so let's look for any phrase with the word omit in it:

```
/omit
If a subroutine is called using the "&" form, the argument list is
optional, and if omitted, no @_ array is set up for the subroutine: the @_
array at the time of the call is visible to subroutine instead. This is
an efficiency mechanism that new users may wish to avoid.
```

The paragraph we find appears to explain exactly what is going on with our subroutine call. So we need to go back and fix our code to explicitly pass a parameter to the wanted function.

Quit the pager using whatever method is most appropriate, probably a simple q, to return to the debugger prompt:

```
q
DB<34>
```

Checking the Proposed Solution

We can see what might happen, before changing any code, by simply calling our wanted subroutine with an explicit argument, and seeing how it behaves. Alongside the action we set up earlier to print out the value that was passed in, we could also print out the return value, for reference. First, let's try it with a couple of special characters:

```
DB<34> p &wanted('pid: [$$]')
    wanted(pid: [$$])
    1
DB<35>
```

Next we might try it without any funny characters to see how that behaves in contrast:

```
DB<35> p &wanted('pid')
    wanted(pid)
    0
DB<36>
```

That about settles it. It is easy to see that the wanted subroutine is not receiving the argument the original programmer thought it was. This will need to be fixed before the program can continue, by passing the (implicit to the while loop) $_ variable directly to the subroutine as an explicit parameter.

Exploring Restart Possibilities

While it is possible to simply redefine this subroutine directly from the debugger command line itself, the fact that the debugger is actually sitting right in the middle of this subroutine currently, and has actions and breakpoints set which affect it, changes the available choices somewhat. It is necessary to step out, or backwards, from the current position and to replace this subroutine with a new definition, otherwise the debugger will get frustrated while it tries to work out where it was, where it is going, and what it's going to do once it gets there.

There are a couple of realistic choices as to how this can be accomplished.

- Start over: Quit, change the source code in the errant file manually (presumably a copy of production code), and start our debugger session completely fresh again from the beginning, trying to remember all the commands we entered to return to our current position.

- Restart: Save our current session, edit the code on-the-fly, use the debugger to restart our session, and let it run a subset of our commands for us to return to this point.

- Rerun: Simply use the built-in rerun [-[n]] command to rerun this session to the current position, or to a particular previous stage in the history list.

Starting over is perhaps the simplest, but the most inelegant and clunky solution, while rerunning demands is merely a passing acquaintance with a couple of debugger commands.

But the debugger is what we're here to learn about, so we'll run through the process of restarting our session completely within the debugger itself.

This has the added advantage that even though we are going the change the code, we still don't have to actually change the source code on disk itself.

Modifying the Code Harmlessly

Even in the debugger, it is not possible to change a single line of code, per se, but we can change a subroutine with comparative ease. If, for example, we wished to change the wanted subroutine, because it's quite short and would easily fit on a single line, we could quite simply type something like this into the debugger command prompt:

```
sub wanted { return 1 if $_[0] =~ /\w+/ }
```

Doing this ensures the subroutine is modified to return every line with an alphanumeric in it. However, because it's the calling routine that needs changing, and firstly the debugger context is currently within the subroutine and secondly we need to change a subroutine of 11 lines, this is going to leave a lot of room for error to creep in by the time we've finished typing it all in. We should really redefine this subroutine in a place where we can access it in a less error-prone fashion.

Note that the debugger will even accept a multi-line command, if the newline is escaped, but if we need to backslash every line of an 11-line subroutine, we're probably going to be here for a while typing this all out cleanly without any errors. The best solution would be to copy the errant subroutine into a separate file, and then to modify it, so that the wanted call looks like this:

```
$data{$f}{$cnt} = $_ if &wanted($_);
```

Next we'll load the entire new subroutine into the debugger, at the appropriate time, with a Perl do statement.

Storing Our Command History and Restarting the Debugger

The first thing to do is to store our current command history set, by using the save fn command, where fn is the filename to save the commands to. For our example we'll use the file current_perldb. If you don't use a filename, the debugger will save your commands to the default .perl5dbrc file instead.

```
DB<36> save current_perldb
DB<37>
```

The file is created and written to, if it does not already exist.

Now that the command history is safe, let's go to another terminal or text editor window, and write the newsub file with the following new definition of the getdata subroutine. You'll notice that only line 8 has changed to include the explicit passing of the $_ parameter to the wanted function call:

```
sub getdata {
    my %files = @_;
    foreach my $f (keys %files) {
        $cnt = 0;
        my $fh = $files{$f};
        while (<$fh>) {
            ++$cnt;
            $data{$f}{$cnt} = $_ if &wanted($_);
        }
    }
};
```

Now we want to use the R command to restart the debugger, and to send it back to the beginning of the current session. We'll be using all the same command line arguments and environment as when we started:

```
DB<37> R
Warning: some settings and command line options may be lost!
Loading DB routines from perl5db.pl version 1.27
Editor support available.
Enter h or 'h h' for help, or 'man perldebug' for more help.
main::(findvars:3):    %INC = ();
  DB<37>
```

You can usually ignore the Warning: some settings ... may be lost! message, because the debugger is actually quite good at resetting all variables to the appropriate values—but it is wise to be cautious all the same.

Rerunning Earlier Debugger Commands

Before we start running the saved debugger commands in the file current_perldb, we should first check that it is actually going to do exactly what we want, not least because we don't wish to end up at exactly the same place as before. Remember, we want to stop just *before* we descend into the getdata subroutine, then we want to *modify* it before running it.

So, it's back into a text editor to remove the last several lines from our command history. We'll remove the lines to the point before we descended into getdata with the s command. The file should now look something like this:

```
l
x \@ARGV
x \%INC
c 9
x \%INC
S (?i:filehan)
n
p $regex
p join(', ', keys %INC)
n
n
n
x \%files
l
c 13
| x %files
.
```

That's a lot to try to remember (and to retype without making a mistake, from memory). Fortunately the debugger can run these commands one after the other, from the beginning of our session automatically, by using the source command. All the commands in the file will be run, and if there was a command which required input, to quit an external pager program for instance (as may be the case in this example), then the appropriate input should be entered at the correct time:

```
DB<37> source current_perldb
>> #source .perl5dbrc
>> l
3==>    %INC = ();
4
5:      use FileHandle;
6
7:      map { eval "require $_;" } @ARGV;
8
9:      my $regex = $ENV{REGEX} || '[\$\@\%\*]&+';
10
11:     map { $files{$_} = FileHandle->new("< $INC{$_}") } keys %INC;
12
>> x \@ARGV
0  ARRAY(0x817d79c)
   0  'CGI'
   1  'MissingModule'
   2  'English'
>> x \%INC
0  HASH(0x8171124)
   'Carp.pm' => '/opt/perl/lib/5.8.5/Carp.pm'
   'Carp/Heavy.pm' => '/opt/perl/lib/5.8.5/Carp/Heavy.pm'
   'Exporter.pm' => '/opt/perl/lib/5.8.5/Exporter.pm'
<...snip...>
   20  'CGI.pm'
21 FileHandle=GLOB(0x8507e0c)
   -> *Symbol::GEN10
         FileHandle({*Symbol::GEN10}) => fileno(18)
>> .
main::(findvars:13):    &getdata(%files);
  DB<54>
```

The commands have all been run, and you can see each command prefixed by the special source command prompt (>>) as it is entered and executed, and then the output of the command then follows. The debugger stops just before the getdata subroutine call at line 13.

Before changing anything, use l getdata to take a listing of the current getdata definition:

```
DB<54> l getdata
   22       sub getdata {
   23:              my %files = @_;
   24:              foreach my $f (sort keys %files) {
   25:                      $cnt = 0;
   26:                      my $fh = $files{$f};
   27:                      while (<$fh>) {
   28:                              ++$cnt;
   29:                              $data{$f}{$cnt} = $_ if &wanted;
   30                       }
```

```
     31                      }
     32        }
DB<55>
```

Now is the time to replace the existing version of the getdata subroutine. Overwrite the definition in the symbol table by running the newsub file that was prepared earlier. Bear in mind, the only reason went through the entire Restart sequence was to avoid having to type.

Remember too, anything that doesn't look like a debugger command is sent to Perl for evaluation. For example, when the do 'newsub' command is entered at the prompt, and this is not recognized as a valid debugger command, Perl gets a chance to evaluate it. Here is the command:

```
DB<55> do 'newsub'
DB<56>
```

Now use the l getdata command to list the code, both to determine what Perl thinks of the new subroutine, and to confirm that the new definition has been accepted:

```
DB<56> l getdata
     Switching to file '../newsub'.
     1          sub getdata {
     2:                 my %files = @_;
     3:                 foreach my $f (keys %files) {
     4:                         $cnt = 0;
     5:                         my $fh = $files{$f};
     6:                         while (<$fh>) {
     7:                                 ++$cnt;
     8:                                 $data{$f}{$cnt} = $_ if &wanted($_);
     9                         }
     10                }
     11        }
DB<57>
```

Our change has taken effect. In the code listing, line 8 of the subroutine now has the explicit parameter passing that was missing from the original version.

At this stage, checking to see exactly the arguments that are being set and received would be sensible, as this will confirm whether the modified code really fixes the problems that we observed. The following command will do this for the newsub subroutine. Note that it is necessary to use the line number 9 here, because the context is currently the newsub file:

```
DB<57> a 8 print "sending($_)\n"
DB<58>
```

Now it would be sensible to return to the findvars context before assigning an action to the code associated with this file. Note that in the more usual case of assigning actions and breakpoints (and so on) to code, this is not an issue, because the files have a namespace and it is possible, and indeed necessary, to use this as the defining context. Simply because we are overwriting code defined in an existing file out of the %INC hash, with code defined in the new subroutine definition file which has suddenly appeared from nowhere (as far as the debugger is concerned), it is necessary to explictly change context. The familiar . command is all that is required to reset the current context:

```
DB<58> .
    main::(findvars:13):    &getdata(%files);
DB<58>
```

This brings the debugger back to the findvars file, and it is now possible to assign the wanted subroutine confirmation message as an action here:

```
DB<58> a 19 print "received(@_)\n"
DB<59>
```

With these two actions defined, it is now possible to run the program and to see exactly what is sent from the findvars program at line 9 (line 28 in the original code), and what is received in the wanted subroutine at line 19. However, if the program simply runs all the way to the end, the output would be huge, so it is better to continue only so far as is necessary to inspect the variables that are interesting in relation to the current problem. This is possible with the c linenumber command, which will tell the debugger to continue until line 19 and to stop there:

```
DB<59> c 19
    sending(package warnings::register ;
    )
    main::wanted(findvars:19): return ($_[0] =
        ~ /$regex/ && $_[0] !~ /^\s*\#/ ? 1 : 0);
    received(package warnings::register ;
    )
DB<60>
```

Now the line the program is sending to the subroutine is correct, and the line that the subroutine is receiving is also correct. Notice that the newline included in the string is pushing the bracket to the next line, and that the complete string read from the file is being used. This should be run and observed a couple more times at least, to ensure the solution is solid:

```
DB<61> c 19
    sending(
    )
    main::wanted(findvars:19): return ($_[0] =~ /$regex/
                               && $_[0] !~ /^\s*\#/
? 1 : 0);
    received(
    )
DB<62>
```

The line returned had only whitespace (the newline) in it, which is a good reason to run this command once more:

```
DB<62> c 19
    sending(our $VERSION = '1.00';
    )
    main::wanted(findvars:19): return ($_[0] =
        ~ /$regex/ && $_[0] !~ /^\s*\#/ ? 1 : 0);
    received(our $VERSION = '1.00';
    )
DB<63>
```

That looks much better. Now would be a reasonable time to run to the end of the file, to ensure that the %data structure is being populated. Since we don't need to see every line passed in and out of the subroutine, and because they are therefore now redundant, use A * to delete all actions:

```
DB<63> A *
    Deleting all actions...
DB<64>
```

Now use L * to list all actions and breakpoints, to check that they have been cleared:

```
DB<64> L *
DB<65>
```

Now run all the way through to line 5, which takes the next file from the %files hash. This way, it will be possible to see if the %data structure is *really* being populated correctly:

```
DB<65> c 5
    main::getdata(newsub:5):                          $cnt = 0;
DB<66>
```

Once the program stops here, it is possible to dump out the %data structure to see what data has been captured. Remember that because the o hashDepth option is still set to the value of 2, only the first couple of values will be printed. If you wish to see all the data, you will want to reset this option to a higher value:

```
DB<66> x \%data
   0  HASH(0x83698a0)
 'warnings/register.pm' => HASH(0x84fe9a4)
    28 => '     my ($bit) = @_ ;
    '
    29 => '     my $mask = "" ;
    '
    ....
DB<67>
```

OK, that looks much better, and this session can be exited, using the now familiar q command.

Checking Your Work

Having seen that the code appears to be fixed (both the regex and the parameter passing problems), and that no other issues appear to have cropped up, now would be a reasonable time to try to run the entire program with the original arguments, without the debugger enabled, to check the output and that the behavior of the code has indeed been corrected. The command and output now look something like this:

```
%> findvars CGI MissingModule English
CGI.pm vars:
    [21]    $CGI::revision = '$Id: 05.pod,v 1.10 2004/11/07 perltut Exp $';
    [22]    $CGI::VERSION=3.04;
    [36]      local $^W = 0;
```

```
    [37]      $TAINTED = substr("$0$^X",0,0);
    [40]    my @SAVED_SYMBOLS;
    <...snip...>
Carp.pm vars:
    [3]     our $VERSION = '1.02';
    [59]    packages explicitly marked as safe by inclusion in @CARP_NOT, or
    [60]    (if that array is empty) @ISA.  The ability to override what
    [61]    @ISA says is new in 5.8.
    [66]    trusts C, then A trusts C.  So if you do not override @ISA
    <...snip...>
English.pm vars:
    [3]     our $VERSION = '1.01';
    [6]     @ISA = (Exporter);
    [17]       if ($ERRNO =~ /denied/) { ... }
    [23]    which get triggered just by accessing them (like $0) will still
    [28]    the C<$/> variable can be referred to either $RS or
    <...snip...>
```

This is exactly what was expected, and it is possible to declare the bugs fixed. Now it is necessary to fix the original source code, too.

Fixing the Source

Locating the problem is not the end of the task. We still need to update the errant production code. Although it would be possible to take the entire, in this case single, file and overwrite the old source code, this approach is not recommended. A better solution is to prepare a diff between the old faulty code and the new corrected code.

Creating a diff may seem unnecessarily complicated for a single file, but for a code base of dozens or hundreds of files, it's crucial. It is essential to have a method by which a single fix may be applied to a single application. If you are using multiple modules, distinct files for separating out functionality by object for example, it is highly likely that several or many files will need to be modified to implement a single bug fix.

Taking a diff and applying a patch is a sweet and elegant solution that many programmers appear to sidestep, for reasons best known to themselves. Again, much akin to the aversion to using a debugger, perhaps the reason is usually that old chestnut: plain old ignorance. Therefore, to do our bit for progress and civilization, here is a short rundown on how to take the diff and apply the patch for the short problem worked through in this chapter.

The diff command takes, in this case, the -u argument that produces a unified diff format, or special output that includes several context lines before and after each actual difference. This can help you to identify exactly which change belongs to which line, in cases where there may be difficulty in identifying the precise line. Also, it can make it easier for people to view the changes, and assess whether they are correct or not, prior to applying the resulting patch.

The rest of the command identifies the original source file, the corrected or fixed code, and finally the output of this command is redirected into a new file, the diff(erence) itself:

```
%> diff -u findvars findvars.fixed > findvars.diff
%>
```

The contents of the `findvars.diff` file should now look something like this:

```
--- findvars 2004-11-07 10:56:17.000000000 +0100
+++ findvars.fixed    2004-11-07 10:35:06.000000000 +0100
@@ -4,9 +4,11 @@
 use FileHandle;
-map { eval "require $_;" } @ARGV;
+map { eval "require $_;"
+    or print STDERR "Warning: unable to require $_: $@"
+} @ARGV;
-my $regex = $ENV{REGEX} || '[\$\@\%\*]&+';
+my $regex = $ENV{REGEX} || '[\$\@\%\*\&]+';
 map { $files{$_} = FileHandle->new("< $INC{$_}") } keys %INC;
@@ -26,7 +28,7 @@
        my $fh = $files{$f};
        while (<$fh>) {
            ++$cnt;
-            $data{$f}{$cnt} = $_ if &wanted;
+            $data{$f}{$cnt} = $_ if &wanted($_);
        }
    }
 }
```

Now to apply the contents of this `diff` file to the original file, you would use the `patch` program with a command somewhat like this:

```
%> patch findvars findvars.diff
```

The `diff` and `patch` commands shown here are very simple ones. Both commands handle multiple files and recursive directory structures, for more complex work. For information on the many options both commands support, and for more advanced usage, see the `diff` and `patch` manpages. In fact, you may find out an interesting bit of trivia about `patch`: It was written over 20 years ago by Larry Wall, three years before he created Perl.

Summary

In this chapter you've learned how to use the debugger to actually enter, control, modify, and debug a simple Perl program.

You should now be able to approach any Perl debugging problem with some confidence. Rather than remaining at the mercy of your code, whether you wrote it or because you are now responsible for maintaining it, you can now use a number of different techniques to completely inspect, instruct, change, and control its execution and behavior. Additionally, you can take a modified source file and find the differences between it and the original, before finally applying the fixes to the original file. You know how to do this in a reliable and predictable sequence, suitable for a production environment.

The rest of the book concentrates less on fixing a particular problem, and more on learning the various techniques available. In particular, the next chapter takes a look at how to approach debugging programs using the tracing facilities of the Perl debugger. You'll use tracing abilities to find out where elements of your program were called from and with what arguments.

■ ■ ■

## CHAPTER 5

Tracing Execution

Give us the tools, and we will finish the job.

—Churchill to Roosevelt in 1941

Having the right tool for the job is essential. It's all very well to have a big, impressive hammer in your toolbox, but if you have a nut and a bolt to put together, you won't get very far unless you have a wrench too.

A *trace* is a report of a program's position in the code execution stack; information for both how it got there, and, in the case of subroutines and methods, the arguments that were passed from the calling subroutine. Tracing is an invaluable tool for describing what your program is doing, which may not be what you *thought* it was doing.

Before we go any further, here is a short sample trace from the middle of executing the charcount program to give you an idea of the sort of information that is available, from the previous chapter. Use the T command at the debugger prompt, and you'll see that the debugger is already tracing code we never even wrote, that is, in this case it is tracing code way up inside the FileHandle and IO::File modules:

```
$ = Symbol::gensym() called from file \
    '/opt/perl/lib/5.8.5/i686-linux/IO/Handle.pm' line 306
$ = IO::Handle::new('FileHandle') called from file \
    '/opt/perl/lib/5.8.5/i686-linux/IO/File.pm' line 145
$ = IO::File::new('FileHandle', '< walrus') called from file \
    'charcount' line 12
```

This is a three-line stack trace, split for ease of viewing, from a single point in the code. It shows the specific line in the specific file we came from to get to this position. It also shows the namespace and subroutine of the current context, and the arguments with which it was called. It even notes that the context is scalar, instead of array (or list), and you can see how this is denoted by the helpful $ sigil on the far left of each line. If it had been an array context, the sigil would have been the familiar @.

The information in a trace can look daunting at first, not least because the information provided is verbose. This chapter explains how to control the amount of information and how to switch tracing on and off.

Options Affecting Trace Information

There are a couple of ways to modify the information that a trace will produce. You can use the maxTraceLen option to determine how many of the subroutine arguments will be printed, and you can also use the frame option, which will control the amount and type of stack data produced. Both methods use dedicated Perl debugger options:

- maxTraceLen: An integer that defines the number of characters of the trace arguments that can be shown per line. We'll discuss and demonstrate this option quite early on in the following examples.

- frame: Defines the information associated with each trace message. There are several frame flags, and each provides different information in the stack trace.

    - 0: Do not display enter or exit messages. This is the default.

    - 1: Show entering subroutines.

    - 2: Show exiting subroutines.

    - 4: Print arguments to subroutines and scalar or array context.

    - 8: Display tied and referenced variables.

    - 16: Print the return value from subroutines.

These numeric values are added together to express the options you want. For example, add options 1, 4, and 16 together to get an option value of 21. Don't worry too much about the frame options right now, as we'll return to them later in the chapter.

Tracing Methods and Control

The first thing to clear up is how to instruct the Perl debugger to turn tracing on and off. There are several ways to do this:

- T: This debugger command produces a one-time stack trace.

- t: This debugger command toggles tracing on and off.

- $DB::trace: This debugger command turns tracing on if set to a true value, and turns it off if set to false (explicitly from within the code). Allows a program to turn debugging on and off while running.

- AutoTrace: This debugger command turns tracing on from the PERLDB_OPTS AutoTrace environment variable.

We'll use the charcount program again, with the walrus file as input, to work through these methods one at a time and to show you how to control tracing of your Perl program.

One-Time Stack Trace: T

When stepping through a program, the most common way to get a stack trace is to use the T command, which will produce a one-time only stack trace. Let's enter the debugger and get acquainted with this command:

```
$> perl -d charcount walrus
Loading DB routines from perl5db.pl version 1.27
Editor support available.
Enter h or 'h h' for help, or 'man perldebug' for more help.
main::(charcount:6):    my $file = $ARGV[0] || '';
DB<1>
```

The debugger stops at the first executable statement, as usual. You can use the one-time trace command at any time, so let's use it now to see what we get:

```
DB<1> T
DB<1>
```

We don't get a lot. This is because the executable stack starts from the main context, and to get any information on it, we have to enter a different layer of execution. In short, we have to go into a subroutine or method. So, let's find a suitable subroutine to try, by using the S command to list all subroutines, but constrain the display to just those subroutines in our main context:

```
DB<1> S main
main::BEGIN
main::parse
DB<2>
```

Good, we found the main::parse subroutine, and we can use the c command to continue straight there:

```
DB<2> c parse
main::parse(charcount:40):              my $str = shift;
DB<3>
```

Now, going from the parse subroutine to the T command should make more sense:

```
DB<3> T
$ = main::parse('The Walrus and The Carpenter by Lewis Carroll.^J',
                '[bcdfghjklmnpqrstvwxyz]') called from file 'charcount' line 22
DB<3>
```

The stack trace clearly tells us that we are in a scalar context, within the main::parse subroutine called from line 22 of the charcount program. It also tells us that the arguments (passed via @_) contained two strings. The first string consists of the first line of our input file:

```
'The Walrus and The Carpenter by Lewis Carroll.'^J'
While the second argument is the regex we are going to test the first string with.
'[bcdfghjklmnpqrstvwxyz]'
```

The maxTraceLen option's default value makes it possible for us to see all of the arguments passed to the subroutine. You can show the current value of this option by querying the option (o) command with the name of the option followed directly by a ?:

```
DB<3> o maxTraceLen?
maxTraceLen = '400'
DB<4>
```

The default value in this case is 400, and though your system *may* be different, it is likely that the minimum default value will be above 100. To see the effect this has on the stack trace, set the maxTraceLen option to a small value:

```
DB<4> o max=10
maxTraceLen = '10'
DB<5>
```

Having done this, call for a single stack trace again:

```
DB<5> T
$ = main::p...(' The ... called from file 'charcount' line 22
DB<5>
```

You can see the output is almost useless with such a small value. The full subroutine name is not even visible, so we definitely won't see any arguments. Do the same thing again with a more reasonable number this time:

```
DB<5> o max=50
maxTraceLen = '50'
DB<6>
```

followed by a single trace once more:

```
DB<6> T
$ = main::parse('The Walrus and The Carpenter by Lewis Carroll.^J', \
    '[bcdfg... called from file 'charcount' line 22
DB<6>
```

That result seems much more reasonable. It is now possible to read both the subroutine name and enough of the arguments to show us that the information is at least of some use to us. The default value, whatever it is on your system, is probably sufficient in most cases, but it should be clear that being able to control the number of characters belonging to the trace arguments can be very useful. In certain cases, you may require to see much more than 400 characters, even several thousand perhaps. Other times, more than 50 characters may swamp your bugfixing exercise with too much detail. For the moment, set the maxTraceLen option back to its default value:

```
DB<6> o max=400
maxTraceLen = '400'
DB<7>
```

Next, before disabling tracing with the t command, let's return from the current subroutine to the main context using the r command:

```
DB<7> r
scalar context return from main::parse: 8
main::(charcount:23):        $i_vows += my $vows = &parse($line, '[aeiou]');
DB<7>
```

Toggle Stack Trace On/Off: t

The t command toggles tracing both on and off. Recall that tracing shows each line of code as it is executed.

To see the effect of running a chunk of code with tracing switched on, we'll execute several statements one after the other. First use the l command to display a code listing for a reminder of our current context and to find a suitable line from which to continue:

```
DB<7> l
23==>        $i_vows += my $vows = &parse($line, '[aeiou]');
24:          $i_spec += my $spec = &parse($line, '[^a-zA-Z0-9\s]');
25:          print sprintf('%6d', $i_cnt).':'.
26               '  hard'.('.'x(8-length($cons))).$cons.
27               '  soft'.('.'x(8-length($vows))).$vows.
28               '  spec'.('.'x(8-length($spec))).$spec;
29:          print $verbose ? "   $line\n" : "\n";
30:          $i_cnt++;
31       }
32
DB<7>
```

Now we'll turn on tracing:

```
DB<7> t
Trace = on
DB<7>
```

Use the c command to continue to line 25:

```
DB<7> c 25
main::parse(charcount:40):          my $str = shift;
main::parse(charcount:41):          my $reg = shift;
main::parse(charcount:42):          my $cnt = my @cnt = ($str =~ /($reg)/g);
main::parse(charcount:43):          return $cnt;
main::(charcount:24):     $i_spec += my $spec = &parse($line, '[^a-zA-Z0-9\s]');
main::parse(charcount:40):          my $str = shift;
main::parse(charcount:41):          my $reg = shift;
main::parse(charcount:42):          my $cnt = my @cnt = ($str =~ /($reg)/g);
main::parse(charcount:43):          return $cnt;
main::(charcount:25):        print sprintf('%6d', $i_cnt).':'.
main::(charcount:26):             '  hard'.('.'x(8-length($cons))).$cons.
main::(charcount:27):             '  soft'.('.'x(8-length($vows))).$vows.
main::(charcount:28):             '  spec'.('.'x(8-length($spec))).$spec;
DB<8>
```

The screen fills with the lines of code being executed. From this output, we can see that the parse subroutine was entered twice, and that each line that was executed is displayed sequentially. Notice how the t display is slightly different from the earlier T example, with slightly less information. Specifically, the called from file ... line ... statement is missing—because it is redundant—now you can see where everything was called from, by following the sequence of traces.

When displaying a stack trace, you have the opportunity to define a number of options in order to see the current context. This is controlled via the stack frame setting mentioned earlier. The default value for frame is 0, which you can see by querying the option:

```
DB<8> o frame?
frame = '0'
DB<9>
```

Make the following examples more convenient to execute by setting a breakpoint. This way we can use c to continue to line 25, by using the while loop to get to the next line in the input file, each time we wish to print out a trace series:

```
DB<9> b 25
DB<10>
```

Now set the frame option to 2, which will display a message each time we enter or exit a subroutine:

```
DB<10> o fr=2
frame = '2'
DB<11>
```

Now use c to continue to the breakpoint we just set:

```
DB<11> c
29:          print $verbose ? "  $line\n" : "\n";
0:  hard.......8  soft.......3  spec.......6
30:          $i_cnt++;
21:          my $line = $_;
22:          $i_cons += my $cons = &parse($line, '[bcdfghjklmnpqrstvwxyz]');
entering main::parse
40:          my $str = shift;
41:          my $reg = shift;
42:          my $cnt = my @cnt = ($str =~ /($reg)/g);
43:          return $cnt;
exited main::parse
23:          $i_vows += my $vows = &parse($line, '[aeiou]');
entering main::parse
40:          my $str = shift;
41:          my $reg = shift;
42:          my $cnt = my @cnt = ($str =~ /($reg)/g);
43:          return $cnt;
exited main::parse
24:          $i_spec += my $spec = &parse($line, '[^a-zA-Z0-9\s]');
entering main::parse
40:          my $str = shift;
41:          my $reg = shift;
42:          my $cnt = my @cnt = ($str =~ /($reg)/g);
43:          return $cnt;
exited main::parse
25:          print sprintf('%6d', $i_cnt).':'.
26:              '  hard'.('.'x(8-length($cons))).$cons.
27:              '  soft'.('.'x(8-length($vows))).$vows.
28:              '  spec'.('.'x(8-length($spec))).$spec;
DB<11>
```

Now, instead of only a list of executed statements, we can also see when we enter and exit each subroutine. This in itself does not offer any more information than we got from the trace using frame=0. But, it does make what is happening clearer and makes it easier to follow the stack trace. Indeed, every chunk of code making up each subroutine can be easily inspected in visual isolation from the rest of the code.

Now let's have a look at setting frame=4, which will display the context and the arguments to the subroutine:

```
DB<11> o fr=4
frame = '4'
DB<12>
```

Again, enter c to continue to the breakpoint at line 25:

```
DB<12> c
29:         print $verbose ? "  $line\n" : "\n";
1:  hard.......0  soft.......0  spec.......0
30:             $i_cnt++;
21:             my $line = $_;
22:             $i_cons += my $cons = &parse($line, '[bcdfghjklmnpqrstvwxyz]');
  in $=main::parse('The sun was shining on the sea^J',
 '[bcdfghjklmnpqrstvwxyz]') from charcount:22
40:         my $str = shift;
41:         my $reg = shift;
42:         my $cnt = my @cnt = ($str =~ /($reg)/g);
43:         return $cnt;
23:             $i_vows += my $vows = &parse($line, '[aeiou]');
  in $=main::parse('Shining with all his might:^J', '[aeiou]')
  from charcount:23
40:         my $str = shift;
41:         my $reg = shift;
42:         my $cnt = my @cnt = ($str =~ /($reg)/g);
43:         return $cnt;
24:             $i_spec += my $spec = &parse($line, '[^a-zA-Z0-9\s]');
  in $=main::parse('He did his very best to make^J',
 '[^a-zA-Z0-9\\s]')
  from charcount:24
40:         my $str = shift;
41:         my $reg = shift;
42:         my $cnt = my @cnt = ($str =~ /($reg)/g);
43:         return $cnt;
25:          print sprintf('%6d', $i_cnt).':'.
26:             '  hard'.('.'x(8-length($cons))).$cons.
27:             '  soft'.('.'x(8-length($vows))).$vows.
28:             '  spec'.('.'x(8-length($spec))).$spec;
DB<12>
```

This time both the arguments and the context are printed. The lines begin with in $=main::parse('... and end with from charcount:.... This is the same setting used by the T command that we saw earlier. Also, the enter and exit markers have changed to in and out, in order to accommodate the request for a different display.

As mentioned earlier, you can combine these frame options together to define the exact information that you require for your particular circumstance. A useful option for this is frame=16, which instructs the stack trace to print out the return value from each subroutine. Let's turn on every stack trace option possible by setting frame=30:

```
DB<12> o fr=30
frame = '30'
DB<13>
```

Enter c to continue to the breakpoint at line 25 and to see the stack traces generated:

```
DB<13> c
29:         print $verbose ? "  $line\n" : "\n";
2:  hard.......4  soft.......3  spec.......1
30:         $i_cnt++;
21:         my $line = $_;
22:         $i_cons += my $cons = &parse($line, '[bcdfghjklmnpqrstvwxyz]');
in  $=main::parse('The billows smooth and bright^J',
 '[bcdfghjklmnpqrstvwxyz]') from charcount:22
40:        my $str = shift;
41:        my $reg = shift;
42:        my $cnt = my @cnt = ($str =~ /($reg)/g);
43:        return $cnt;
out $=main::parse('The billows smooth and bright^J',
'[bcdfghjklmnpqrstvwxyz]')
from charcount:22
scalar context return from main::parse: 5
23:         $i_vows += my $vows = &parse($line, '[aeiou]');
in  $=main::parse('And this was odd, because it was^J', \
'[aeiou]') from charcount:23
40:        my $str = shift;
41:        my $reg = shift;
42:        my $cnt = my @cnt = ($str =~ /($reg)/g);
43:        return $cnt;
out $=main::parse('And this was odd, because it was^J', '[aeiou]')
from charcount:23
scalar context return from main::parse: 5
24:         $i_spec += my $spec = &parse($line, '[^a-zA-Z0-9\s]');
in  $=main::parse('And this was odd, because it was^J', \
'[^a-zA-Z0-9\\s]') from charcount:24
40:        my $str = shift;
41:        my $reg = shift;
42:        my $cnt = my @cnt = ($str =~ /($reg)/g);
43:        return $cnt;
out $=main::parse('And this was odd, because it was^J', '[^a-zA-Z0-9\\s]')
from charcount:24
```

```
scalar context return from main::parse: 1
25:         print sprintf('%6d', $i_cnt).':'.
26:             '   hard'.('.'x(8-length($cons))).$cons.
27:             '   soft'.('.'x(8-length($vows))).$vows.
28:             '   spec'.('.'x(8-length($spec))).$spec;
DB<13>
```

Generating this amount of data for every program with a bug is overkill. However, it can be useful in some situations. For instance, tracing the arguments that appear to be changing between calling a subroutine and actually running the subroutine can be quite enlightening. Equally, when you are uncertain which object is calling which method, this approach can settle the argument without the need for conjecture and assumptions.

So far, we've been looking at some of the many options available to control the type of information you can request from a stack trace, and how to switch the tracing on and off from within the debugger itself. Next we describe how to tell the debugger to print stack traces, both from your code and the command line.

The $DB::trace Variable

If you have a particular chunk of code you wish to trace, perhaps conditionally, you can use the $DB::trace variable in your code. DB is the Perl debugger namespace, and $DB::trace is one of the package variables that control the debugger's behavior.

To demonstrate this, we can modify the charcount code, by inserting a $DB::trace = 1 if $line =~ /rude/ statement at line 22, which will make the code look like this:

```
19 # parse the file
20 while (<$FH>) {
21     my $line = $_;
22     $DB::trace = 1 if $line =~ /rude/;
23     $i_cons += my $cons = &parse($line, '[bcdfghjklmnpqrstvwxyz]');
24     $i_vows += my $vows = &parse($line, '[aeiou]');
25     $i_spec += my $spec = &parse($line, '[^a-zA-Z0-9\s]');
26     $DB::trace = 0;
27     print sprintf('%6d', $i_cnt).':'.
```

Line 22 sets $DB::trace=1 only if it matches the regex /rude/, while line 26 always sets $DB::trace=0 for the remaining run of the program. This sort of conditional use of the $DB::trace variable is one of the very powerful ways you can control debugger output, either on-the-fly, or by hardwiring directly into your code at a point that you are particularly interested in.

What if your program isn't running under the debugger? Setting $DB::trace will create a new DB namespace with $trace as its only variable. And, since the debugger isn't running, the $DB::trace is ignored, and your program will continue with no inadvertent side-effects:

```
$> perl -d charcount walrus
Loading DB routines from perl5db.pl version 1.27
Editor support available.
Enter h or 'h h' for help, or 'man perldebug' for more help.
main::(charcount:6):    my $file = $ARGV[0] || '';
DB<1>
```

Having started the debugger, use c to continue with no restraint, and the debugger will simply run off the end of the program:

```
DB<1> c
 0:   hard......8   soft......3   spec......6
 1:   hard......0   soft......0   spec......0
 2:   hard......4   soft......3   spec......1
 3:   hard......5   soft......5   spec......1
 4:   hard......0   soft......1   spec......0
 5:   hard......4   soft......2   spec.....10
 6:   hard......6   soft......3   spec......8
 7:   hard......0   soft......0   spec......0
 8:   hard......7   soft......4   spec......5
 9:   hard......8   soft......8   spec.....10
10:   hard......0   soft......0   spec......1
11:   hard.....21   soft.....20   spec.....21
12:   hard......0   soft......0   spec......0
main::(charcount:23):                    $i_cons += my $cons = &parse($line,
            [bcdfghjklmnpqrstvwxyz]');
main::parse(charcount:42):          my $str = shift;
main::parse(charcount:43):          my $reg = shift;
main::parse(charcount:44):          my $cnt = my @cnt = ($str =~ /($reg)/g);
main::parse(charcount:45):          return $cnt;
main::(charcount:24):      $i_vows += my $vows = &parse($line, '[aeiou]');
main::parse(charcount:42):          my $str = shift;
main::parse(charcount:43):          my $reg = shift;
main::parse(charcount:44):          my $cnt = my @cnt = ($str =~ /($reg)/g);
main::parse(charcount:45):          return $cnt;
main::(charcount:25):      $i_spec += my $spec = &parse($line, '[^a-zA-Z0-9\s]');
main::parse(charcount:42):          my $str = shift;
main::parse(charcount:43):          my $reg = shift;
main::parse(charcount:44):          my $cnt = my @cnt = ($str =~ /($reg)/g);
main::parse(charcount:45):          return $cnt;
main::(charcount:26):              $DB::trace = 0;
13:   hard......4   soft......1   spec......4
...
```

Bearing in mind that charcount counting starts at 0, you can see that the $DB::trace variable turned tracing on at line 14 of the input file, and immediately turned it off again for the next line of processing. Programmatic, and therefore conditional, control of the stack trace can be very useful when you do not wish to involve yourself in the manual process of stepping through and then switching the tracing input on and off.

The next option takes this concept even further.

AutoTrace

The AutoTrace option is a special startup option that you can place in the PERLDB_OPTS environment variable. Before running your program, the debugger inspects the environment variable for relevant options. You can place any debugger option in this variable, because it is parsed at startup as a sequence of `o optname [=optval]` commands. In addition, there are a couple of startup options specifically dedicated to tracing, in addition to the aforementioned `frame` option:

- `AutoTrace`: This option switches tracing on if defined, similar to using `t`.

- `LineInfo`: This option defines the name of a file for all trace output to be sent to.

- `NonStop`: This option runs through the entire program under the debugger without waiting for human intervention.

You don't have to use all of these options at one time, but they often mesh well together. This example uses all of them at once to show how this works. First we export all the options into the environment variables:

```
$> export PERLDB_OPTS="Line=trace.out auto=1 Non frame=4"
```

Note how the option names are case-insensitive, and that it is not important to write out the entire name. It is sufficient to define the uniquely identifying part of the option. Also, just defining `Non` is the same as specifying `NonStop=1`.

Now run the debugger against the program and input data:

```
$> perl -d charcount walrus
 0:  hard.......8  soft.......3  spec.......6
 1:  hard.......0  soft.......0  spec.......0
 2:  hard.......4  soft.......3  spec.......1
 3:  hard.......5  soft.......5  spec.......1
...
60:  hard......33  soft......26  spec.......1
61:  hard.......0  soft.......0  spec.......0
62:  hard.......1  soft.......0  spec.......1
63:  hard.......0  soft.......1  spec.......0
total:  hard      411  soft      221  spec      325
$>
```

The program, along with the debugger, runs through its entire execution stack, printing out its usual report to `STDOUT`, and then finishes. All the trace data has gone into the `trace.out` file specified as the argument to the `LineInfo` option. Now we can take a look at the trace output using any suitable method. Here we use the `cat` program to examine `trace.out`:

```
$> cat trace.out
in  $=CODE(0x8180e9c)() from charcount:3
3:    use strict;
in  $=strict::import('strict') from charcount:3
28:       shift;
29:       $^H |= @_ ? bits(@_) : $default_bits;
in  $=CODE(0x8180ecc)() from charcount:4
4:    use FileHandle;
in  $=CODE(0x822d4dc)() from /opt/perl/lib/5.8.5/FileHandle.pm:3
3:    use 5.006;
...
```

Because AutoTrace=1 was specified in PERLDB_OPTS, the debugger has switched tracing on from the very beginning of the run. The $DB::trace=1 at line 22 will not have any effect the first time through the program, until the $DB::trace=0 kicks in at line 26:

```
17:      my $i_spec = 0;
20:      while (<$FH>) {
21:          my $line = $_;
22:          $DB::trace = 1 if $line =~ /rude/;
23:          $i_cons += my $cons = &parse($line, '[bcdfghjklmnpqrstvwxyz]');
in  $=main::parse('The Walrus and The Carpenter by Lewis Carroll.^J', \
       '[bcdfghjklmnpqrstvwxyz]') from charcount:23
42:          my $str = shift;
43:          my $reg = shift;
44:          my $cnt = my @cnt = ($str =~ /($reg)/g);
45:          return $cnt;
24:          $i_vows += my $vows = &parse($line, '[aeiou]');
in  $=main::parse('^J', '[aeiou]') from charcount:24
42:          my $str = shift;
43:          my $reg = shift;
44:          my $cnt = my @cnt = ($str =~ /($reg)/g);
45:          return $cnt;
25:          $i_spec += my $spec = &parse($line, '[^a-zA-Z0-9\s]');
in  $=main::parse('The sun was shining on the sea,', \
       '[^a-zA-Z0-9\\s]') from charcount:25
42:          my $str = shift;
43:          my $reg = shift;
44:          my $cnt = my @cnt = ($str =~ /($reg)/g);
45:          return $cnt;
26:          $DB::trace = 0;
```

Now $DB::trace=0 takes effect, even though we started with AutoTrace on, and the rest of the program is untraced except for the call to main::parse itself. When the input $line contains a match against the /rude/ regex specified on line 22, the printing of the stack trace starts again:

```
in  $=main::parse('Shining with all his might:^J', \
       '[bcdfghjklmnpqrstvwxyz]') from charcount:23
in  $=main::parse('He did his very best to make^J', \
       '[aeiou]') from charcount:24
in  $=main::parse('The billows smooth and bright^J', \
       '[^a-zA-Z0-9\\s]') from charcount:25
23:          $i_cons += my $cons = &parse($line, '[bcdfghjklmnpqrstvwxyz]');
in  $=main::parse('And this was odd, because it was^J', \
       '[bcdfghjklmnpqrstvwxyz]') from charcount:23
42:          my $str = shift;
43:          my $reg = shift;
44:          my $cnt = my @cnt = ($str =~ /($reg)/g);
45:          return $cnt;
24:          $i_vows += my $vows = &parse($line, '[aeiou]');
```

```
in  $=main::parse('The middle of the night.^J', '[aeiou]') from charcount:24
42:        my $str = shift;
43:        my $reg = shift;
44:        my $cnt = my @cnt = ($str =~ /($reg)/g);
45:        return $cnt;
25:        $i_spec += my $spec = &parse($line, '[^a-zA-Z0-9\s]');
in  $=main::parse('^J', '[^a-zA-Z0-9\\s]') from charcount:25
42:        my $str = shift;
43:        my $reg = shift;
44:        my $cnt = my @cnt = ($str =~ /($reg)/g);
45:        return $cnt;
...
```

The control over this process is quite flexible, and allows for any number of variations in approach. This makes it very simple to choose the most suitable method to trace your program, depending on what you are trying to find out, and which bit of executing code, with corresponding arguments and context, you wish to inspect.

The `Devel::Trace` **Module**

Throughout this chapter you have learned how to use the debugger to generate stack traces. Usually, it's not possible to get a stack trace unless you are using the debugger. An exception is to use one of the debugging hooks that Perl provides for the debugger itself, which are covered in Chapter 12. This is what the `Devel::Trace` module, available from CPAN, does. By using this module, you can get stack traces without using the debugger at all.

Here is an example using the `Devel::Trace` module, which traces the point that the charcount program begins to loop through the input file:

```
$> perl -d:Trace charcount walrus
>> charcount:6: my $file = $ARGV[0] || '';
>> charcount:7: my $verbose = $ARGV[1] || 0;
>> charcount:9: unless (-f $file) {
>> charcount:12: my $FH = FileHandle->new("< $file") or \
die("unable to open file($file): $!");
>> /opt/perl/lib/5.8.5/i686-linux/IO/File.pm:141:    my $type = shift;
>> /opt/perl/lib/5.8.5/i686-linux/IO/File.pm:142:    my $class = \
ref($type) || $type || "IO::File";
>> /opt/perl/lib/5.8.5/i686-linux/IO/File.pm:143:    @_ >= 0 && @_ <= 3
>> /opt/perl/lib/5.8.5/i686-linux/IO/File.pm:145:
            my $fh = $class->SUPER::new();
>> /opt/perl/lib/5.8.5/i686-linux/IO/Handle.pm:304:    my $class = \
ref($_[0]) || $_[0] || "IO::Handle";
>> /opt/perl/lib/5.8.5/i686-linux/IO/Handle.pm:305:
            @_ == 1 or croak "usage: new $class";
>> /opt/perl/lib/5.8.5/i686-linux/IO/Handle.pm:306:    my $io = gensym;
>> /opt/perl/lib/5.8.5/Symbol.pm:102:    my $name = "GEN" . $genseq++;
>> /opt/perl/lib/5.8.5/Symbol.pm:103:    my $ref = \*{$genpkg . $name};
>> /opt/perl/lib/5.8.5/Symbol.pm:103:    my $ref = \*{$genpkg . $name};
```

```
>> /opt/perl/lib/5.8.5/Symbol.pm:104:      delete $$genpkg{$name};
>> /opt/perl/lib/5.8.5/Symbol.pm:105:      $ref;
>> /opt/perl/lib/5.8.5/i686-linux/IO/Handle.pm:307:     bless $io, $class;
>> /opt/perl/lib/5.8.5/i686-linux/IO/File.pm:146:     if (@_) {
>> /opt/perl/lib/5.8.5/i686-linux/IO/File.pm:147:        $fh->open(@_)
>> /opt/perl/lib/5.8.5/i686-linux/IO/File.pm:158:       @_ >= 2 && @_ <= 4 or \
          croak 'usage: $fh->open(FILENAME [,MODE [,PERMS]]
)';
>> /opt/perl/lib/5.8.5/i686-linux/IO/File.pm:159:       my ($fh, $file) = @_;
>> /opt/perl/lib/5.8.5/i686-linux/IO/File.pm:160:       if (@_ > 2) {
>> /opt/perl/lib/5.8.5/i686-linux/IO/File.pm:176:       open($fh, $file);
>> /opt/perl/lib/5.8.5/i686-linux/IO/File.pm:150:       $fh;
>> charcount:14: my $i_cnt  = 0;
>> charcount:15: my $i_cons = 0;
>> charcount:16: my $i_vows = 0;
>> charcount:17: my $i_spec = 0;
>> charcount:20: while (<$FH>) {
>> charcount:21:     my $line = $_;
>> charcount:22:     $i_cons += my $cons =
          &parse($line, '[bcdfghjklmnpqrstvwxyz]');
>> charcount:40:     my $str = shift;
>> charcount:41:     my $reg = shift;
>> charcount:42:     my $cnt = my @cnt = ($str =~ /($reg)/g);
>> charcount:43:     return $cnt;
...
```

The standard output is extremely verbose, and although the output is not quite as versatile as the debugger stack traces, the module can be tweaked and controlled in several ways. For example, you can turn tracing on and off for specific chunks of code programmatically using a module variable that looks a lot like $DB::trace:

```
$Devel::Trace::TRACE = 1;
```

Or you can do the same thing using the Devel::Trace::trace subroutine:

```
Devel::Trace::trace('off')
```

To learn more about this very useful module, see the CPAN search site, http://search.cpan.org/dist/Devel-Trace/.

Summary

In this chapter you've learned how to use the debugger to conditionally trace your programs, and even your individual statements. You've learned how tracing can reveal to you the inner workings of libraries and modules, by the use of customized stack traces, not only your code, but also code which your program uses and that you have never even seen, let alone written.

The next chapter explores several specialized breakpoint commands for working with multiple libraries and modules, and teaches you to access and control chunks of code at both runtime and compiletime.

CHAPTER 6

■ ■ ■

Debugging Modules

Twas brillig, and the slithy toves did gyre and gimble in the wabe.

—"The Jabberwocky" by Lewis Carroll

Much like Carroll's interesting use of familiar words to create new, plausible, but expressive words such as *brillig* and *slithy*, the Perl debugger has several commands specifically designed for debugging multiple libraries. At first sight, several of these commands appear to be both familiar and similar to one another, but on closer inspection are found to be distinct and to have different meanings. We explore several of these commands in this chapter.

Multiple Modules

As you've probably noticed, a large part of this book is concerned with demonstrating Perl debugger usage while working with a single file. However, most programs use multiple libraries or modules for any but the simplest of tasks, and these libraries may be use'd or require'd, done, or even eval'd, presenting differing situations dependent on whether the code is included at compile-time or runtime. There may be many situations in which, for example, you might wish to set a breakpoint when a file is loaded, when a module is first used, when a subroutine is compiled or first entered, or when a file is brought in via a do or eval command.

The %INC Hash

Examining the contents of the %INC hash of any running Perl program will show a long list of modules you probably didn't even know existed (as well as the paths to the files they were loaded from), much less realized that your program was already using.

To demonstrate the number of modules a simple program might import, let's take a look at the %INC hash of a Perl program that relies solely on the Data::Dumper module:

```
%> perl -MData::Dumper -e 'print Dumper(\%INC)'
$VAR1 = {
          'warnings/register.pm' =>
                        '/opt/perl/lib/5.8.4/warnings/register.pm',

          'bytes.pm' => '/opt/perl/lib/5.8.4/bytes.pm',
```

```
            'Carp.pm' => '/opt/perl/lib/5.8.4/Carp.pm',
            'XSLoader.pm' => '/opt/perl/lib/5.8.4/i686-
                                        linux/XSLoader.pm',
            'Exporter.pm' => '/opt/perl/lib/5.8.4/Exporter.pm',
            'warnings.pm' => '/opt/perl/lib/5.8.4/warnings.pm',
            'overload.pm' => '/opt/perl/lib/5.8.4/overload.pm',
            'Data/Dumper.pm' => '/opt/perl/lib/5.8.4/i686-
                                        linux/Data/Dumper.pm'
        };
%>
```

As you can see, there are eight libraries already loaded! This is a good thing, because it demonstrates that core libraries distributed with the Perl source are written modularly, and we all benefit from the fact that the Perl distribution is built from a core of stable central code—a foundation we can build on. Nevertheless, in this example you can see how many libraries have been pulled in without us really noticing.

Learning how to navigate throughout these libraries with the debugger is the subject of this chapter. For the moment, use the q command to quit, then we can return to the discussion of our breakpoints.

Special Breakpoint Commands

The Perl debugger expressly supports the debugging of multiple libraries and modules, at both compilation time and time of execution, in addition to the usual movement and data inspection commands described elsewhere in this book. However, there are certain breakpoint commands that this section will explore. A list of them can be found in Table 6-1.

Table 6-1. *Some Commands and Descriptions*

Command	Description
b [line] [condition]	Sets a breakpoint conditionally on the given or current line.
b subname [condition]	Sets a breakpoint conditionally on the first line of the given subroutine.
b compile subname	Sets a breakpoint at the first executable statement encountered after the given subroutine has been compiled.
b postpone subname [condition]	Sets a breakpoint at the first executable statement of the subroutine given after the subroutine has been compiled, conditionally.
b load filename	Sets a breakpoint at the first executable statement of the filename given after the file has been compiled.

At first sight, in the standard documentation, these breakpoint commands and their descriptions may all look confusingly similar, and the specific purpose of each may be unclear. Closer inspection shows distinct variations between each command and we have chosen the similar wording purposefully to expose the differences between each breakpoint form in Table 6-1.

Setting a breakpoint is typically done using either the first or the second command in the previous list. That is, we usually find ourselves setting a breakpoint on a line or a subroutine in a runtime context. These first and second forms have been discussed earlier, namely in Chapter 3. Therefore, in this chapter we're concerned with the rest, specifically with the b compile, b postpone, and b load commands, each of which deals with compiletime context.

Example Code

In this section, we'll present the code listings used in the examples demonstrated throughout this chapter. Listing 6-1 displays the program usereq, which we use as our entry point to load and run our library code, and is the program executed at runtime.

Listing 6-1. *The* usereq *Program*

```perl
#!/usr/bin/perl
use strict;
use NoArg qw(noargs);
use FileHandle;
print __FILE__." loaded\n";
if (noargs(@ARGV)) {
    print __FILE__." has no arguments\n";
} else {
    require Args;
    my $o_args = Args->new;
    print __FILE__." arguments: ".$o_args->format('all');
}
exit;
BEGIN {
    print __FILE__." begun\n";
}
__END__
=head1 NAME
usereq - print the command line args
=head1 SYNOPSIS
usereq arg1 argn
=head1 DESCRIPTION
A short program used as an entry point to load and run Args.pm
=cut
```

The NoArg.pm script (Listing 6-2) is a utility module for deciding if there are (not) any command line arguments. It is loaded at compiletime via use.

Listing 6-2. NoArg.pm

```perl
package NoArg;
use strict;
require Exporter;
use vars qw(@ISA @EXPORT_OK);
```

```
@ISA = qw(Exporter);
@EXPORT_OK = qw(noargs);
print __FILE__." loaded\n";
sub noargs {
    print __FILE__." running noargs()\n";
    return (scalar(@_) == 0 ? 1 : 0);
}
1;
BEGIN {
    print __FILE__." begun\n";
}
__END__
=head1 NAME
NoArg.pm - are there any args
=head1 SYNOPSIS
print "yup\n" if NoArg::noargs(@ARGV);
=head1 DESCRIPTION
Decide if there are any arguments on the command line
=cut
```

The Args.pm script (Listing 6-3) is a module that captures the command line arguments via new() and returns them via a format() function. It is loaded at runtime via require.

Listing 6-3. Args.pm

```
package Args;
use strict;
print __FILE__." loaded\n";
sub new {
    my $class = shift;
    print __FILE__." running new()\n";
    my $self = {
        _args => require 'getargs',
    };
    die("Failed to find 'getargs' $@") unless
                    ref($self->{_args}) eq 'ARRAY';
    bless($self, $class);
}
sub format {
    my $self  = shift;
    my $index = shift;
    print __FILE__." running format()\n";
    my $str;
    if ($index eq 'all') {
        $str = join("<-\n  ->", @{$self->{_args}});
    } elsif ($index =~ /^\d+$/) {
        $str = $self->{_args}[$index];
```

```
    } else {
        print "Error: unrecognized index($index)\n";
    }
    return "\n  ->$str<-\n";
}
1;
BEGIN {
    print __FILE__." begun\n";
}
__END__
=head1 NAME
Args.pm - capture the command line args.
=head1 SYNOPSIS
print Args->new->format('all');
=head1 DESCRIPTION
A module to get the command line arguments
=cut
```

The getargs script (Listing 6-4) is a short piece of code that takes care of clearing @ARGV and returning the original contents, and is loaded at runtime via an explicit do statement.

Listing 6-4. *The* getargs *Script*

```
#!/usr/bin/perl
use strict;
print __FILE__." loaded\n";
my @ARGS = @ARGV;
while (@ARGV) {
    print __FILE__." running: ".shift(@ARGV)."\n";
}
print __FILE__." done\n";
\@ARGS;
BEGIN {
    print __FILE__." begun\n";
}
__END__
=head1 NAME
getargs - print command line args
=head1 SYNOPSIS
getargs one two three
=head1 DESCRIPTION
A module to display the command line arguments
=cut
```

These code examples are fairly simple, and are here to demonstrate the concepts of loading multiple libraries in various fashions. This way we can practice using the debugger to control when and where we stop program execution, and the inspection and interaction with our environment.

Print Statements in the Code

In each of the preceding code examples, usearg, Args.pm, NoArg.pm, and getargs, take note of the various print statements making up a substantial part of the code. These listings will keep you informed of the current position of the program or module at any given time.

As a reference, the print statements found in the code follow in Table 6-2. Note that __FILE__ is a special Perl literal that will be replaced with the current filename at runtime.

Table 6-2. *Reference to Print Statements Found in the Code*

Statement	Description
print __FILE__." begun\n"	The code is compiled and is in a BEGIN block.
print __FILE__." loaded\n"	The code is compiled and ready to execute the first executable statement.
print __FILE__." running\n"	The code is running, these are mostly in subroutines being called.
print __FILE__." done\n"	The code has completed execution.

Running the Code

Running the usereq program with no arguments produces the following output:

```
%> perl ./usereq
NoArg.pm begun
NoArg.pm loaded
./usereq begun
./usereq started
./usereq running
NoArg.pm running noargs()
./usereq has no arguments
./usereq done
```

Running the usereq program with one or more arguments produces something like the following output:

```
%> perl ./usereq arg1 argn
NoArg.pm begun
NoArg.pm loaded
./usereq begun
./usereq started
NoArg.pm running noargs()
Args.pm begun
Args.pm loaded
Args.pm running new()
getargs begun
getargs loaded
```

```
getargs running: arg1
getargs running: argn
getargs done
Args.pm running format()
./usereq arguments: ->arg1<- ->argn<-
./usereq done
```

Tracing Compiletime Code

Before we tackle our breakpoints, it's worth mentioning that one perfectly good way to find out what is going on for all the Perl code executed at both compiletime and runtime is to turn tracing on.

Although tracing has been covered in Chapter 5, we're just going to cover some of the ground here again as it applies to our particular situation, for the sake of completeness.

Using `PERLDB_OPTS` to Turn Tracing On

Turning tracing on may be done in a number of ways, and to demonstrate how the tracing mechanism works across files and packages, we can simply set an environment variable, such as `PERLDB_OPTS`, to set `AutoTrace=1` and get something like this:

```
%> export PERLDB_OPTS="AutoTrace=1 NonStop=1 LineInfo=dbgr.out"
```

Let's review each part of this environment variable:

- `AutoTrace=1`: Turn tracing on.

- `NonStop=1`: Do not stop, even where there is a debugger command or variable telling the debugger to stop, just keep going.

- `LineInfo=dbgr.out`: Put all debugger output into the file `dbgr.out`. This can be any valid filename.

Now run the debugger as before:

```
%> perl -d ./usereq one two three
```

This will display output similar to that shown in the previous example. In addition to this, we now have a file `dbgr.out` with around 2500 lines of tracing information. Although it wouldn't be fair to say that tracing each line of code always generates 300 lines of tracing information, as you can see in the following output, it can be quite a verbose process—if you're not careful.

The Traced Output

To start, let's have a filtered look at some of that `dbgr.out` file:

```
1 main::CODE(0x81803ec)(./usereq:4):
2 4:  use strict;
3 main::CODE(0x81803ec)(./usereq:4):
4 4:  use strict;
<...snip...>
2461 strict::import(/opt/perl/lib/5.8.4/strict.pm:29):
```

```
2462 29:      $^H |= @_ ? bits(@_) : $default_bits;
2463 Args::CODE(0x838dcc8)(Args.pm:36):  print __FILE__." begun\n";
2464 Args::(Args.pm:6):  print __FILE__." loaded\n";
2465 Args::(Args.pm:33): 1;
2466 main::(./usereq:14):        my $o_args = Args->new;
<...snip...>
2496 Args::format(Args.pm:24):      $str = join("<-\n  ->", @{$self->{_args}});
2497 Args::format(Args.pm:30):       return "\n  ->$str<-\n";
2498 main::(./usereq:18):    exit;
```

We can see code being described right up into the core of the strict program, but it's too much detail for our purposes in this section. A pragma is a hint to the Perl compiler to help with optimizing or checking your Perl code, before running it. Coming back to the code, it would be very easy for us to get lost amongst this useful but verbose output, particularly in a more realistic program with multiple libraries and many code branches.

Another reason not to trace without regard to context, is that the execution of each print statement for every line, whether to screen or to file, takes a comparatively long time to execute. This can eat up quite a bit of memory, and slow down your program. Tracing is, like the debugger itself, just one more useful item in your repertoire of troubleshooting tools, and like all good tools, should be treated with respect and only used when it's appropriate.

■Note For a full explanation of all the good things you can do with tracing and the debugger, see Chapter 5.

We wish to fine-tune our approach here, and be more selective about what we get when we call a trace. We also wish to have more control over our environment, which brings us back to the special breakpoint commands mentioned in Table 6-1.

Setting Breakpoints on Compiletime or Runtime Code

In the following examples, you will learn how to use the debugger to set breakpoints in runtime code (the usual scenario). You will also learn set breakpoints in compiletime code, or breakpoints in code that hasn't been executed. The latter can be useful particularly when dealing with modules that use overloading to redefine subroutines and methods.

We'll start with the more usual case of setting a breakpoint on a subroutine.

The b subname [condition]

This command sets a conditional breakpoint on the first line of the given subroutine at runtime.

We can see how to set a breakpoint on a subroutine by using the usereq program and running it under the debugger. In this case, we do not require any arguments for the usereq program, and so it can be simply run directly:

```
%> perl -d usereq
Loading DB routines from perl5db.pl version 1.27
Editor support available.
Enter h or 'h h' for help, or 'man perldebug' for more help.
NoArg.pm begun
NoArg.pm loaded
usereq begun
main::(usereq:8):       print __FILE__." loaded\n";
  DB<1>
```

We've stopped at the first executable statement in our file, namely the print __FILE__."
loaded\n" print statement in usereq.

Inspecting Our Environment

Now we can have a look at our environment to see which subroutines are available at the present time. Because we know we are using the NoArg module, we can restrict the subroutine names returned by using a pattern as an argument to S. In this case, by using Arg, a subset of those characters:

```
DB<1> S Arg
    NoArg::BEGIN
    NoArg::noargs
DB<2>
```

OK, so we now have two subroutines to choose from. Let's have a look at NoArg::noargs using the l command:

```
DB<2> l NoArg::noargs
    Switching to file 'NoArg.pm'.
    13      sub noargs {
    14:             print __FILE__." running noargs()\n";
    15:             return (scalar(@_) == 0 ? 1 : 0);
    16      }
DB<3>
```

Now we want to set a breakpoint on the noargs subroutine. Note that although noargs would have given us the same results on its own, because it has been exported to our namespace already, it is always a good idea to explicitly state which package your subroutine belongs to:

```
DB<3> b NoArg::noargs
DB<4>
```

As you can see, the debugger doesn't even confirm it has done anything, but we can use the L command to view a list of currently set breakpoints, actions, and watch-expressions. Let's use L to verify whether or not our command has actually been executed correctly:

```
DB<4> L
    NoArg.pm: 14:               print __FILE__." running noargs()\n";
    break if (1)
DB<4>
```

We don't have any actions or watch-variables, so all we see is the confirmation that our breakpoint has been set. We might also use the L b form of this command, if we are only interested in breakpoints at this point, because it would only display the breakpoints that are currently set:

```
DB<4> L b
   NoArg.pm:
    14:             print __FILE__." running noargs()\n";
 break if (1)
DB<5>
```

Now we use c to continue until reaching our breakpoint:

```
DB<5> c
   usereq loaded
   NoArg::noargs(NoArg.pm:14):           print __FILE__." running noargs()\n";
DB<5>
```

We appear to have stopped at the first line of the subroutine, and we can check this by asking for a one-time trace using T:

```
DB<5> T
   $ = NoArg::noargs() called from file 'usereq' line 10
DB<5>
```

Sometimes it is just a good idea to be explicit, and to ask for the trace to confirm what we assume to be correct. From the trace we can see that we got here via usereq from line 10.

Returning from the Subroutine

Let's use r to return from this subroutine to our calling context, as explained in Chapter 3:

```
DB<5> r
   NoArg.pm running noargs()
   scalar context return from NoArg::noargs: 1
   main::(usereq:11):          print __FILE__." has no arguments\n";
DB<5>
```

OK, we're back in usereq, and it's a good time to look around. We'll use l at our current position to see the code that will be executed next, and to reorient ourselves.

```
DB<5> l
   11==>           print __FILE__." has no arguments\n";
   12      } else {
   13:             require Args;
   14:             my $o_args = Args->new;
   15:             print __FILE__." arguments: ".$o_args->format('all');
   16      }
   17
   18:     exit;
   19
   20      BEGIN {
DB<5>
```

We can see that the Args module would be called in the other branch. The program has some arguments in this other branch, and we might want to see the subroutines that are available in that package.

Setting a Breakpoint in Another Module

At this point, we could try to install a breakpoint on one of the subroutines in the Args module, format() subroutine:

```
DB<5> b Args::format
    Subroutine Args::format not found.
DB<6>
```

Hmmm, that didn't work—the debugger hasn't found the subroutine. We may have misspelled the name, and a quick way to check would be to look for any subroutine in the Args package. We might use a command like this:

```
DB<6> S Args
DB<7>
```

Still nothing! If you're wondering why the S Arg command showed several subroutines earlier and the S Args command doesn't show anything now, check out the difference between Arg and Args commands. We've added an "S" accidentally. There are subroutines in the currently loaded code that have Arg in the subroutine name, but none have Args in the subroutine name yet. It may be obvious when stated like that, but very often, that is what debugging is all about. Don't *assume*, look!

Loading an UnUsed Module

Now we can see that it's not surprising that there weren't any subroutines found. The code hasn't been loaded yet, and it's only going to be require'd in the other branch at runtime. If we really want to inspect this code, with this debugger instantiation, we can still load the module manually:

```
DB<7> use Args
    Args.pm begun
    Args.pm loaded
DB<8>
```

Now have another look, by rerunning the S Args command, and this time we should find several subroutines defined:

```
DB<8> S Args
    Args::BEGIN
    Args::format
    Args::new
DB<9>
```

That's better. We can now list and inspect the newly loaded code. At this point, we should quit and move onto the next breakpoint command, where we explain how to get the debugger to stop once Perl has compiled the subroutine:

```
DB<9> q
    %>
```

The b compile subname

The b compile command sets a breakpoint at the first executable statement encountered after the given subroutine has been compiled. In this example, because we wish to stop as soon as the subroutine has been compiled, we have to give the program several arguments. This way the usereq program will execute the else statement that involves the Args module. Note that we bypassed this code in the preceding example.

We'll run the debugger on the usereq program with several arguments:

```
%> perl -d usereq one two three
Loading DB routines from perl5db.pl version 1.27
Editor support available.
Enter h or 'h h' for help, or 'man perldebug' for more help.
NoArg.pm begun
NoArg.pm loaded
usereq begun
main::(usereq:8):        print __FILE__." loaded\n";
  DB<1>
```

The debugger stops again at the first executable statement, and this time our first command will be to set a breakpoint against the compile of the Args::format subroutine.

```
DB<1> b compile Args::format
DB<2>
```

Unfortunately, the debugger still doesn't give us any information about this, and we'll just have to just assume it was successful. We could try listing the subroutine, using the l subname form, perhaps Perl knows something we do not?

```
DB<2> l Args::format
    Switching to file ''.
    Subroutine Args::format not found.
DB<3>
```

Well, I guess not. The debugger has neither given us feedback when we set the compiletime breakpoint, or found the subroutine against which it apparently set the breakpoint. This is because the debugger knows it is working with a breakpoint that has yet to be compiled, and therefore working with information it does not have yet.

Checking Postponed Breakpoints

We can confirm whether a breakpoint is postponed by checking if we have our breakpoint. Do this using the L command to list all breakpoints, actions, and watch-expressions:

```
DB<3> L
    Postponed breakpoints in subroutines:
    Args::format    compile
DB<3>
```

In the returned listing, we can see by the Postponed keyword that the Args::format breakpoint has the special compile hint next to it. This is exactly what we are looking for! Now we know that the next time the debugger compiles this subroutine it will set a breakpoint at the first executable statement it encounters—after finishing the compiling of the subroutine.

Now issue the c command to simply continue to the next breakpoint where the debugger is told to stop:

```
DB<4> c
    usereq loaded
    NoArg.pm running noargs()
    Args::CODE(0x83d2960)(Args.pm:36):              print __FILE__." begun\n";
DB<4>
```

We're stopped in the BEGIN block—after all of the Args code has been compiled, but before any of it has been run. In other words, at the first line of executable code *after* the subroutine has been compiled. Even the BEGIN block has not been run yet, as can be seen from our print __FILE__." begun\n" statement. The first BEGIN block of the Args module is *about* to be run.

This can be very useful when a module uses BEGIN blocks to control or set up program behavior. Problems with uninitialized variables can be problematic to debug using print statements encountered before and after the BEGIN block, because the BEGIN blocks get executed at compiletime and the print statements at runtime.

Now we can check where we are, and how we got there, by asking for a once-only trace again:

```
DB<3> T
    $ = Args::BEGIN() called from file 'Args.pm' line 37
    $ = eval {...} called from file 'Args.pm' line 37
    $ = require 'Args.pm' called from file 'usereq' line 13
DB<3>
```

Let's take the customary look around the environment, using the l subname command, to reorient ourselves:

```
DB<3> l Args::format
    18      sub format {
    19:             my $self  = shift;
    20:             my $index = shift;
    21:             print __FILE__." running format()\n";
    22:             my $str;
    23:             if ($index eq 'all') {
    24:                     $str = join("<-\n  ->", @{$self->{_args}});
    25             } elsif ($index =~ /^\d+$/) {
    26:                     $str = $self->{_args}[$index];
    27             } else {
DB<4>
```

We can now see which subroutines have been defined in this namespace (at this point in the runtime of the program), by using the S Args command again. We should then see the appropriate defined Args::* subroutines:

```
DB<4> S Args
    Args::BEGIN
    Args::format
    Args::new
DB<5>
```

Viewing Variables in Another Package

Note that there is nothing to stop us from looking at variables that belong to another package. We can simply use the V package command to see them:

```
DB<5> V NoArg
    @ISA = (
                        0  'Exporter'
    )
    @EXPORT_OK = (
                        0  'noargs'
    )
DB<6>
```

For a reminder of where you are, and to reset the code listing display pointer, use

```
DB<6> .
    Args::CODE(0x83d2948)(Args.pm:36):   print __FILE__." begun\n";
DB<6>
```

Now execute the next line of code (in our case, the single line in the BEGIN block), by using the n command to step to the next statement:

```
DB<6> n
    Args.pm begun
    Args::(Args.pm:6):      print __FILE__." loaded\n";
DB<6>
```

which brings us into the body of the Args module. Note that this is nothing like stopping in the subroutine. However, if this module did a series of setup actions inside the BEGIN block, we could debug them here, before the entire code in the module was executed. This is a very useful command to know when multiple modules or libraries are used, and when you want to get to the code in the module, *before* a single line of it has been run.

Having interacted with our environment, and learned how the b compile subname command works, we can continue to the end of the program:

```
DB<6> c
    Args.pm loaded
    Args.pm running new()
    getargs begun
    getargs loaded
    getargs running: one
    getargs running: two
    getargs running: three
    getargs done
    Args.pm running format()
    usereq arguments:
->one<-
->two<-
```

```
->three<-
    Debugged program terminated.  Use q to quit or R to restart,
use O inhibit_exit to avoid stopping after program termination,
h q, h R or h O to get additional info.
DB<6>
```

The b compile subname (with a Restart)

This command will set a breakpoint at the first executable statement encountered after the given subroutine has been compiled. To understand why this is useful, consider the previous example. Of course, the previous example doesn't help us if we wanted to set a compiletime breakpoint in the NoArg::noargs subroutine, because it is already loaded in the current session. In this case, we would have to restart the debugger session. Note that if we quit and restart a similar debugging session with the same arguments, all of our breakpoint information will be lost. However if we use the R (for restart) command, our breakpoint information will be stored and restored across the restart on our behalf, by the debugger itself.

Let's start by setting up a new debugger session to work with. To do this, we can use the same command as in the most recent example:

```
%> perl -d usereq one two three
Loading DB routines from perl5db.pl version 1.27
Editor support available.
Enter h or 'h h' for help, or 'man perldebug' for more help.
NoArg.pm begun
NoArg.pm loaded
usereq begun
main::(usereq:8):       print __FILE__." loaded\n";
  DB<1>
```

At this point, as you can see from the messages printed, the code in the NoArg module is already compiled, so we can't get to it directly, but we can set a compiletime breakpoint which will take effect the next time around, and effectively take us to a point to which we've already been and is currently behind us in sequence:

```
DB<1> b compile NoArg::noargs
DB<2>
```

Because we don't receive any feedback from the debugger on this, we should check it to make sure it took effect:

```
DB<2> L
    Postponed breakpoints in subroutines:
     NoArg::noargs  compile
DB<2>
```

Restarting the Session

Because the breakpoint listing looks fine (with the compiletime hint), now we can choose to restart the debugger session from the beginning using the R command:

```
DB<2> R
    Warning: some settings and command line options may be lost!
Loading DB routines from perl5db.pl version 1.27
Editor support available.
Enter h or 'h h' for help, or 'man perldebug' for more help.
NoArg::CODE(0x82e361c)(No
rg.pm:21):
21:                print __FILE__." begun\n";
  DB<2>
```

Note first of all that we receive the warning

```
Warning: some settings and command line options may be lost!
```

This is normal, and happens every time you use the R command to restart a debugger session. Although most settings and command line options will be carried across sessions, the warning is still worth noting, even if only to remain on the paranoid side. This message is just keeping you on your toes. Essentially the restart code in the debugger has not changed substantially between Perl version 5.005_3, when it first appeared, and the current version 5.8.5, and has proved consistently reliable. There have been a couple of *tweaks* however; for instance, -T (taint) and -A (assertion) flags have been added, as well as editor (vi or emacs) support. In normal usage, and in most unusual cases too, the debugger will faithfully reproduce the initial state of the session for a restart.

Returning to our restarted session, we can see that this time, the debugger has stopped just after the subroutine has been compiled, and as we saw in the previous example, the BEGIN routine has not been run yet. We are now inside the use code, which our program has called in its own compilation phase.

We can check our position with a once-only trace command using T:

```
DB<2> T
    $ = NoArg::BEGIN() called from file 'NoArg.pm' line 22
    $ = eval {...} called from file 'NoArg.pm' line 22
    $ = require 'NoArg.pm' called from file 'usereq' line 5
    $ = main::BEGIN() called from file 'NoArg.pm' line 22
    $ = eval {...} called from file 'NoArg.pm' line 22
DB<2>
```

Note that it is confirmed by the trace that we are in the NoArg::BEGIN subroutine. Now we can return from this code using the r command:

```
DB<2> r
    NoArg.pm begun
    scalar context return from CODE(0x82e361c): 1
    NoArg::CODE(0x81813a8)(NoArg.pm:6):
    6:      require Exporter;
DB<2>
```

We'll use the r command again to bring us back out to the top level usereq context, where the debugger helpfully reminds us what our next line of code is; the use FileHandle statement on line 6:

```
DB<3> r
    NoArg.pm loaded
    scalar context return from CODE(0x81813a8): ''
    main::CODE(0x8181420)(usereq:6):        use FileHandle;
DB<3>
```

Identifying Loaded Subroutines

We can demonstrate that our usereq program has not finished compilation yet by looking for any FileHandle subroutines. These subroutines have not been loaded yet, because the usereq program is still in the middle of the compilation process, and therefore no FileHandle subroutines should be loaded at this time:

```
DB<4> S FileHandle
DB<5>
```

Nothing there yet. Now we can execute the next line by using the n command:

```
DB<5> n
    FileHandle::CODE(0x8181420)(/opt/perl/lib/5.8.4/FileHandle.pm:5):
    5:      our($VERSION, @ISA, @EXPORT, @EXPORT_OK);
DB<5>
```

This time we use S FileHandle, we are shown the list of available FileHandle subroutines:

```
DB<5> S FileHandle
    FileHandle::BEGIN
    FileHandle::import
    FileHandle::pipe
DB<6>
```

As you have just seen, it is possible to get the debugger to stop at the first executable line of a library of code during runtime, while also directing it to stop compilation of any more code as soon as a particular subroutine has been compiled. This ability to do stop code in the middle of the compilation phase can be very powerful, when you wish to observe the behavior of a program without the interference of a use'd library or module. With the breakpoint commands demonstrated in this chapter, you have complete control over the execution of your Perl program at both compiletime and runtime.

Lets quit out of our program and move on to the next case.

The b postpone subname [condition]

The b postpone command sets a breakpoint at the first executable statement of the subroutine given after the subroutine has been compiled. Of course this is only effective if you intend to actually *run* the subroutine, in direct contrast to the previous b compile command. The subroutine in this case doesn't need to be already loaded.

For this example, we should run the debugger on the program with several arguments again:

```
%> perl -d usereq one two three
Loading DB routines from perl5db.pl version 1.27
Editor support available.
```

```
Enter h or 'h h' for help, or 'man perldebug' for more help.
NoArg.pm begun
NoArg.pm loaded
usereq begun
main::(usereq:7):          print __FILE__." loaded\n";
  DB<1>
```

Now we can set a breakpoint to be postponed until the next time this subroutine is called:

```
DB<1> b postpone Args::format
DB<2>
```

This time, because we used the postponed form, the debugger does not complain about not being able to find the relevant subroutine in the list of compiled code. Instead, it quietly notes the breakpoint for future reference.

All the same, let's check to see that it has been set with our trusty L command:

```
DB<2> L
    Postponed breakpoints in subroutines:
     Args::format    break +0 if 1
DB<2>
```

Note how the break +0 if 1 statement is given as the *default* condition if one isn't explicitly supplied. Now continue until we hit a stopping command or breakpoint:

```
DB<2> c
    usereq loaded
    NoArg.pm running noargs()
    Args.pm begun
    Args.pm loaded
    Args.pm running new()
    getargs begun
    getargs loaded
    getargs running: one
    getargs running: two
    getargs running: three
    getargs done
    Args::format(Args.pm:19):               my $self  = shift;
DB<2>
```

The debugger has stopped on the first line of the Args::format subroutine. We can see how we were called by asking for a stack trace using the T command:

```
DB<2> T
    $ = Args::format(ref(Args), 'all') called from file 'usereq' line 14
DB<2>
```

Looking Around the Local Environment

While we are here, we can have a proper look at our argument list passed to the subroutine by dumping a reference to it with the x command:

```
DB<2> x \@_
    0  ARRAY(0x823aeb4)
  0  Args=HASH(0x81fa690)
    '_args' => ARRAY(0x81fa720)
        0  'one'
        1  'two'
        2  'three'
  1  'all'
DB<3>
```

We can also list the code at the current location. It's always a good idea to reorient ourselves—there's nothing worse than executing a debugger command only to realize that you weren't where you thought you were, and have just run off the end of the program, or gone past the critical point. Better safe than sorry, I always say, it doesn't take long to have a quick look around. Remember that the ==> pointer shows where we are in the code:

```
DB<3> l
    19==>b          my $self  = shift;
    20:             my $index = shift;
    21:             print __FILE__." running format()\n";
    22:             my $str;
    23:             if ($index eq 'all') {
    24:                 $str = join("<-\n  ->", @{$self->{_args}});
    25              } elsif ($index =~ /^\d+$/) {
    26:                 $str = $self->{_args}[$index];
    27              } else {
    28:                 print "Error: unrecognised index($index)\n";
DB<3>
```

Now let's walk through the code one line at a time:

```
DB<3> n
    Args::format(Args.pm:20):              my $index = shift;
DB<3>
```

Let's move ahead to the next line so that our $index variable will be defined from our subroutine argument list:

```
DB<3> n
    Args::format(Args.pm:21):              print __FILE__." running format()\n";
DB<3>
```

Now that the $index variable has been defined in this context, we can print it out for reference:

```
DB<3> p $index
    all
DB<4>
```

Finally we can return from the subroutine, which (if the $PrintRet option is set) will also print out the return value or values and the context in which we are returning:

```
DB<4> r
    Args.pm running format()
    scalar context return from Args::format: '
->one<-
->two<-
->three<-
        '

    usereq arguments:
->one<-
->two<-
->three<-
    main::(usereq:17):      exit;
DB<4>
```

Viewing Code Elsewhere

It's worth remembering that you can always view the code in another module or library, which can be defined in any file anywhere on the system, with the single proviso that this code has been compiled.

Before we quit the usereq program, let's have a quick look at the NoArg::noargs subroutine:

```
DB<4> l NoArg::noargs
    Switching to file 'NoArg.pm'.
    13      sub noargs {
    14:             print __FILE__." running noargs()\n";
    15:             return (scalar(@_) == 0 ? 1 : 0);
    16      }
DB<5>
```

We're not restricted to reviewing only the code we've written; we can also look at third-party code. Let's have a look at the import subroutine in the FileHandle module, which is part of the core Perl distribution:

```
DB<5> l FileHandle::import
    Switching to file '/opt/perl/lib/5.8.4/FileHandle.pm'.
    69      sub import {
    70:         my $pkg = shift;
    71:         my $callpkg = caller;
    72:         require Exporter;
    73:         Exporter::export($pkg, $callpkg, @_);
    74
    75          #
    76          # If the Fcntl extension is available,
    77          #  export its constants.
    78          #
DB<6>
```

The next l continues listing code from the last position at which it was set, still in the FileHandle module:

```
DB<6> l
    79:            eval {
    80:                require Fcntl;
    81:                Exporter::export('Fcntl', $callpkg);
    82:            };
    83:        }
    84
    85        ##################################################
    86        # This is the only exported function we define;
    87        # the rest come from other classes.
    88        #
DB<6>
```

Resetting the Display

To bring the display pointer back to our current position, use the . command:

```
DB<6> .
    main::(usereq:8):        print __FILE__." loaded\n";
DB<6>
```

We've explored enough for now; let's quit and move on to the next breakpoint case:

```
DB<6> q
    %>
```

The b Load **Filename**

The b Load command sets a breakpoint at the first executable statement of the filename given after the file has been compiled. Again, we run the debugger on our program with the predictable arguments, to keep things consistent, and so that we are familiar with the code and its behavior:

```
%> perl -d usereq one two three
Loading DB routines from perl5db.pl version 1.27
Editor support available.
Enter h or 'h h' for help, or 'man perldebug' for more help.
NoArg.pm begun
NoArg.pm loaded
usereq begun
main::(usereq:7):        print __FILE__." loaded\n";
  DB<1>
```

■**Note** This command will set a breakpoint when the file is require'd.

In this case we want to set a breakpoint when we load our file, for example via a `require` statement:

```
DB<1> b load getargs
    Will stop on load of 'getargs'.
DB<2>
```

This time at least we get some feedback from the debugger. What a relief! However, because we're careful people, let's take a look anyway at our breakpoint list, just to make sure, using the familiar L b command:

```
DB<2> L b
    Breakpoints on load:
     getargs
DB<2>
```

Sure enough, there it is, this time with the on load debugger note.

Running to the Breakpoint

Now we're going to just run through the program and see where we end up. We can watch everything go through the BEGIN and load steps as we continue to the next stopping position. This is when our file gets loaded via the `require` statement from within the new method of the Args class.

Use the c command to let the debugger continue until it hits a breakpoint:

```
DB<2> c
    usereq loaded
    NoArg.pm running noargs()
    Args.pm begun
    Args.pm loaded
    Args.pm running new()
    getargs begun
    'getargs' loaded...
    Args::new(getargs:5):        print __FILE__." loaded\n";
DB<2>
```

Let's have a look at the code following our current position, to get feedback on where we are, by using the l command:

```
DB<2> l
    5==>     print __FILE__." loaded\n";
    6
    7:       my @ARGS = @ARGV;
    8
    9:       while (@ARGV) {
    10:              print __FILE__." running: ".shift(@ARGV)."\n";
    11:      }
    12
    13:      print __FILE__." done\n";
    14
DB<2>
```

We can take a look at how we were called via the once-only stack `backtrace` command:

```
DB<2> T
    $ = require 'getargs' called from file 'Args.pm' line 11
    $ = Args::new('Args') called from file 'usereq' line 13
DB<2>
```

Now let's use the c command with a line number for an argument to run down to line 13 of getargs:

```
DB<2> c 13
    getargs loaded
    getargs running: one
    getargs running: two
    getargs running: three
    Args::new(getargs:13):        print __FILE__." done\n";
DB<3>
```

To inspect the work the code has done, we should examine our input arguments to see that the array was actually cleaned. We use the dump-value command x with a reference to our @ARGV:

```
DB<3> x \@ARGV
    0  ARRAY(0x817d6ec)
      empty array
DB<4>
```

While we're here, let's also have a look at the variable we use internally to ensure we have carried over the correct values, again, using the x command:

```
DB<4> x \@ARGS
    0  ARRAY(0x81fa708)
        0  'one'
        1  'two'
        2  'three'
DB<5>
```

We're done, and we just need to take a last visual check of the code using l, before we allow the code to return.

Visual Checks Before Returning from a Subroutine

All these visual checks may seem unnecessary, but think of it along the lines of a last look over your shoulder before executing a change of direction maneuver on a motorbike. The times you don't remember to look are usually the times you wish you had.

Use the l command to list the code at our current position:

```
DB<5> l
    13==>    print __FILE__." done\n";
    14
    15:        \@ARGS;
    16
```

```
17      BEGIN {
18:              print __FILE__." begun\n";
19      }
DB<5>
```

Return and Continue

Finally, we can return from the file context in a similar fashion to returning from a subroutine by using the r command. This will bring us back to our usereq code:

```
DB<5> r
    getargs done
    scalar context return from Args::new: '_args' => ARRAY(0x81fa708)
 0  'one'
 1  'two'
 2  'three'
    main::(usereq:14):              print __FILE__.
        " arguments: ".$o_args->format('all');
DB<5>
```

As we return, the return arguments and context are printed out for our reference, and then we can continue off the end of the program using the c command:

```
DB<5> c
    Args.pm running format()
    usereq arguments:
->one<-
->two<-
->three<-
    Debugged program terminated.  Use q to quit or R to restart,
use O inhibit_exit to avoid stopping after program termination,
h q, h R or h O to get additional info.
DB<5>
```

and quit:

```
DB<5> q
    %>
```

Summary

In this chapter you have learned how to use the special breakpoint setting commands within the debugger, and used these commands to control program execution across multiple libraries at both compiletime and runtime.

You can use these commands to stop a program, not just at the first executable line of your main program, but also before it has even been loaded completely. You can do this before a BEGIN block has been run, or inside a BEGIN block of another module or library. You can gain control of the program in order to debug it, and any libraries it uses, thoroughly.

The next chapter explores the special case of debugging a program with recursive or otherwise complex functions.

CHAPTER 7

■■■

Debugging Object-Oriented Perl

It is indicative of inflexible procedural design if you find yourself using conditional statements to distinguish between object types.

—Sriram Srinivasan, *Advanced Perl Programming*

That statement is a gem that is too often ignored in Object-Oriented (OO) Perl programming. There are a number of programming practices that are specific to OO coding, and if you are not familiar with them, they can make debugging OO code quite complicated.

Yet debugging OO code should be no more complicated than debugging any other sort of code. At the end of the day, it's all just code and OO is simply a different way of expressing a programmer's intention from procedural code. By the time it gets to the machine level, the OO code may even be identical to the procedural version. OO is a useful way for a programmer to do a task in a clear, efficient, and reusable manner, and is just one more technique for getting the job done.

In this chapter, we will assume you are familiar with OO techniques and will show you several methods for handling OO Perl code. In particular, we'll look at ways of dealing with the following types of coding constructs:

- Objects: Code that describes a thing or process, usually with defined behavior and implicit relationships to other objects.

- Object member variables: Variables belonging to a particular object instance.

- Inheritance and Overloaded Methods: Child object methods that replace, redefine, or extend the code from parent objects.

- Autoloaded Methods: methods to call when no explicit subroutine code can be found for a particular object class.

First of all, we'll need some example code. The following Objects.pm module generates several simple objects for us to work with, all of which rely on each another. Each object provides several methods or member variables, which the object expects to be called in a particular manner. Each object will also respond to unknown method calls, or unrecognized member variable requests, in a manner that it believes is suitable for its object type.

Sample Program

The Objects.pm module (shown in Listing 7-1) is a small library that defines several related objects, in order to demonstrate the code constructs referred to previously. It provides the code to create a base Object, which in turn has an AUTOLOAD method for returning instance member variables and may be inherited from another (at this point unknown) object. The library provides a Book object, which it inherits from this Object, but also allows itself to be inherited by further objects, should the programmer require them. Lastly there are the Fiction and NonFiction objects, which use the Book object as a source of inheriting methods and for redefining certain behavior.

Listing 7-1. *The* Objects.pm *Module*

```
1 package Object;
2
3 use strict;
4 use vars qw($AUTOLOAD);
5
6 sub new {
7       my $class = shift;
8       bless {
9               _name    => ref($class) || $class,
10              _desc    => 'A thing',
11              _unknown => 'unknown attribute',
12      }, $class;
13 }
14
15 sub AUTOLOAD {
16      my $self = shift;
17      return if $AUTOLOAD =~ /DESTROY/;
18      my $attr = $AUTOLOAD;
19      $attr =~ s/^.+?([a-zA-Z]+)$/$1/;
20      return ($self->{"_$attr"} || $self->{_unknown}.": $attr");
21 }
22
23 1;
24
25 package Book;
26
27 use strict;
28 use base qw(Object);
29 $Book::VERSION = "1.02";
30 my $publisher = 'Apress';
31
32 sub new {
33      my $class = shift;
34      my $name  = shift;
35      my $self  = Object->new;
```

```
36        $self->{_name}    = $name;
37        $self->{_desc}    = 'A book';
38        $self->{_contents} = \@_;
39        $self->{_unknown}  = 'unknown book attribute';
40        bless $self;
41 }
42
43 sub linecount {
44        my $self = shift;
45        return scalar @{$self->{_contents}};
46 }
47
48 1;
49
50 package Fiction;
51
52 use strict;
53 use base qw(Book);
54 use vars qw($AUTOLOAD);
55
56 sub new {
57        my $class = shift;
58        my $self = Book->new(@_);
59        $self->{_desc} = 'A story book';
60        bless $self;
61 }
62
63 sub linecount { # Use the current process ID
64        return $$; # to simulate line counts.
65 }
66
67 sub AUTOLOAD {
68        my $self = shift;
69        return if $AUTOLOAD =~ /DESTROY/;
70        my $sub = $AUTOLOAD;
71        $sub =~ s/.*:://;
72        if ($sub =~ /^[aeiou]/) {
73                return "Making this up as we go along($sub)";
74        } else {
75                $sub = "SUPER::$sub";
76                return $self->$sub();
77        }
78 }
79
80 1;
81
82 package NonFiction;
83
```

```
84 use strict;
85 use base qw(Book);
86
87 sub new {
88     my $class = shift;
89     my $self = Book->new(@_);
90     $self->{_desc} = 'A true tale';
91     $self->{_bibliography} = 'substantial';
92     bless $self;
93 }
94
95 1;
96
97 __END__
98
99 =head1 NAME
100
101 Objects.pm - several objects
102
103 =head1 DESCRIPTION
104
105 Simple Object packages providing various Book-like objects for manipulation.
106
107 =cut
```

Next, there is the Perl code that calls the Objects.pm module (shown in Listing 7-2), and is contained in the file called objects. This code uses the objects available in the Objects.pm module to loop over the arguments given from the command line. As it loops over each argument, it prints the result, demonstrating how each object will respond to each object method call, and how it will react to an unknown method provided on the command line.

Listing 7-2. *The* objects *Script*

```
1 #!/usr/bin/perl -w
2
3 use Objects;
4 use strict;
5
6 unless (@ARGV) {
7     die("Usage: $0 method [names+]");
8 }
9
10 my @contents = ('first line', 'second line', 'third line', 'fourth line');
11 foreach my $obj (qw(Object Book NonFiction Fiction)) {
12     foreach my $meth (qw(name desc linecount), @ARGV) {
13         my $o_obj = $obj->new("A $obj title", @contents);
14         eval {
15             print sprintf('%-25s', ref($o_obj)."->$meth: ").
                       $o_obj->$meth()."\n";
```

```
16                };
17                if ($@) {
18                        print $@;
19                }
20        }
21      print "\n";
22 }
23
24 exit 0;
25
26 __END__
27
28 =head1 NAME
29
30 objects - some object code
31
32 =head1 SYNOPSIS
33
34      objects method_name
35
36 =head1 DESCRIPTION
37
38 Given one or more method names, passes them to each known Object, and calls
39 them in turn, printing out the result.
40
41 =cut
```

The code will pass to each object in turn, using the arguments name, desc, and linecount as methods to call, followed by whatever arguments are given on the command line. The name of the object and method called will be printed on the left-hand side, and the result will be shown on the right.

Executing the Code

Executing the objects program, with a single argument of bibliography from the command line, will produce output similar to the following:

```
$> perl ./objects bibliography
Object->name:          Object
Object->desc:          A thing
Object->linecount:     unknown attribute: linecount
Object->bibliography:  unknown attribute: bibliography
Book->name:            A Book title
Book->desc:            A book
Book->linecount:       4
Book->bibliography:    unknown book attribute: bibliography
NonFiction->name:      A NonFiction title
NonFiction->desc:      A true tale
NonFiction->linecount: 4
```

```
NonFiction->bibliography: substantial
Fiction->name:           A Fiction title
Fiction->desc:           A story book
Fiction->linecount:      2579
Fiction->bibliography:   unknown book attribute: bibliography
```

Note how each object responds to the method call in a different manner. In this simple case, it is possible to read the code in the Objects.pm module and to systematically work out the result for each particular case.

In real life, when an input file may have several million lines, and there may be a considerable number of variables and multiple interrelated objects involved, the output may not be so simple to foresee. We need strategies and tools to help us inspect the data at specific times and in certain cases, and to determine what each case will produce. This is an expedient way to discover where and why a particular problem (bug) is occurring. We'll use this code and command line to take a look at the possibilities that are available to you through the Perl debugger.

Debugging the Code

Now repeat exactly the same command you just ran, but this time using the –d switch to take it through the debugger:

```
$> perl -d objects bibliography
Loading DB routines from perl5db.pl version 1.27
Editor support available.
Enter h or 'h h' for help, or 'man perldebug' for more help.
main::(objects:6):    unless (@ARGV) {
DB<1>
```

The debugger stops at the first executable line, line 6. Although we have not executed any of the code in the objects program, the Objects.pm library has already been loaded. This means we can already look at the code that has been loaded, and what methods are available to each object type, before we go any further.

To see the code generated from the Objects.pm module, we can take a look with the f command, which tells the debugger we wish to view a file, by giving it an argument of Objects. The debugger will helpfully print out the first WindowSize lines of the file as we enter it. WindowSize is an option that we can modify to suit our working environment or situation:

```
DB<1> f Objects
Choosing /home/perltut/code/Objects.pm matching 'Objects':
1       package Object;
2
3:      use strict;
4:      use vars qw($AUTOLOAD);
5
6       sub new {
7:              my $class = shift;
8:              bless {
9                       _name    => ref($class) || $class,
10                      _desc    => 'A thing',
DB<2>
```

To see the next 15 lines of the Objects.pm file, use the l command with the appropriate argument. To see all the available options for the l command, type h l:

```
DB<2> l +15
11                      _unknown => 'unknown attribute',
12              }, $class;
13      }
14
15      sub AUTOLOAD {
16:             my $self = shift;
17:             return if $AUTOLOAD =~ /DESTROY/;
18:             my $attr = $AUTOLOAD;
19:             $attr =~ s/^.+?([a-zA-Z]+)$/$1/;
20:             return ($self->{"_$attr"} || $self->{_unknown}.": $attr");
21      }
22
23:     1;
24
25      package Book;
26
DB<3>
```

This code listing includes the package Book line, which informs Perl that the following code belongs to a different Book package. This is the extent of the Object code in the file.

Listing Methods

We can also retrieve a listing of methods for any object or class. To see all the available methods for an Object object, use the m command against the class name. This demonstrates that you do not need an actual object instance—rather you can work just as easily with the class name too:

```
DB<3> m Object
AUTOLOAD
new
via UNIVERSAL: VERSION
via UNIVERSAL: can
via UNIVERSAL: ISA
DB<4>
```

The VERSION, can, and ISA methods are generic to *all* Perl objects. This is because the UNIVERSAL class, from which all Perl objects are descended, provides them. The two remaining methods AUTOLOAD and new are of particular interest. We can also obtain a listing of the new method by specifying it as the argument to the l command:

```
DB<4> l Object::new
6       sub new {
7:              my $class = shift;
8:              bless {
9                       _name   => ref($class) || $class,
10                      _desc   => 'A thing',
```

```
11                        _unknown => 'unknown attribute',
12              }, $class;
13      }
DB<5>
```

We can do the same for the Book::new method to see both the differences and the similarities:

```
DB<5> l Book::new
31      sub new {
32:             my $class = shift;
33:             my $name  = shift;
34:             my $self  = Object->new;
35:             $self->{_name}     = $name;
36:             $self->{_desc}     = 'A book';
37:             $self->{_contents} = \@_;
38:             $self->{_unknown}  = 'unknown book attribute';
39:             bless $self;
40      }
DB<6>
```

On line 34 a new Object is created. This object is then modified over the following four lines, by having various instance member variables defined. Finally, at line 39, it is blessed into the Book class. The blessed object is what is returned from the Book::new method as the Book object and now considers itself to be both a Book and an Object.

Dumping a new Object

We can also take a look at the contents of a typical Object by using the x command to instantiate an instance of Object, and then dump it:

```
DB<6> x Object->new
0  Object=HASH(0x81fd47c)
'_desc' => 'A thing'
'_name' => 'Object'
'_unknown' => 'unknown attribute'
DB<7>
```

We can do the same with a Book object, but in this case, instead of simply throwing away the returned object, we will store it in the $o variable for future reference. You might want to keep this object handy, so that you can refer to it later. Eventually, you will use the i command to inspect the inheritance tree for an instance of this particular object. You might also want to keep a reference for this object, in order to track the effect of a piece of code on it, or to see how it has been affected by program behavior elsewhere during the debugging session:

```
DB<7> x my $o = Book->new
0  Book=HASH(0x83fd1ac)
'_contents' => ARRAY(0x827a060)
empty array
'_desc' => 'A book'
'_name' => undef
'_unknown' => 'unknown book attribute'
DB<8>
```

Note how the _desc member variable was reset within the Book::new method to A book. Also, you'll notice that the name undef is reflecting the incorrect usage of the Book::new method (this method expects a book name and contents as arguments). In this case, it is only the usage of the object method in the debugger that we have called incorrectly; the code in the previous example program is fine. This demonstrates how it can be useful to actually run the code, perhaps calling a subroutine multiple times with different arguments, to see what it actually does, and the value it returns, rather than to simply assume you know. The _unknown attribute has also changed, but we'll come across that shortly.

The Inheritance Tree

It can be useful to know the inheritance tree of a particular object. To see the classes and various version numbers for the newly created Book object, we can use the i command:

```
DB<8> i $o
Book 1.02, Object -1, set by base.pm
DB<9>
```

The Book object has a VERSION number (1.02). The plain Object has the special -1 number that has been set by base.pm, indicating it has not been assigned an explicit VERSION number yet.

Inspecting Package Variables

The V command is very useful for inspecting packaging variables because it will dump out all the variables in the given package. In a real-world scenario, this listing is likely to be very long and would usually benefit from being filtered through with a pager program using the | command (such as | V Book, for example). In this case, Book is such a small package that there is no point, and we can simply dump all known variables:

```
DB<9> V Book
@ISA = (
0  'Object'
)
$VERSION = 1.02
DB<10>
```

The V command takes a package name and an optional regex as arguments. The regex is applied to the name of the variables to dump, so to restrict the arguments dumped we could have used a regex like this (note the ~):

```
DB<10> V Book ~Ver
DB<11>
```

That did not produce any matching variables because the regex is wrong, or rather we should say if we wanted to find $VERSION it was wrong. A regex is case-sensitive, unless we explicitly make it case-insensitive:

```
DB<11> V Book ~(?i:Ver)
$VERSION = 1.02
DB<12>
```

Notice that this command will not find any lexical variables that have been declared using my. For that you need to use the y command.

The y command has two rules. First, it uses the PadWalker module to find these lexical variables, so PadWalker must be installed on your system. PadWalker didn't come with Perl by default until Perl 5.8.6, so you may have to install it from CPAN. Second, it will only find lexical variables in *higher* scopes. That means you cannot simply execute y at the beginning of your program and expect to find all lexicals in the main package; it is necessary to be at least at one subroutine depth. We'll do this in a moment.

Taking a Moment to Think About the Situation

We've already discovered quite a lot about the objects that have been generated from the Objects. pm module, despite not having proceeded beyond the first line of code. This shows just how much information is available to the programmer and debugger from the very beginning of program execution. Many times, you can find out all you need to fix a bug well before the entire program has completed.

Just knowing which object methods are available may be enough to figure out why a program is failing. Perhaps an object has not been properly initialized, and therefore critical member variables are not in place. Maybe an object cannot see the methods that you planned to use, perhaps because these desired methods have been assigned to another object, or have been overloaded at a later stage.

Such scenarios are not uncommon. Sometimes the problem is that the programmer has simply *assumed* something about the code, and has not taken the trouble to have a look while the code is running. Making the time to take a breath, perhaps drink a cup of coffee, or take a short walk (whatever helps you find your particular thinking hat) is an important part of the successful debugging strategy.

Lexical Variables

As mentioned previously, to get the debugger to dump lexical variables via the y command, we need to be at least one subroutine deep. Use the c command to continue to the first known subroutine:

```
DB<12> c Object::new
Object::new(/home/perltut/code/Objects.pm:7):
7:              my $class = shift;
DB<13>
```

Now use the y command to print out all lexical variables (by default y prints the lexicals from one level up):

```
DB<13> y
DB<13>
```

Alas, we find nothing in the Object namespace. Proceed to the next object and do the same again:

```
DB<13> c Book::new
Object->name:           Object
Object->desc:           A thing
Object->linecount:      unknown attribute: linecount
Object->bibliography:   unknown attribute: bibliography
```

```
Book::new(/home/perltut/code/Objects.pm:33):
33:                my $class = shift;
DB<14>
```

The Object navigated through the preset and command line arguments, and showed the results. Now the debugger has stopped in the Book::new method as instructed. Use the y command again:

```
DB<14> y
$publisher = '$publisher'
DB<14>
```

The lexical $Book::publisher variable, along with its value, is dumped so that it may be inspected. It's quite exciting to see all your lexicals at once, but sometimes just looking at the available data is not enough. There are times when it is necessary, or even simply useful, to be able to walk through the code, line by line, as it executes. This can be particularly useful with object methods, especially when you are unfamiliar with the object code in question, and wish to understand it better.

Stepping Through an Object Method Call: s

We will use the s command to step through a short method call. To make clear what's going on, and to ensure we can set a breakpoint at a relevant line of code, return to the main context by using the r command:

```
DB<14> r
scalar context return from Book::new: '_contents' => ARRAY(0x81fd0f8)
0  'first line'
1  'second line'
2  'third line'
3  'fourth line'
'_desc' => 'A book'
'_name' => 'A Book title'
'_unknown' => 'unknown book attribute'
main::(objects:14):                   eval {
DB<14>
```

Because the PrintRet option is set (by default) using the r command, the return value from the Book::new method call, including the context, is printed. The execution of the program stops again, and now it is possible to set a conditional breakpoint on line 14. The conditions, in this case, are that the $obj variable must be equal to NonFiction and the $meth variable should include the word count, which will stop the program just before it calls the linecount() method:

```
DB<14> b 14 $obj eq 'NonFiction' && $meth =~ /count/
DB<15>
```

Before running this, we can also set a pre-prompt Perl command using the < command. This will display the values of the various variables each time the debugger offers us a prompt, thus giving us constant feedback on the variables that concern us at the moment:

```
DB<15> < print "obj: ".($obj||'')." meth: ".($meth||'')." o_obj: ".($o_obj||'')."\n"
DB<16>
```

We use the ($obj||'') construct to avoid annoying Use of uninitialized value in concatenation... warnings when this line is printed out. Now use the c command to continue until the debugger hits the breakpoint at line 14:

```
DB<16> c
Book->name:           A Book title
Book->desc:           A book
Book->linecount:      4
Book->bibliography:   unknown book attribute: bibliography
NonFiction->name:     A NonFiction title
NonFiction->desc:     A true tale
main::(objects:14):                        eval {
obj: NonFiction meth: linecount o_obj: NonFiction=HASH(0x8458a20)
DB<16>
```

The program runs through the rest of the Book object methods and begins executing the NonFiction method calls, stopping when it reaches line 14 and the conditional breakpoint conditions are met. Now it is possible to use the s command to single-step through the Perl code, and view one executable statement after the next:

```
DB<16> s
main::(objects:15): print sprintf
        ('%-25s', ref($o_obj)."->$meth: ").$o_obj->$meth()."\n";
obj: NonFiction meth: linecount o_obj: NonFiction=HASH(0x8458a20)
DB<16>
```

The s command took the debugger into the eval{} statement. Typing s again will take us into the next subroutine: the $meth() call:

```
DB<16> s
Book::linecount(/home/perltut/code/Objects.pm:44):
44:              my $self = shift;
obj:  meth:  o_obj:
DB<16>
```

It is clear from the LineInfo displayed by the debugger that the program has stopped at the first line of the Book::linecount subroutine, at line 44. This is where the $self variable is assigned from the first argument shifted off the subroutine parameter list. Typing s again will take us one step further:

```
DB<16> s
Book::linecount(/home/perltut/code/Objects.pm:45):
45:              return scalar @{$self->{_contents}};
obj:  meth:  o_obj:
DB<16>
```

The subroutine is about to return the scalar value of the _contents member variable. Before it does this, it must evaluate the expression given in a list context (the @{...} construct), thus making it a two-step process, and allowing us to see this line twice.

Note that because the most recent command was an s, it is possible to use either an s again, or to repeat the s command by simply pressing Enter and sending a CR (Carriage Return) to the debugger. This also works for the n command:

```
DB<16> <CR>
Book::linecount(/home/perltut/code/Objects.pm:45):
45:             return scalar @{$self->{_contents}};
obj:  meth:  o_obj:
DB<16>
```

Notice also how the obj, meth, and o_obj variables are all empty in the current context. Now enter one more CR:

```
DB<16> <CR>
NonFiction->linecount:    4
main::(objects:17):                       if ($@) {
obj: NonFiction meth: linecount o_obj: NonFiction=HASH(0x8458a20)
DB<16>
```

The final result from the Book::linecount method is printed—and it's the integer 4. This confirms that calling linecount() on a NonFiction object will actually use Book::linecount. Sometimes single-stepping through the code can help a great deal in the seemingly endless hunt for that last (?) elusive bug.

Another very useful approach to dealing with methods called on objects, and confirming how they may be used, is to trace them, on the fly.

Tracing an Object Method Call: t expr

Because objects can call one another in so many ways, it can be helpful to trace them as they call a particular method. It's good to know that Perl searches for object methods using a depth-first search. The depth-first search Perl uses works through the class names in the @ISA array, from left-to-right and depth-first. That is, it starts at the leftmost object and goes as deep as it can, before taking a look at the next class to the right, and going deep again. If you trace the call, you can see for yourself exactly which path Perl chooses when it searches through the @ISA array for the correct method to call.

Use the t expr command to trace the execution of the desc method on the current Book object. Include a print statement to see the final result:

```
DB<16> t print $o_obj->desc
main::((eval 28)[/opt/perl/lib/5.8.5/perl5db.pl:620]:3):
3:      print $o_obj->desc;
Object::AUTOLOAD(/home/perltut/code/Objects.pm:16):
16:             my $self = shift;
Object::AUTOLOAD(/home/perltut/code/Objects.pm:17):
17:             return if $AUTOLOAD =~ /DESTROY/;
Object::AUTOLOAD(/home/perltut/code/Objects.pm:18):
18:             my $attr = $AUTOLOAD;
Object::AUTOLOAD(/home/perltut/code/Objects.pm:19):
19:             $attr =~ s/^.+?([a-zA-Z]+)$/$1/;
Object::AUTOLOAD(/home/perltut/code/Objects.pm:20):
20:             return ($self->{"_$attr"} || $self->{_unknown}.": $attr");
A true tale
DB<17>
```

The trace confirms that this method call will use the `Object::AUTOLOAD` subroutine and returns the `A true tale` value. Using a variant on the conditional breakpoint from earlier, we can set up the debugger to stop when our $obj turns into a `Fictional` one:

```
DB<17> b 14 $obj eq 'Fiction'
DB<18>
Use c to continue to the breakpoint to pick up the new object.
DB<18> c
NonFiction->bibliography: substantial
main::(objects:14):                      eval {
obj: Fiction meth: name o_obj: Fiction=HASH(0x81fd0e8)
DB<18>
```

The program has completed the `NonFiction` object calls, and has stopped the first time the $obj has turned into `Fiction`. This is confirmed by the handy pre-prompt `Perl` we set up earlier. Now trace the same statement as before:

```
DB<18> t print $o_obj->desc
main::((eval 32)[/opt/perl/lib/5.8.5/perl5db.pl:620]:3):
3:      print $o_obj->desc;
Fiction::AUTOLOAD(/home/perltut/code/Objects.pm:68):
68:             my $self = shift;
Fiction::AUTOLOAD(/home/perltut/code/Objects.pm:69):
69:             return if $AUTOLOAD =~ /DESTROY/;
Fiction::AUTOLOAD(/home/perltut/code/Objects.pm:70):
70:             my $sub = $AUTOLOAD;
Fiction::AUTOLOAD(/home/perltut/code/Objects.pm:71):
71:             $sub =~ s/.*:://;
Fiction::AUTOLOAD(/home/perltut/code/Objects.pm:72):
72:             if ($sub =~ /^[aeiou]/) {
Fiction::AUTOLOAD(/home/perltut/code/Objects.pm:75):
75:                 $sub = "SUPER::$sub";
Fiction::AUTOLOAD(/home/perltut/code/Objects.pm:76):
76:                 return $self->$sub();
Object::AUTOLOAD(/home/perltut/code/Objects.pm:16):
16:             my $self = shift;
Object::AUTOLOAD(/home/perltut/code/Objects.pm:17):
17:             return if $AUTOLOAD =~ /DESTROY/;
Object::AUTOLOAD(/home/perltut/code/Objects.pm:18):
18:             my $attr = $AUTOLOAD;
Object::AUTOLOAD(/home/perltut/code/Objects.pm:19):
19:             $attr =~ s/^.+?([a-zA-Z]+)$/$1/;
Object::AUTOLOAD(/home/perltut/code/Objects.pm:20):
20:             return ($self->{"_$attr"} || $self->{_unknown}.": $attr");
A story book
DB<19>
```

There's a whole lot more going on there. Instead of going straight to the `Object::AUTOLOAD` method, this time Perl has looked in the available `NonFiction::AUTOLOAD` method. Then this

NonFiction code, after working on the parameters a bit, has passed control (at line 76) to its SUPER class, before returning the A story book value. This is a case of AUTOLOAD calling AUTOLOAD via object inheritance.

Other Approaches

There are other techniques you can use with objects in the debugger. These include using the documented can method, which will return a reference to a subroutine if the object can calls a particular method. Let's take a look at the return value and see if the object can will call a method called linecount:

```
DB<19> print $o_obj->can(linecount)
CODE(0x83041ec)
DB<20>
```

As you can see, it's not simply a true value, but a code reference that gets returned. We can dump this to see what it points to:

```
DB<20> x $o_obj->can(linecount)
0   CODE(0x83041ec)
-> &Fiction::linecount in /home/perltut/code/Objects.pm:63-65
DB<21>
```

Hmmm, let's take a look at that Fiction::linecount subroutine, using the l command to list the code:

```
DB<21> l Fiction::linecount
Switching to file '/home/perltut/code/Objects.pm'.
63      sub linecount {
64:             return $$;
65      }
DB<22>
```

which brings us full circle to where we started, looking at and reading the code. As you can see, debugging OO Perl uses many of the techniques used to debug procedural code, and as always, remember to observe the behavior and assume nothing.

For more information on using OO programming techniques with Perl, see the following related perldocs: perlboot, perlobj, perltooc, and perltoot.

Summary

In this chapter you have learned how to use the Perl debugger to walk through an object-oriented Perl program, and how to find the methods available to you for each object. You've also learned how to inspect the call tree, via a stack trace on an expression, which allows you to see what will happen when an object is called with an apparently unrecognized method or argument.

In the next chapter we'll take a look at how you can use the Perl debugger as a shell and how to use it to experiment with code constructs on the fly.

CHAPTER 8

■ ■ ■

Using the Debugger As a Shell

If the gods had meant us to be naked, we would be born that way . . .

—Anonymous

We can paraphrase this line to read, "If Perl had intended for us to have a Perl shell, it would always have been there." Interestingly, in both of these quotes we can find an extant truth. Perl has always had an interactive shell, in the form of the debugger, which has been shipped with Perl since the first incarnation, way back in the 1980s. Most, people however, have turned to using modules to realize a Perl shell, which is okay too, because, as we know, there is always more than one way to do things. In this chapter, however, we're going to focus on using the debugger as a shell.

One of Perl's strengths is its interactive nature. It is very good at letting you try out ideas and quickly see whether they'll work. You can write a small program in a text file and execute it immediately, or you can specify a complete mini-program by using the -e switch, possibly multiple times, when calling Perl on the command line. The debugger lets you take this even further by acting as an interactive command shell, interfacing directly with the Perl interpreter, and trying out code and constructs as quickly as you can think of them. In this chapter we're going to look at some of the ways you can use the debugger as a Perl shell, and offer some hints and tips for making that experience a pleasant and rewarding one.

Interactive Shell Power

A shell is an interactive, command-based environment for interacting with the operating system. This means that it does not run and immediately exit; instead it runs the given command, and once completed, it waits for the next one. The Unix login shell and the Windows/DOS command prompt are general purpose shells, but there are many different Perl modules that provide specialized shells for specialized tasks. In each case, the ability to type commands into the shell and have them executed immediately can make it much faster than having to write entire programs to try out simple commands.

For example, the shell in the `DBI::Shell` module makes it simple to interact with databases and try out DBI functionality, without having to write a completely new program. This can save hours of time when you're debugging a Perl program, which uses the DBI, because you can send the relevant SQL (Structured Query Language) of the database in question, directly to the database, and see if the problem lies in the database or in the code.

The Perl debugger can be used directly as a Perl shell, and when used this way it enables you to leverage all of its power in a running, and effectively persistent, instance of the Perl interpreter. In fact, you are already in a Perl shell as soon as the debugger is running interactively. Anything you type will be sent to Perl directly and executed as a Perl command, unless it can be interpreted as a debugger command first. Also, all the power of the debugger is there at your fingertips—you can trace through an expression, set a breakpoint in a distant subroutine and call it, and so on.

Let's start a session to examine some debugger command line features that will affect how statements execute within the debugger shell. First, start a Perl shell session with the debugger using 0 as the target program, and given via the -e command line option as an indicator of what code to use:

```
> perl -d -e 0
Loading DB routines from perl5db.pl version 1.27
Editor support available.
Enter h or 'h h' for help, or 'man perldebug' for more help.
main::(-e:1):   0
DB<1>
```

You find yourself in a simple loop in the debugger. From now on, everything you type will be executed by either the debugger or by Perl itself. Let's print out the value of the current process ID using the venerable print command:

```
DB<1> print "current process id: $$\n"
current process id: 2839
DB<2>
```

If your command is ambiguous in any way, or you wish to make certain that the debugger will ignore your command and pass it immediately on to Perl, simply prefix the command with ; or +. Another approach would be to surround the command with braces. To demonstrate this feature, let's do the same as the previous command using the debugger command p instead of the Perl print command:

```
DB<2> p "current process id: $$\n"
current process id: 2839
DB<3>
```

As you can see, that works fine, because the debugger has a p command, which although it simply translates this to print internally, the p is still the relevant command. However, if we force the debugger to pass this command directly to Perl, we get a very different result. This time, prefix the command with + to force this behavior, and see what happens:

```
DB<3> +p "current process id: $$\n"
String found where operator expected at (eval 21) [/opt/perl/lib/5.8.5/
    perl5db.pl:620] line 2, near "p "current process id: $$\n""
at (eval 21)[/opt/perl/lib/5.8.5/perl5db.pl:620] line 2
eval '($@, $!, $^E, $,, $/, $\, $^W) = @saved;
    package main; $^D = $^D | $DB::db_stop;
+p "current process id: $$\\n";
;' called at /opt/perl/lib/5.8.5/perl5db.pl line 620
DB::eval called at /opt/perl/lib/5.8.5/perl5db.pl line 3292
DB::DB called at -e line 1
```

```
(Do you need to predeclare p?)
at (eval 21)[/opt/perl/lib/5.8.5/perl5db.pl:620] line 2
eval '($@, $!, $^E, $,, $/, $\\, $^W) = @saved;
    package main; $^D = $^D | $DB::db_stop;
+p "current process id: $$\\n";
;' called at /opt/perl/lib/5.8.5/perl5db.pl line 620
DB::eval called at /opt/perl/lib/5.8.5/perl5db.pl line 3292
DB::DB called at -e line 1
syntax error at (eval 21)[/opt/perl/lib/5.8.5/perl5db.pl:620] line 2,
    near "p "current process id: $$\n""
DB<4>
```

Now there's an error message to be proud of. Clearly p `"current process id: $$\n"` is not a Perl command!

This is consistent with what we know and merely confirms for us how stupid computers can be. Computers only do what we tell them to do, precisely. It may appear sometimes that they do not DWIM (Do What I Mean), but they always DWIS (Do What I Say). Debugging is the continual process of finding out what you told the computer to do, and replacing it with what you *should* have told the computer to do.

Perl is particularly good at interpreting the DWIM approach to programming, and this is one of the reasons it's such a good language to learn and to use for many purposes. Because you can use the Perl debugger as a Perl shell, it can be used as a powerful environment for trying out new constructs, testing ideas, and experimenting with code. This makes it ideal for the typically one-off type of commands often used in a shell environment.

Creating a Workaround

Because this is Perl, we can create our own commands to work around the issue demonstrated previously. Let's extend or change the debugger's standard p command by creating a new p command for just this one session. We'll do this by declaring a subroutine, on the fly, which prints its arguments surrounded by a pair of arrows:

```
DB<4> sub p { print "->@_<-\n" }
DB<5>
```

The arrows will help display visually exactly which parameters were given to the p command in the first place. Now run the same command as earlier, prefixing the p with the plus sign (+), so as to explicitly pass the command directly to Perl, and make sure it doesn't get interpreted as a debugger command:

```
DB<5> +p "current process id: $$\n"
->current process id: 2932
<-
DB<6>
```

Now we've done away with the previous extensive error message, and we can now see the newline given in the arguments to the call. This kind of approach can be very useful for determining the arguments that were *actually* sent to the subroutine, and not the arguments that you thought were sent to the subroutine.

Earlier, we talked about how even the debugger uses the revered print statement, at least by wrapping it in the p command. In this example, we've done it again and used the print statement to good purpose, extending its functionality and producing a solution to the current issue by using the tools at our disposal. The point with debugging, as in all programming, is know precisely what you want to do, and to make the computer do that, and nothing else.

Before proceeding, let's take a quick detour and see how you can call out to the system shell too.

Calling the Shell

In addition to using the debugger as a Perl shell, you can call the system shell without ever leaving your debugger session. The standard command for doing this is by using the ShellBang option, or !. Unfortunately, this is the same character used by the RecallCommand option. This means that the debugger has a clunky workaround, which is to use both options together, or !!, to indicate that you want to call a shell command:

```
DB<6> !!date
Fri Feb 25 11:16:39 CET 2005
DB<7>
```

This being Perl, (nearly) everything is possible and we can change the command used to call the shell from !! to, let's say, the forward slash: /. There are several benefits to doing this. For one thing the commands are completely distinct and therefore not so easily confused by either man or computer. Also, we find that we only have to use a single keystroke. You can choose any convenient character, but as the / is not used in the debugger elsewhere, it is an ideal candidate for the replacement.

Creating a Command Alias

In this case, the command to alias the ShellBang command to the forward slash looks like this:

```
DB<7> = / !!
/       = !!
DB<8>
```

The option change is confirmed from the debugger, and now you can simply call / shell-command to execute any shell command of your choosing:

```
DB<8> / ls -ltr /var/log/
total 7763
drwxr-xr-x   2 root     root          48 2003-09-23 19:18 ircd
drwxr-x---   2 news     news         136 2003-11-09 19:04 news
-rw-r--r--   1 root     root           0 2003-11-09 19:14 ntp
...
DB<9>
```

Not having to leave your session to interact with the system is a powerful tool. For example, you might wish to remove log files, or check that particular files and directory structures are in place, before proceeding with a debugging session. The possibilities are endless.

Capturing Output

Another way the debugger interacts with your operating system is when you use the doc or man commands to invoke the perldoc program, in order to examine the installed documentation. The output from these calls is piped through the pager of your choice. Although the default pager is usually less or more (on Unix-compatible systems), you can change this with the pager option command (see h o).

You can pass the output of any debugger command to your pager if the output is likely to exceed the limits of your current session view. Just precede your command with the pipe symbol, or |. This is particularly useful when you have an object or data structure in Perl. Try it when dumping the %INC hash:

```
DB<10> | x \%INC
0   HASH(0x8171ea4)
'AutoLoader.pm' => '/opt/perl/lib/5.8.5/AutoLoader.pm'
'Carp.pm' => '/opt/perl/lib/5.8.5/Carp.pm'
'Carp/Heavy.pm' => '/opt/perl/lib/5.8.5/Carp/Heavy.pm'
'Config.pm' => '/opt/perl/lib/5.8.5/i686-linux/Config.pm'
'DynaLoader.pm' => '/opt/perl/lib/5.8.5/i686-linux/DynaLoader.pm'
'Exporter.pm' => '/opt/perl/lib/5.8.5/Exporter.pm'
'File/Glob.pm' => '/opt/perl/lib/5.8.5/i686-linux/File/Glob.pm'
'IO.pm' => '/opt/perl/lib/5.8.5/i686-linux/IO.pm'
...
DB<11>
```

Now you can use the appropriate quit command for the pager to exit back into the debugger session:

```
q
DB<12>
```

Using the Debugger As a Laboratory

A useful thing to note about using the debugger as a Perl shell comes when you realize that anything you type will be passed to Perl for execution in an internal eval statement. You can safely experiment with different code constructs to find the best solution to a particular problem, knowing that any major problems will be caught for you, and that you can leisurely examine the error messages provided in $@. Take the case of capturing the output from a regex match. You might quite reasonably write or review code similar to the following line, which builds the hash on the left from the matched word characters found in the string:

```
DB<11> %hash = "this and  that in  a string" =~ /\w+\s*/g
DB<12>
```

When you dump the structure with the x command, though, you find that most of the keys and values have, along with the word characters, also absorbed the spaces between the words and stuck them on the end in each case:

```
DB<12> x \%hash
0   HASH(0x84f34c8)
'a ' => 'string'
```

```
'that ' => 'in  '
'this ' => 'and  '
DB<13>
```

A quick fix for this is to modify the match to include capturing parentheses. It's simple to try out on the debugger command line:

```
DB<13> %hash = "this and  that in  a string" =~ /(\w+)\s*/g
```

Now the match will return a list of what was captured into the hash, not just what was greedily matched. You can see this by dumping out the new structure:

```
DB<14> x \%hash
0  HASH(0x84ecea8)
'a' => 'string'
'that' => 'in'
'this' => 'and'
DB<15>
```

You can see how useful this can be in simply experimenting with different regexes until the right combination is found. If you are unsure about a construct, just try it out. You don't need to start up a new Perl interpreter with each call (as you would if you used a command like perl -e '$str =~ /regex/'). Instead you can just modify the regex within the session and try again.

Here's an example of how you might extend this to learn more about what was matched in each attempt. First let's set up a string against which to match a regex:

```
DB<15> $str = 'user.name@an.ip-domain.org'
DB<16>
```

Now set up a regex in an attempt to separate the words to suit our purposes. In this case we want everything before the @ to be one word, and everything following the @ to be separated by a period (.):

```
DB<16> $regex = '([^@]+)\@([^.]+).([^.]).([^.]+)'
DB<17>
```

You can see what will be captured into the $1, $2, $3, etc. variables, by dumping the result in the debugger, using the x command:

```
DB<17> x $str =~ /$regex/
0  'user.name'
1  'an'
2  'i'
3  '-domain'
DB<18>
```

That doesn't look quite like what was expected, as the i and the -domain values should have been assigned to the single $3 variable. Looking closely at the regex you can see that the third set of parentheses has no multiplier (+), or plus sign, next to it, so the regex correctly returned *one* character instead of *one or more* characters.

Change the regex to include the missing plus sign:

```
DB<18> $regex = '([^@]+)\@([^.]+).([^.]+).([^.]+)'
DB<19>
```

Try dumping out the results of the regex a second time:

```
DB<19> x $str =~ /$regex/
0  'user.name'
1  'an'
2  'ip-domain'
3  'org'
DB<20>
```

This is a quick approach to working with a regex. For a really detailed work through of debugging regexes, see Chapter 11 and the re, perlre, and perlretut perldocs.

Scoping Issues in the Debugger

A small *gotcha* when you are declaring variables to work with in the debugger session is that a my variable will simply disappear. Any statement executed from the debugger command line is evaled in an implicit scope, and any lexical variable created in one scope will not be seen by the next.

This means that although you can see and work with both my and our variables declared in your program's scope, and you can see and work with our, local, and global variables under the debugger, the debugger will simply not recognize a my variable declared from its own command line. For example, you might be tempted to declare a $var using my and assigning the $str we have been using to it:

```
DB<20> my $var = $str
DB<21>
```

Use p to print the value of the $var variable and you will see it will yield nothing, because the my $var which existed just a moment ago no longer exists:

```
DB<21> p $var
DB<22>
```

To see the difference between types of variable scoping, declare a $var using our, and assign $str to it:

```
DB<22> our $var = $str
DB<23>
```

Now use p again to print out the value of the $var:

```
DB<23> p $var
user.name@an.ip-domain.org
DB<24>
```

As you can see, the our variable is quite visible, in the same way as a local variable would be. The safest, or simplest, thing to do in most cases, is to simply declare the variable bare, without any my or our functions at all. This may not seem a particularly critical piece of information, but if you've spent some time creating my variables from the debugger command line and have dealt with the weirdness that comes from these variables mysteriously disappearing—now you know why.

Tracing an Expression

We looked at tracing under the debugger fairly extensively in Chapter 5, but there was a variant we did not discuss there. The debugger also supports the ability to trace an expression on-the-fly. The syntax looks like

```
t expr
```

where expr may be any valid Perl expression. We can take a clean CGI object, give it a few parameters and a trace execution of just the new method, which parses the input from the CGI environment or the arguments supplied. But, first we must ensure the CGI module is loaded:

```
DB<24> use CGI
DB<25>
```

Now we can execute a CGI->new() statement along with some additional arguments, and trace it to see exactly what happens:

```
DB<25> t CGI->new( { arg1 => this, arg2 => that } )
main::((eval 36)[/opt/perl/lib/5.8.5/perl5db.pl:620]:3):
3:      CGI->new( { arg1 => this, arg2 => that } );
CGI::new(/opt/perl/lib/5.8.5/CGI.pm:299):
299:       my($class,@initializer) = @_;
CGI::new(/opt/perl/lib/5.8.5/CGI.pm:300):
300:       my $self = {};
CGI::new(/opt/perl/lib/5.8.5/CGI.pm:302):
302:       bless $self,ref $class || $class || $DefaultClass;
<...533 lines snipped here>
CGI::init(/opt/perl/lib/5.8.5/CGI.pm:624):
624:           $self->save_request unless defined $initializer;
CGI::new(/opt/perl/lib/5.8.5/CGI.pm:330):
330:       return $self;
DB<26>
```

Behind that simple statement are more than 550 lines of code, which saves you an enormous amount of work with regard to parsing both the CGI input and the environment your web handlers may have to deal with. It's no wonder the CGI module is one of the most popular Perl modules on the CPAN—this volume of data is an ideal candidate for piping through a pager by using the pipe command described previously.

Remember, also, that it is not necessary to trace the entire expression through to the end without stopping, because we can also stop midway during the execution of our t expr statement. First you need to use the b command to define a breakpoint at the start of the CGI::init() subroutine:

```
DB<26> b CGI::init
DB<27>
```

Now when we execute the trace command we only run through 25 lines of code before stopping at the CGI::init() subroutine at the new breakpoint:

```
DB<27>  t CGI->new( { arg1 => this, arg2 => that } )
main::((eval 20)[/opt/perl/lib/5.8.5/perl5db.pl:620]:3):
```

```
3:      CGI->new( { arg1 => this, arg2 => that } );
CGI::new(/opt/perl/lib/5.8.5/CGI.pm:299):
299:     my($class,@initializer) = @_;
CGI::new(/opt/perl/lib/5.8.5/CGI.pm:300):
300:     my $self = {};
CGI::new(/opt/perl/lib/5.8.5/CGI.pm:302):
302:     bless $self,ref $class || $class || $DefaultClass;
CGI::new(/opt/perl/lib/5.8.5/CGI.pm:303):
303:     if (ref($initializer[0])
304:         && (UNIVERSAL::isa($initializer[0],'Apache')
305:             ||
306:             UNIVERSAL::isa($initializer[0],'Apache::RequestRec')
307:            )) {
CGI::new(/opt/perl/lib/5.8.5/CGI.pm:310):
310:     if (ref($initializer[0])
311:         && (UNIVERSAL::isa($initializer[0],'CODE'))) {
CGI::new(/opt/perl/lib/5.8.5/CGI.pm:314):
314:     if ($MOD_PERL) {
CGI::new(/opt/perl/lib/5.8.5/CGI.pm:328):
328:      $self->_reset_globals if $PERLEX;
CGI::new(/opt/perl/lib/5.8.5/CGI.pm:329):
329:      $self->init(@initializer);
CGI::init(/opt/perl/lib/5.8.5/CGI.pm:439):
439:     my $self = shift;
DB<<28>>
```

At this point we can inspect the program variables at our leisure. We'll decide if the CGI object is being initialized properly, and make whatever decisions are relevant based on absolute knowledge of the internal workings of the program. As you can see, the internal workings may include code that someone else has written, as well as code that you have written. The only thing we can safely assume is that there is *code* to work with and to inspect.

Now we can remove the b CGI::init breakpoint by using the B * command to erase all breakpoints:

```
DB<<28>> B *
DB<<29>>
```

Finally two r commands return us to the previous scope.

Stepping Through an Expression

Similar to tracing over a subroutine call, the debugger also supports stepping through an expression using the s command—as you might step through a subroutine call. While you're tracing through a call, each line of code is printed, but you don't have control over the program unless you have previously set a breakpoint for it to stop against. In the midst of stepping, however, you can always set a breakpoint, inspect a variable, or continue, as necessary. You have complete control. The syntax for this variation of the stepping command is

```
s expr
```

In this case we use an almost identical command to the previous tracing example, replacing the t with an s. To demonstrate this, let's take several steps through a CGI-new method call:

```
DB<28> s CGI->new( { arg1 => this, arg2 => that } )
main::((eval 52)[/opt/perl/lib/5.8.5/perl5db.pl:620]:3):
3:      CGI->new( { arg1 => this, arg2 => that } );
DB<<29>>
```

The command supplies the code to the debugger, and declares this as the next statement to be executed. Now, having used the s command once, you can use a carriage-return (CR), or submit an empty command as a short cut for repeating the last command. This will take us to the first line of the CGI::new() method:

```
DB<<29>> <CR>
CGI::new(/opt/perl/lib/5.8.5/CGI.pm:299):
299:    my($class,@initializer) = @_;
DB<<29>>
```

Here are the $class and @initializer arguments being passed into the CGI::new() method. Another carriage-return steps the program one statement further on:

```
DB<<29>> <CR>
CGI::new(/opt/perl/lib/5.8.5/CGI.pm:300):
300:    my $self = {};
DB<<29>>
```

Now we have an empty CGI object in the $self variable constructed from a hash reference and can move to the next line of code:

```
DB<<29>> <CR>
CGI::new(/opt/perl/lib/5.8.5/CGI.pm:302):
302:    bless $self,ref $class || $class || $DefaultClass;
DB<<29>>
```

Another carriage-return and the CGI object is blessed into the appropriate class based on the arguments supplied, or the $DefaultClass:

```
DB<<29>> <CR>
CGI::new(/opt/perl/lib/5.8.5/CGI.pm:303):
303:    if (ref($initializer[0])
304:        && (UNIVERSAL::isa($initializer[0],'Apache')
305:        ||
306:        UNIVERSAL::isa($initializer[0],'Apache::RequestRec')
307:        )) {
DB<<29>>
```

In this step we can see the $initializer array being inspected for the number of dedicated Apache or Apache::RequestRec values demonstrating central support for the Apache web server and the mod_perl interface. This exercise demonstrates the possibility of stepping through any code that you call because the inner workings of all modules and libraries are available to you in their entirety. At this point, we can simply return from this method, rather than step through the 545 remaining statements. Use the r command to finish execution of the subroutine and return to the enclosing scope:

```
DB<<29>> r
list context return from CGI::new:
0   CGI=HASH(0x846ec04)
'.charset' => 'ISO-8859-1'
'.fieldnames' => HASH(0x8601eac)
empty hash
'.parameters' => ARRAY(0x8601f00)
0   'arg2'
1   'arg1'
'arg1' => ARRAY(0x8412dc0)
0   'this'
'arg2' => ARRAY(0x837d090)
0   'that'
'escape' => 1
DB<29>
```

The r command has the bonus benefit of printing, or dumping the return context and value (data structure) of the subroutine, as long as the PrintRet option is set. It is possible to see the name of the parameters given in the .parameters array as well as the keys and values in the CGI object itself, confirming that the input arguments were correctly parsed.

As you can see, it is possible to have a lot of fun with the debugger in shell mode. The debugger is effectively always in shell mode, but it's up to you to decide whether to use it interactively, or as a non-interruptible autotrace program by using the AutoTrace=1 and NonStop=1 options. For more information on these options see Chapters 5 (tracing) and 6 (multiple libraries), as well as perldoc perldebug and the h o command.

Summary

In this chapter you've discovered how to use the Perl debugger as a shell for executing arbitrary and varied commands, as well as how to call the system shell from within a debugger session. You've seen how this can be useful in experimenting with and exploring the different possibilities which may be available, to arrive at the best coding solution for a particular set of circumstances.

In the next chapter we'll take a look at debugging a plain CGI program locally, using the debugger inside a mod_perl enabled apache web server. Well also learn how to approach debugging a remote Perl program running on a different machine altogether.

CHAPTER 9

■■■

Debugging a CGI Program

"Go Web, go!"

—Spider-Man, while learning to swing (*Spider-Man*, 2002)

This chapter discusses using the Perl debugger to dissect a web-based Perl program, showing you how to debug programs running under plain CGI and mod_perl. You'll learn how to debug programs running both locally and on a remote machine. In particular, we concentrate on the cases where you might try to debug your Perl program in one of the following typical configurations:

- Where your program is running under the CGI protocol:

    - Using the debugger from the command line

    - Using the debugger from the command line using CGI -debug

    - Using the debugger via a web server from the command line

    - Where your program is running under mod_perl (with Apache) and using Apache::DB with the debugger

- Where your program is running on a remote machine:

    - Using the debugger from the command line using PERLDB_OPTS

    - GUI (Graphical User Interface) method using the ptkdb debugger

Using the standard perl -d calling syntax is usually fine for local programs. However, the introduction of a networked environment can introduce new challenges. For example, how would one efficiently debug programs responsible for communicating with remote machines, or those embedded within a web server process (as per Apache mod_perl for instance)?

To add to the confusion, there may be multiple languages being used, multiple IN, OUT, and ERROR filehandles passed about, and various processes passing client requests to and from system buffers at any one time. All of this just makes things harder to follow what exactly is going on at any one moment. Many people try the standard debugger syntax, get frustrated when it doesn't work right away, and give up too quickly. In these cases, don't despair—you usually just need to jump through a couple of minor hoops to get past these problems.

For starters, let's have a look at a typical scenario by examining a program that is using the CGI module.

Running Under the CGI Protocol

For this example we'll examine a simple CGI program that prints out the parameters that were passed to it. Place the code found in Listing 9-1 in a file called example.cgi.

Listing 9-1. *The* example.cgi *Script*

```perl
#!/usr/bin/perl -d
use CGI qw(:standard);
my $o_cgi = CGI->new();
print
    header,
    start_html('Perl Debugger Tutorial - CGI example'),
    "<h3>Params:</h3><hr><ul>\n"
;
foreach my $p ($o_cgi->param) {
    print "\t<li>$p: ".join(', ', $o_cgi->param($p))."\n";
}
print "</ul><hr>\n", end_html;
exit;
__END__
=head1 NAME
example.cgi - short cgi program
=head1 SYNOPSIS
%> perl -d ./example.cgi this=that this=theother a=param
=head1 DESCRIPTION
Print out the parameters given.
=cut
```

For this to work, you will need to make sure that the program is placed in an executable directory under your web server root, and that the web server has been instructed to execute the program using the Perl interpreter. See your web server documentation for information on how to do this.

We will use the w3m (http://w3m.sourceforge.net/) web browser program for the purposes of this demonstration, because of its command line convenience.

The w3m web browser will retrieve and format the HTML as ASCII text, suitable for viewing in a plain terminal window. The advantage of using this particular program is that the content won't be a distraction—you can view the raw output as plain (partially-formatted) text. Furthermore, sometimes it's good to know, or to remember, how to walk before trying to run. If we had used wget, another versatile program for downloading web pages, we would have the actual HTML itself, and the unformatted tags would also get in the way of the examples. Note that the functionality of the example program is unchanged—using w3m is simply a visual as well as a publishing convenience.

We can retrieve the output of this program using a URL similar to this:

```
%> w3m http://192.168.0.7/example.cgi?this=that\&this=theother\&a=param
```

The w3m program renders the HTML in plain text format, but as close to a graphical web page as possible. Typically, the output will be similar to this:

```
Params:
-------------------------------------------------------------------------
* this: that, theother
* a: param
-------------------------------------------------------------------------
```

Debugging from the Command Line: `perl -d`

To debug a CGI application, we can use the familiar syntax. To do so we just need to convert the URL into a command line by giving the path to the program, and then separating the arguments by whitespace. Note that because we are using the CGI module, which provides explicit support for this sort of debugging, we can send arguments to our program separated by whitespace (or by ampersands as they're often seen in URLs). CGI will internally translate these into the appropriate input for our program, which is expecting a POST or GET request (see the CGI documentation for more info). Note that if you decide to use the ampersand version, you will need to quote the string so that the shell doesn't place the program in the background.

Let's debug the example.cgi script, passing in a few parameters in order to achieve a real-world scenario:

```
%> perl -d ./example.cgi this=that this=theother a=param
Loading DB routines from perl5db.pl version 1.27
Editor support available.
Enter h or 'h h' for help, or 'man perldebug' for more help.
main::(./example.cgi:5):        my $o_cgi = CGI->new();
  DB<1>
```

The debugger stops at the first executable line, in our case where the CGI object is initialized, and waits for further instruction. At this point, we can step to the next statement using the n command:

```
DB<1> n
    main::(./example.cgi:7):    print
    main::(./example.cgi:8):     header,
    main::(./example.cgi:9):     start_html('Perl Debugger Tutorial - CGI example',
    main::(./example.cgi:10):             "<h3>Params:</h3><hr><ul>\n"
DB<1>
```

Note how the next chunk of executable code is in fact distributed over several lines, even though there are two function calls, header() and start_html() included. This is because the debugger rightfully recognizes the next four lines as a single executable statement and will treat them as such.

The CGI object has been instantiated via its new() method, and has absorbed all the incoming arguments, so the debugger is now at the point where it can look at the parameter names via the CGI object, by calling the param() method:

```
DB<1> x $o_cgi->param
    0  'this'
    1  'a'
DB<2>
```

From this, it can be seen that the parameters were passed cleanly via the command line, and that we can also interact with the debugger in our CGI program. We can now continue and run to the end of the program:

```
DB<2> c
    Content-Type: text/html; charset=ISO-8859-1
<?xml version="1.0" encoding="iso-8859-1"?>
<!DOCTYPE html
        PUBLIC "-//W3C//DTD XHTML 1.0 Transitional//EN"
         "http://www.w3.org/TR/xhtml1/DTD/xhtml1-transitional.dtd">
<html xmlns="http://www.w3.org/1999/xhtml" lang="en-US" xml:lang="en-US">
<head><title>Perl Debugger Tutorial - CGI example</title>
</head><body><h3>Params:</h3><hr><ul>
        <li>this: that, theother
        <li>a: param
</ul><hr>
Debugged program terminated.  Use q to quit or R to restart,
  use O inhibit_exit to avoid stospping after program termination,
  h q, h R or h O to get additional info.
  </body></html>
  DB<2>
```

And finally use q to quit the debugger session. Notice that although w3m may have interpreted the HTML output into ASCII text on our behalf, the debugger allows anything printed to STDOUT, the default output of the program, to be printed normally to the screen. Also bear in mind, that the </body></html> string located just before the previous DB<2> debugger prompt, may be concatenated together in the terminal output, resulting in the output being somewhat mixed up visually. This is due to buffering and will occasionally be a tad confusing, just remember this is what is happening and it won't disturb your debugging sessions too much.

Debugging from the Command Line Using CGI: -debug

There may be times when it is useful to be able to manually adjust the parameters that your program receives on the command line. In these cases, you can use the -debug pragma with the CGI module. Using a command line similar to the previous example, we give an empty parameter list, and instead are prompted (via the -debug switch) for our input when the CGI object is initialized:

```
%> perl -MCGI=-debug -d ./example.cgi
Loading DB routines from perl5db.pl version 1.27
Editor support available.
Enter h or 'h h' for help, or 'man perldebug' for more help.
main::(./example.cgi:5):        my $o_cgi = CGI->new();
  DB<1>
```

Once we step to the next line, we are asked for our parameters:

```
DB<1> n
    (offline mode: enter name=value pairs on standard input;
     press ^D or ^Z when done)
```

Having entered our parameters

```
(offline mode: enter name=value pairs on standard input; press ^D or ^Z
 when done)
this=that
this=those
etc
```

we can enter ^D to return to the debugger prompt:

```
^D
main::(./example.cgi:7):    print
main::(./example.cgi:8):      header,
main::(./example.cgi:9):        start_html('Perl Debugger Tutorial - CGI example'),
main::(./example.cgi:10):             "<h3>Params:</h3><hr><ul>\n"
  DB<1>
```

Now we can inspect the CGI parameter list:

```
DB<1> x $o_cgi->param
    0  'this'
    1  'etc'
DB<2>
```

and take a look at the contents of the this parameter:

```
DB<3> x $o_cgi->param('this')
    0  'that'
    1  'those'
DB<4>
```

For purposes of experimentation, and to see how much control we have over our environment, let's modify the parameter list:

```
DB<4> $o_cgi->param('this', 'arg')
DB<5>
```

We can see the result by inspecting the parameter once more:

```
DB<5> x $o_cgi->param('this')
    0  'arg'
DB<6>
```

Again, at this point we can use c to run to the end of our program and review the results:

```
DB<4> c
    Content-Type: text/html; charset=ISO-8859-1
<?xml version="1.0" encoding="iso-8859-1"?>
<!DOCTYPE html
        PUBLIC "-//W3C//DTD XHTML 1.0 Transitional//EN"
          "http://www.w3.org/TR/xhtml1/DTD/xhtml1-transitional.dtd">
<html xmlns="http://www.w3.org/1999/xhtml" lang="en-US" xml:lang="en-
S"><head><title>Perl Debugger Tutorial - CGI example</title>
```

```
</head><body><h3>Params:</h3><hr><ul>
        <li>this: arg
        <li>etc:
</ul><hr>
Debugged program terminated.  Use q to quit or R to restart,
  use O inhibit_exit to avoid stopping after program termination,
  h q, h R or h O to get additional info.
</body></html>
  DB<4>
```

The modified parameters are reflected in the content output by the program.
Finally, let's quit the debugger:

```
DB<4> q
  %>
```

For more information and tips on debugging with the CGI module, see the CGI documentation and the references in Chapter 16.

Debugging via a Web Server

So far the examples have been initiated from the command line, which is fine for getting a general feel for debugging something *in principle*, and can be very successful in finding the majority of bugs. However, this approach isn't really practical because it does not occur in the same environment in which the program is actually intended to run.

To do that of course we need to run the program under a web server. Most people don't do this, even though the technique is remarkably simple. Essentially all we need to is to get the web server to run in *single-user* mode.

Normally, Apache runs multiple processes, with each new request going to a subprocess. Two requests in a row may not even go to the same subprocess. For debugging in single-user mode, we pass the -X parameter when starting the server. Each request is handled by one process, which we can debug.

Use a command line similar to this for Apache:

```
%> httpd -X -f ./conf/httpd.conf
```

Note that with the -X command, instead of returning with a new command line prompt, the httpd process has apparently hung up somewhere. In fact it is doing exactly what we asked it to do, and it is providing us with an interface once the web server receives a request. But, we'll return to this matter in a moment.

Now from another command line we can run exactly the same command as the previous example by using w3m to perform our request (substituting the IP address of the machine that our standalone Apache is running on):

```
%> w3m http://192.168.0.7/example.cgi?this=that\&this=theother\&a=param

...

192.168.0.7 contacted. Waiting for reply...
```

Note that this time it is the w3m process that appears to hang with the Waiting for reply...
message.

Returning to our original prompt, from where we started Apache with the -X command, we can see what we were waiting for—a comfortably familiar debugger prompt:

```
%> httpd -X -f ./conf/httpd.conf
Loading DB routines from perl5db.pl version 1.27
Editor support available.
Enter h or 'h h' for help, or 'man perldebug' for more help.
main::(/home/perltut/code/example.cgi:7):
7:      my $o_cgi = CGI->new();
  DB<1>
```

If you don't get a debugger prompt, there is a problem with your setup. Either you've used an incorrect httpd.conf file or the Apache::DB module was not initialized properly. Don't worry, there should be some output in the Apache error logfiles, which should help you to determine the cause of the problem.

Once our output looks like the previous prompt, we know that Apache has handed over control to Perl. Perl is now running under the control of the debugger, and we can debug our single request as necessary. We'll start by printing out information about the web server:

```
DB<1> p $ENV{SERVER_SOFTWARE}
    Apache/1.3.31 (Unix)
DB<2>
```

Naturally we will also want to check the parameters that were passed in the URI:

```
DB<2> p $ENV{REQUEST_URI}
    /example.cgi?this=that&this=theother&a=param
DB<3>
```

Now we should step across the next line to initialize the CGI object:

```
DB<3> n
    main::(/home/perltut/code/example.cgi:9):
    9:      print
    10:             header,
    11:             start_html('Perl Debugger Tutorial - CGI example'),
    12:             "<h3>Params:</h3><hr><ul>\n"
DB<4>
```

Initializing the CGI object allows us to see which parameters we have access to when using the Dump method of the CGI object:

```
DB<5> p $o_cgi->Dump
    <ul>
    <li><strong>this</strong></li>
    <ul>
    <li>that</li>
    <li>theother</li>
    </ul>
    <li><strong>a</strong></li>
    <ul>
    <li>param</li>
```

```
        </ul>
        </ul>
DB<6>
```

Remember, using a simple c command to continue at the conclusion of the program will not return control to the web browser, it will bring this instantiation of the debugger to an end:

```
DB<6> c
    Debugged program terminated.  Use q to quit or R to restart,
use O inhibit_exit to avoid stopping after program termination,
h q, h R or h O to get additional info.
DB<6>
```

The default behavior of the Perl debugger is to *not* fall off the end of the program being debugged. This way, for instance, you can restart it whenever you like, and to stop you have to explicitly quit the debugger session. In other words, you actually have to use the quit command to finally return the resulting data (web page) to the browser:

```
DB<1> q
```

At this point, the web server process appears to hang once more because it is waiting for more input. However, if we return to the w3m request terminal window, we can see our process has completed and the data has been served:

```
Params:
-------------------------------------------------------------------------------
* this: that, theother
* a: param
-------------------------------------------------------------------------------
```

At this point, it is possible to generate another request, and come back to the Apache window where the debugger is once again waiting patiently for our input.

Using this technique makes debugging your web applications much easier than printing to error logs or the web page itself. Debugging in this manner is all the more powerful because it can be done remotely from the client. The next technique we cover follows that idea.

Debugging from a Remote Machine

The previous example used a local command line to take the place of the possibly remote web server. However, it could be argued that because it's a local alternative, that example is not a true debugging session of the actual process running under the web server itself.

This next example will use the same program, running on one machine under command of a web server, while we enter commands and interact with the debugger from another machine.

Debugging from the Command Line: PERLDB_OPTS

Returning to the command line once more, another approach to debugging a remote program would be to use PERLDB_OPTS with the RemotePort option. To use the RemotePort option, we require a process on the other:end, where *other* is a hostname and *end* is a port number, to both respond to our request for a connection, and to be a conduit for the debugger session controlling input/output. For this process, we will use an extremely simple program called helloworld, provided in Listing 9-2.

Listing 9-2. *The* helloworld *Program*

```
#!/usr/bin/perl
print "Hello World\n";
exit;
__END__
=head1 NAME
helloworld - :-)
=head1 SYNOPSIS
    helloworld
=head1 DESCRIPTION
    Simply print "Hello World\n"
=cut
```

The syntax for setting this debugger option is

```
RemotePort=host:portno
```

You might use it on the command line like this:

```
%> PERLDB_OPTS="RemotePort=192.168.0.7:21" perl -d program args...
```

Before we jump in, it should be clear that in this particular example we should receive an instant failure, because the other end is not prepared for us yet. Let's verify this, using our helloworld program:

```
%> PERLDB_OPTS="RemotePort=192.168.0.7:21" perl -d helloworld
Unable to connect to remote host: 192.168.0.7:12345
Connection refused
Compilation failed in require.
        main::BEGIN() called at /opt/perl/lib/5.8.4/perl5db.pl line 0
        eval {...} called at /opt/perl/lib/5.8.4/perl5db.pl line 0
BEGIN failed--compilation aborted.
Can't use an undefined value as a symbol reference at
opt/perl/lib/5.8.4/perl5db.pl line 7174.
        DB::print_help('Debugged program terminated.  Use B<q> to quit
r B<R> to res...')
            called at /opt/perl/lib/5.8.4/perl5db.pl line 1886
        DB::DB called at /opt/perl/lib/5.8.4/perl5db.pl line 8580
        DB::fake::at_exit() called at /opt/perl/lib/5.8.4/perl5db.pl
line 8174
        DB::END() called at helloworld line 0
        eval {...} called at helloworld line 0
END failed--call queue aborted.
%>
```

You *should* have received this error, if you didn't, start again from the top.

Using the remoteport Program

The point here is that we need to have a mechanism at the remote host that can pick up the requested connection on the specified port, and also handle the debugger interaction from the command line. This isn't so difficult, and to solve this we can use the remoteport program displayed in Listing 9-3.

We could use netcat here, but to reduce dependencies on external programs, and to give you a better idea as to what is happening behind the scenes, we provide this solution instead. If you prefer to use netcat, that's fine too. Note also that whichever program you choose as the listener, you will need to select a port number higher than 1024 unless you're running as root (not a good idea) on that machine.

Listing 9-3. *The* remoteport *Program*

```perl
#!/usr/bin/perl -w
use strict;
use Getopt::Long;
use IO::Socket;
use Term::ReadLine;
use constant BIGNUM => 65536;
our $previous_input;

# Set host and port.
my $host = shift || 'localhost';
my $port = shift || 12345; # over 1024 please
die("Usage: $0 hostname portno") unless ($host =~ /\w+/ && $port =~
^\d+$/);
print "listening on $host:$port\n";
my $term = new Term::ReadLine 'local prompter';
my $OUT;
{
  # strict subs complains about STDOUT, so turn it off for the moment.
  no strict 'subs';
  $OUT = $term->OUT || STDOUT;
}
$OUT->autoflush(1);

# Open the socket the debugger will connect to.
my $sock = new IO::Socket::INET(
                    LocalHost => $host,
                    LocalPort => $port,
                    Proto     => 'tcp',
                    Listen    => SOMAXCONN,
                    Reuse     => 1);
$sock or die "no socket :$!";
my $new_sock = $sock->accept();

# Try to pick up the remote hostname for the prompt.
my $remote_host = gethostbyaddr($sock->sockaddr(), AF_INET) || 'remote';
my $prompt = "($remote_host)> ";
my ($buf, $input);
```

```
# Read output from the debugger, then read debugger input.
while (1) {
   # Drop out if the remote debugger went away.
   exit 0 unless sysread($new_sock, $buf, BIGNUM);
   print $OUT $buf;

# Drop out if we got end-of-file locally (warning: this
# causes the remote Perl to drop dead because the socket goes away).
exit 0 unless defined($input = $term->readline($prompt));
print { $new_sock } munge_input($input);

# Add the line to the terminal history.
$term->addhistory($input) if $input =~ /\S/;
    }

# The debugger interaction can get all confused if the string it gets
# passed is just a null. We clean this up here.
sub munge_input {
  my $actual_input = shift;
  $actual_input = "\n" unless defined $actual_input;
}
__END__

=head1 NAME

remoteport - connect to a remote Perl debugger

=head1 SYNOPSIS

# default to host: localhost and port: 12345

# specify the same:
remoteport localhost 12345

# Use a specific host ip and port:
remoteport 192.168.0.7 17284

=head1 DESCRIPTION

C<remoteport> allows you to set up a remote telnet-like session
with a Perl debugger using the C<RemotePort> option.  You can specify
the host (default localhost) and the port (default 12345) you'd
like to use, as in the previous examples.
```

```
=head1 NOTES

Note that this program doesn't attempt to get the correct IPip
address for you,but its advantage is that it should run on most
machines I<out of the box>.  C<Net::Ifconfig::Wrapper> is probably
the correct module to use, if you wanted to extend this to handle
guessing your ip address correctly, even on Windows or a Mac.  Also,
remember this is a bit basic and somewhat rough on the edges, so
please be kind.  Occasionally it may unexpectedly die on you (in
which case just restart it).  Also sometimes you will need to send
it an extra newline to get it to register a command properly; for
an example try using C<h> and C<h h>.  Hey, what do you want?  It's
a demo program, not a production system!

=cut
```

Having acquainted ourselves with the comments in the program, let's try it out.

Running the `remoteport` Program

First we set up the `remoteport` program on the remote host, so that we will have something to attach to. You may choose any port number you have permissions to open, though normally one chooses a number above *1024* because these are not implicitly reserved by the system. For this example we'll use `localhost` for our current machine (with an ip address of 192.168.0.7), and *12345* for our port number:

```
%> ./remoteport localhost 12345
listening on localhost:12345
...
```

Attaching to the Remote Port

The command line of our debugger server appears to hang. This is appropriate though, because this is where we will be offered our debugger prompt later on, and we have not connected anything to work with it yet. Next we'll go to our remote host (with an IP address of 192.168.0.3), and open a client debugger session as we did previously:

```
%> PERLDB_OPTS="RemotePort=192.168.0.7:12345" perl -d helloworld
...
```

Taking Control of the Program

This also hangs, as it did previously, because the debugger server now has control of the client session from the remote machine. If we go back to our original `remoteport` server session, we will see the debugger prompt:

```
%> ./remoteport localhost 12345
listening on localhost:12345
Loading DB routines from perl5db.pl version 1.27
(192.168.0.3)>
```

The program on the client side is now running under the control of the debugger, which is running on the server specified host and port. As mentioned previously, the code is for demonstration purposes only, so you might need to enter a second carriage-return occasionally (indicated by CR), to flush the prompt:

```
(192.168.0.3)> <CR>
Editor support available.
Enter h or 'h h' for help, or 'man perldebug' for more help.
main::(helloworld:3):   print "Hello World\n";
  DB<1> (192.168.0.3)>
```

That looks better. Now we could try listing our code with the l command:

```
  DB<1> (192.168.0.3)> l
    3==>     print "Hello World\n";
    4
    5:       exit;
    6
DB<1> (192.168.0.3)>
```

We could step over the next line with an n command:

```
DB<1> (192.168.0.3)> n
DB<1> (192.168.0.3)>
```

Now that's strange, because as we can see, the n command should have taken us across the line that said print "Hello World\n";. So, where is it? Well, we know it got printed and that the output went to the STDOUT of the original program (which you will remember is on the client machine). It's simple enough to go have a look:

```
%> PERLDB_OPTS="RemotePort=192.168.0.7:12345" perl -d helloworld
Hello World
```

Sure enough, there it is. If this is a web server and we have requested a page from one machine, we don't actually want the requested page to suddenly appear on another machine, even if we're debugging it, do we?

Remember that the STDIN (the original input), STDOUT (the client display), STDERR (client logfiles, typically) filehandles all remain untouched. We do have control over the Perl program itself, via DB::IN (our server command line), with all debugger output going to DB::OUT (our server terminal), as you'd expect.

All we have to do here is to keep a beady eye on anything going to STDOUT, and we won't sway off track. To demonstrate how the debugger behaves in this context we can print something to STDOUT, such as the default output filehandle unless one is explicitly provided. To do this, we'll use the standard Perl print command:

```
DB<1> (192.168.0.3)> print "process id($$)\n"
    main::(helloworld:5):   exit;
DB<1> (192.168.0.3)>
```

This will appear in the display on our other machine:

```
%> PERLDB_OPTS="RemotePort=192.168.0.7:12345" perl -d helloworld
Hello World
process id(2798)
```

However, if we use a *debugger* command, the default output for this will be a special file-handle called DB::OUT. Let's do something similar with the p command:

```
DB<1> (192.168.0.3)> p "processID($$)\n"
DB<2> (192.168.0.3)>
    processID(2798)
DB<3> (192.168.0.3)>
```

Here we see our own output in the control window in our server process. You've seen how you can debug a Perl program from a remote machine using PERLDB_OPTS, so let's quit now and return to our server system prompt:

```
DB<3> (192.168.0.3)> q
    %>
```

Because we've exited the remoteport program entirely, the Perl process we were debugging at the other end of the connection also dies and, in this case, returns control to the client system prompt:

```
%> PERLDB_OPTS="RemotePort=192.168.0.7:12345" perl -d helloworld
Hello World
process id(2798)
%>
```

Configuring mod_perl

For mod_perl debugging we can use the Apache::DB module. Before proceeding however, let's quickly review the mod_perl installation procedure. To install Apache's mod_perl from source, you will need to install mod_perl, which will require the Apache source tree to be accessible. Next you'll need to install Apache itself. The entire task can be done painlessly from the mod_perl directory with a single command:

```
%> perl Makefile.PL DO_HTTPD=1 USE_APACI=1 APACHE_PREFIX=/usr/local/apache
%> make test install
```

Now verify that mod_perl installed correctly. You can see this by looking at the information provided by Apache when listing the compiled in modules, using the -l flag:

```
%> httpd -l
Compiled-in modules:
  http_core.c
  mod_env.c
  mod_log_config.c
  mod_mime.c
  mod_negotiation.c
  mod_status.c
  mod_include.c
  mod_autoindex.c
  mod_dir.c
  mod_cgi.c
  mod_asis.c
  mod_imap.c
```

```
mod_actions.c
mod_userdir.c
mod_alias.c
mod_access.c
mod_auth.c
mod_setenvif.c
mod_perl.c
%>
```

Note the mod_perl.c at the end of the list, and realize that without this there is no mod_perl installation.

For our example, let's use a program which just prints out a couple of environment variables, so that we can see ourselves running under mod_perl, and embed it inside a typical mod_perl handler method used via a module. We'll use MyMod.pm, displayed in Listing 9-4.

Listing 9-4. *The* MyMod.pm *Module*

```
package MyMod;
sub handler {
    my $r = shift;
print $r->content_type('text/plain');
print $r->send_http_header;
print "<h3>A couple of environment variables:</h3><hr><ul>\n";
foreach my $e (qw(SERVER_SOFTWARE MOD_PERL GATEWAY_INTERFACE)) {
    $DB::single=2;
    print "\t<li>$e: $ENV{$e}\n";
}
print "</ul><hr>\n";
    }
1; # <- satisfy module rules
__END__
=head1 NAME
MyMod.pm - A mod_perl module
-head1 SYNOPSIS
PerlRequire /home/perltut/code/MyMod.pm
PerlHandler MyMod
=head1 DESCRIPTION
An Apache module to print out several mod_perl or http related
environment
variables
=cut
```

There are a couple of things we need to do to make sure we are running in the correct environment and that mod_perl can find our module. Lucky for you, we're going to be pedantic about explaining these.

Place the MyMod.pm file somewhere within Apache's document root. Naturally, in your own installation, it will reside somewhere else, but as can be seen from the previous httpd.conf entry, ours resides at /home/perltut/code/MyMode.pm.

Modifying the `httpd.conf` File

Make sure that there is an appropriate entry in the `httpd.conf` file so that Apache knows both which Perl file will provide the content handler for this entry, and how to access this server. Essentially, this means that for a web-based request (via `port 80`) on the server identified by the IP address `192.168.0.7`, Apache will call the `MyMod::Handler` method. This is defined in the `MyMod.pm` module to handle the request, as shown in Listing 9-5.

Listing 9-5. *The* `httpd.conf` *Entry*

```
# httpd.conf section
PerlRequire /home/perltut/code/MyMod.pm
<Location /mymod>
    SetHandler  perl-script
    PerlHandler MyMod
</Location>
<VirtualHost 192.168.0.7:80>
    DocumentRoot /home/perltut/code/
    ServerName perltut
    ErrorLog /home/perltut/logs/error_log
    CustomLog /home/perltut/logs/access_log common
</VirtualHost>
```

Starting the Apache Process

It should now be possible to start the Apache web server with a short command that specifies the `httpd.conf` file referred to in the previous example:

```
%> httpd -f ./conf/httpd.conf
```

At this point, assuming all is well and that we have a fully functional Apache web server running on `port 80` on our server, we should be able to check this by requesting a page from it.

Executing a Content Request

To make a request for some content, we can use the `w3m` program from earlier in the chapter and request it to return an HTML response for the `mymod` URI, such as

```
%> w3m http://192.168.0.7/mymod
```

The output should look something like this:

```
  A couple of environment variables:
  ------------------------------------------------------------------
* SERVER_SOFTWARE: Apache/1.3.31 (Unix) mod_perl/1.29
* MOD_PERL: mod_perl/1.29
* GATEWAY_INTERFACE: CGI-Perl/1.1
  ------------------------------------------------------------------
```

If the returned content does *not* include the string `mod_perl/`$x.xx$, where $x.xx$ is the `mod_perl` version number, you have a problem. You're not running `mod_perl`, and you must start again from the top, from the section "Configuring `mod_perl`." Please do not be tempted to continue until you have this working successfully. There is absolutely no point in saying "Z doesn't work!" if you already know that X and Y are not fully functional.

Presuming that our content looks ok, and that we have mod_perl running properly, we can proceed to looking at the Apache::DB module. Again, we're going to step through the additional steps one by one.

The Apache::DB Initializer File

The very short, but essential file db.pl (shown in Listing 9-6), uses the Apache::DB module and then initializes it with a call to the Apache::DB::init() method. This file needs to be placed somewhere where Apache can find it. We'll put it next to our module in the /home/perltut/code/ directory.

Listing 9-6. *The* db.pl *File*

```
# db.pl
use Apache::DB;
Apache::DB->init;
```

Modifying httpd.conf

A couple of extra lines should now be added to the httpd.conf file that we used earlier. We need to explicitly require the db.pl file from Listing 9-6, and we need to FixUp our Perl to be handled by Apache::DB. This is shown in Listing 9-7.

Listing 9-7. *The* httpd.conf Apache::DB *Entry*

```
PerlRequire /home/perltut/code/db.pl
<Location /mymod>
    PerlFixUpHandler +Apache::DB
</Location>
```

Starting Apache in Single-User Mode

Apache needs to start up in single-user mode so that it can interact with the debugger as a single process. Otherwise, running multiple processes will confuse the debugger. To start Apache in *single-user* mode we need to pass the -X flag as an argument:

```
%> httpd -X -f ./conf/httpd.conf
...
```

Just like the CGI example earlier, the prompt does not return, but appears to hang. This is okay and is expected behavior, because at this point we need to have another terminal window before continuing.

Working with a Content Request

Now, from another command line, we can make a request for the content by using the command line we used earlier:

```
%> w3m http://192.168.0.7/perltut/mymod

...

192.168.0.7 contacted. Waiting for reply...
```

Again, the process will appear to hang, while waiting for input at the command line from which we started Apache. This time the input is being controlled from the Perl debugger, and this prompt will return to us only when the debugger is finished with it.

Using the Perl Debugger Running Under mod_perl

Returning to our earlier command line window, we should see the familiar sight of the debugger starting up, and waiting at the first line of executable code for input:

```
%> httpd -X -f ./conf/httpd.conf
Loading DB routines from perl5db.pl version 1.27
Editor support available.
Enter h or 'h h' for help, or 'man perldebug' for more help.
MyMod::handler(/home/perltut/code/MyMod.pm:4):
4:              my $r = shift;
  DB<1>
```

If you've gotten to this point, and can see the debugger prompt, well done! You've cracked it! You now have a fully functional Perl debugger running inside a mod_perl environment—this is no small feat and very exciting.

We can check out the environment by looking at the $ENV{SERVER_SOFTWARE} environment variable. The good thing about choosing this variable is that it enables us to double-check that mod_perl is indeed running inside Apache, because the string returned contains both the actual text string mod_perl and the version of it that we are currently running:

```
DB<1> p $ENV{SERVER_SOFTWARE}
    Apache/1.3.31 (Unix) mod_perl/1.29
DB<2>
```

Interestingly, if we execute a once-only backtrace command, it will show both that we are in the MyMod::handler method, and that we have been called via an Apache object, coming from the file /dev/null, via an eval:

```
DB<2> T
    $ = MyMod::handler(ref(Apache)) called from file '/dev/null' line 0
    $ = eval {...} called from file '/dev/null' line 0
DB<2>
```

■Note Remember that being called from /dev/null is a *feature* of the implementation.

We now have complete control over the Perl environment. which is successfully running under mod_perl in all the usual ways offered by the Perl debugger. Thus, we can continue to debug as usual. We hope you can see how simple this strategy is to use, and that you will not only find it fun, but indispensable. Thanks are due to Doug MacEachern, for a very neatly integrated solution.

That's enough for now, let's quit, and let someone else use the web server.

Debugging Using `ptkdb`

A *GUI-based* alternative, if you're using the X Windows system, or X11 on Mac OS X, might be to use the Perl/Tk debugger known as `ptkdb`. The `ptkdb` is covered here briefly for several reasons. First, it has a reputation for being the most generic of the GUI debuggers available. Also, it has a Perl-based interface, written to use the Tk windowing system

---

■**Note** GUI-based Perl debuggers, and where to get them from, are discussed in Chapter 14.

This example assumes you already have a working Perl/Tk installation, *and* a functional `ptkdb` installation. While the former is a large library of GUI support modules and the latter is a single module, both can be installed via CPAN distributions. You can test this fairly easily by using a command like

```
%> perl -d:ptkdb -e 'print "looks ok\n";'
```

This should, as in the following example, produce a Tk window with the Perl debugger running inside it, with no error messages, and then print to the terminal the short feedback message:

```
looks ok
%>
```

Here is a typical CPAN command line for installing both the Tk and `ptkdb` modules:

```
%> perl -MCPAN -e shell -e install('Tk', 'Devel::ptkdb');
```

Running `ptkdb`

You can test whether it works by using this simple command line (`ptkdb`). It should create a basic Perl/Tk window for you (as shown in Figure 9-1), with an empty debugger session ready and waiting, so that you can explore the application interface:

```
%> perl -d:ptkdb -e 0
```

The interface to the `ptkdb` is a little different from the standard debugger, because it uses mouse and menu commands, but there are no major shocks in store for the average user.

Having quit the previous session, we can now set `ptkdb` up on the *server* host to perform its duties of accepting input from, and sending output to, a remote or client machine. To do this, we use the DISPLAY environment variable to define the host and screen identifiers.

An example session could be created in the bash shell like this:

```
%> DISPLAY="192.168.0.7:0.0" perl -d:ptkdb -e 0
```

At this point, the command prompt should appear to hang while the window, which appeared in the previous example, will now appear on the client machine (the host identified with the IP address 192.168.0.7, in this case). *All* debugger input and output will be channeled through the remote Perl/Tk window.

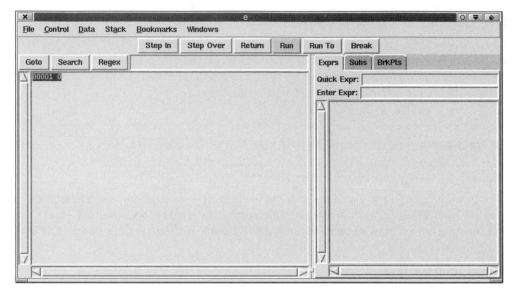

Figure 9-1. *The initial* ptkdb *window*

The DISPLAY Environment Variable

We can see how this works with our program from earlier, by modifying the first line to use the ptkdb debugger module. It should now look something like this:

```
#!/usr/bin/perl -d:ptkdb
```

If we continue by inserting a similar BEGIN block to this one (which sets the DISPLAY environment variable to point to a particular host:display combination), we will be able to view the ptkdb interface on any machine or display we are connected to:

```
sub BEGIN {
    $ENV{DISPLAY} = '192.168.0.7:0.0'
}
```

Here we have diverged from the "*no code changes*" rule. Although there are many ways to set the DISPLAY variable to the appropriate value (including another approach we show next), sometimes enabling the -d:ptkdb line is much more difficult in a real-life scenario without bending the rules and changing the code directly.

As promised, this next command line example shows how to execute precisely the same command as the one we just went over (as long as your OS supports it). In this case we do not change any code at all:

```
%> DISPLAY=192.168.0.7:0.0 perl -d:ptkdb program_name args
```

Running ptkdb via an HTTP Request

Whichever method is chosen, we can now use a web browser to take a look at the program:

```
%> w3m http://192.168.0.7/example.cgi?this=that\&this=theother\&a=param
```

Our Perl/Tk window will appear on our client machine, as shown in Figure 9-2.

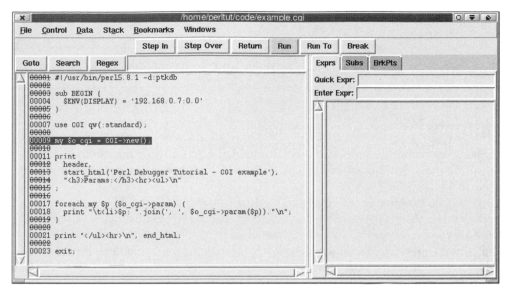

Figure 9-2. *The* ptkdb *window with the debugger stopped*

The web server process on the host machine is now frozen and is waiting for debugger input/output and control as a part of its content delivery mechanism.

Nearly the entire debugger command set is available through the ptkdb GUI interface, in addition to several rather neat features. For example, after holding the cursor over a variable for a short period of time, the dumped value of the variable will appear in a pop-up window.

There is also an evaluation window on the right hand side of the screen (as shown in Figure 9-3), where any expression typed in will be evaluated in the current context.

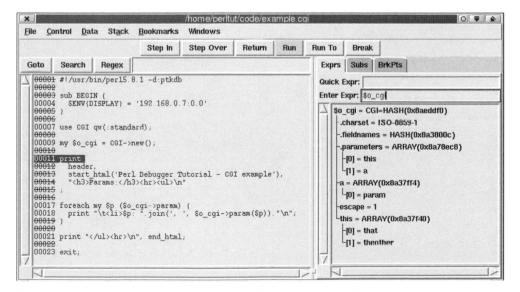

Figure 9-3. *A dump of the* $o_cgi *variable in the expression window*

Quit the ptkdb interface by using the File::Quit menu command.

■**Note** For more information on using the Perl Tk debugger, see the Devel::ptkdb documentation.

Summary

In this chapter, we have learned how to approach debugging a Perl program when running on both local and remote machines. We've learned to do this with both a vanilla *CGI* program, and under mod_perl using Apache::DB.

We have also explored several methods for diverting control of the debugger process to a remote host, via the DISPLAY environment variable, and remoteport debugger options. This frees us from the necessity of having to work on the same server as our program.

The next chapter explores the special cases of working with fork()ed Perl processes and threads.

CHAPTER 10

■ ■ ■

Perl Threads and Forked Processes

"There are a couple of provisos, quid pro quos..."

—The genie in the lamp in Walt Disney's *Aladdin*

Debugging forked or threaded processes are special cases that require Perl to deal with the duplication of multiple and the possible sharing of variables, all the while maintaining control and clarity at all times. The Perl debugger can do this successfully in certain cases, but as we're told by the Genie in the opening quotation, there are a couple of things we need to keep in mind and sometimes you need to give the debugger a bit of help.

In this chapter we're going to show you what the debugger can do with either forked or threaded processes. We're also going to look at POE programs, because POE is a multitasking solution that has much in common with forking and threads. First, let's take a look at what a forked program is, and how threads fit into the picture.

The Similarities and the Differences

People can become confused when trying to see the differences between fork()ed processes, threads, and POE. The examples in this section should make you quite capable of debugging any multitasking Perl program you are likely to come across.

Forks

Each time a Perl program forks when running inside the debugger, both the operating system and Perl fight for control of the various STDIN, STDOUT, and STDERR filehandles. This, as you can imagine, makes for a very interesting pile of spaghetti, because the debugger has to make an explicit open of each of the appropriate filehandles and open new terminals as necessary.

In certain environments, the Perl debugger provides support for the special needs of a forked program, but in most it doesn't and everything around it gets hopelessly entangled, and often hangs. Functional support is currently provided on Unix-based platforms, when the user is using an xterm, and on OS/2. As of the time of writing a KDE window is not supported, for example; and to use it you have to manually open an xterm in the KDE window and work from within that. We'll explain how to do this later in this chapter.

Threads

Functional threads have been available since Perl version 5.6.0, but the user interface only since version 5.8.0. Using threads under Perl will create a new Perl interpreter for each thread. This is similar to a fork in some ways, except that the operating system only sees a single Perl process, and the interpreter is duplicated internally only, and in an efficient manner.

If you're running any version of the debugger prior to Perl version 5.8.5, you won't have any idea which thread you are currently executing, and you will probably find it fairly unmanageable to use, because the debugger steps from one thread to the next continually. This should be regarded as a bug, and was fixed in the most recent versions. An example of this aberrant threads behavior is given later in this chapter, so that you know what you're up against.

POE

As defined in the POE documentation, POE is a framework for cooperative, event-driven multitasking in Perl. POE doesn't implement either threading or fork, although everything is handled within a single process that could be said to nearly *emulate* threading for all its tasks.

■**Note** Using POE::Wheel::Run demands a working fork() implementation—it appears there is no truly free lunch after all!

Why Would I Want to Use fork(), Threads, or POE?

You can put fork(), threads, or POE to many programmatic uses. For example, you might want to use a forking technique to handle a task in a child process while the parent process continues with some other work. Web servers, such as Apache, run a parent process to initially handle incoming requests, and then fork off child processes to do the actual work. You could also design a multitasked feed processor to chop an enormous file into many smaller chunks for complex, parallel, and fast data manipulation.

Any task, in fact, that could be improved by being chopped up into smaller pieces, in order to spread the load for better resource management and use a divide-and-conquer approach to ensure completion in shorter time, could probably be programmed using either the forking, threading, or POE strategies. The strategy you choose is based on the supported features of your Perl version and operating system. For instance, if your operating system doesn't support the fork command at the system level, then clearly you can only choose from using threads or POE. If your version of Perl has not been compiled with threads support, then you need to consider using fork or POE. In all cases, you can probably use POE (but keep in mind the previous comment about Wheel::Run). By the end of this chapter you should have a better idea of what's available and the best way to use the various facilities provided by Perl for multitasking programs.

Using Forks

To demonstrate both forking behavior and how the debugger handles it, we can use a program called forker using the code offered in Listing 10-1.

■**Note** The prefixed numbers are for referring to the code in the text.

Listing 10-1. *The* forker *Program*

```perl
01 #!/usr/bin/perl
02
03 use strict;
04 use POSIX ':sys_wait_h';
05
06 my $DEBUG = $ENV{DEBUG} || 0;
07 my $file  = $ARGV[0] || '';
08 my $count = $ARGV[1] || 10;
09 die("Usage: $0 filename [divisor]") unless -r $file && $count =~ /^\d+$/;
10
11 $|=1;
12
13 $SIG{CHLD} = 'IGNORE';
14 sub process { print length($_[0]).($DEBUG?"\t->@_<-\n":"\t") };
15
16 my ($tot) = grep(/\S+/, split(/\s+/, 'wc $file'));
17 my $num = sprintf('%d', $tot / $count);
18 print "$file: splitting $tot lines into $count main chunks of $num lines\n";
19
20 open(FH, "< $file") or die("$0 unable to open file: $file $!");
21 print "$file: opened...\n";
22 my @lines;
23 my $pid = 1;
24
25 while (<FH>) {
26     push(@lines, $_);
27     if ((scalar(@lines) == $num) || eof FH) {
28         chomp(@lines);
29         my $processid;
30         if ($processid = fork) {
31             $pid++;
32             print "[$$] passed ".@lines." lines to number $pid($processid)
                   for processing\n";
33             waitpid($processid, WNOHANG);
34             @lines = ();
35         } else {
36             die "$0 cannot fork: $!" unless defined $processid;
37             sleep 3; # short pause
38             print "Process [$pid] $$ processing ".@lines." lines...\n";
39             foreach my $line (@lines) {
40                 process($line);
41             }
```

```
42              print "\n" unless $DEBUG;
43              exit 0;
44          }
45      }
46 }
47
48 close FH && print "$file: closed => $0($$) done\n";
49
50 exit 0;
51
52 __END__
53
54 =head1 NAME
55
56 forker - Perl program using fork
57
58 =head1 SYNOPSIS
59
60     %> perl ./forker inputfilename 3
61
62 =head1 DESCRIPTION
63
64 A program which takes a filename and splits it into the optionally given
65 number (or 10) chunks for manipulation via that many forked process.
66
67 =cut
68
```

This forker program is called with a filename as an argument and splits the file into a number of chunks for further processing by forked (child) processes. The number of chunks can be defined as the second argument to the program, but otherwise the default value of 10 will be used. As we loop through the file, we fork off a child process to handle the data each time we reach the appropriate number of chunks in our buffer.

At this point the child process pauses for several seconds, giving the parent time to print its message first, allowing the parent process to continue to the end of its execution, and enabling us to see the child processes all run together independently afterwards. This is really just a clunky mechanism to allow the output to make more sense visually, and it affects neither the logic of the program or the purpose of the example.

Our minimal process handler defined merely prints the length of the given line to show we've been there. To see the actual line of data, set the DEBUG environment variable to a true value.

For purposes of demonstration, we'll use the same walrus input file we have used in previous chapters and try to split it into seven chunks.

Program Output

Before we run this program under the debugger, let's take a moment to review sample output of the forker program using the walrus file as input:

```
%> perl forker walrus 7
walrus: splitting 128 lines into 7 main chunks of 18 lines
walrus: opened...
[2565] passed 18 lines to number 2(2567) for processing
[2565] passed 18 lines to number 3(2568) for processing
[2565] passed 18 lines to number 4(2569) for processing
[2565] passed 18 lines to number 5(2570) for processing
[2565] passed 18 lines to number 6(2571) for processing
[2565] passed 18 lines to number 7(2572) for processing
[2565] passed 18 lines to number 8(2573) for processing
[2565] passed 2 lines to number 9(2574) for processing
walrus: closed => forker(2565) done
%>
```

As we can see from the previous output, we get an extra child process to handle the remaining 2 lines, because the total number of lines (128) doesn't divide evenly into seven equal chunks, as we requested. You can also see from the messages that the input file has been opened, that the child processes are spawned to handle each chunk of input given to them. The file is closed before the child processes go to work three seconds later:

```
%> Process [1] 2567 processing 18 lines...
46      0       31      27      28      29      32      24      0
29      27      31      22      34      28      0   32      26
Process [2] 2568 processing 18 lines...
34      24      29      27      0       28      27      30      24
33      31      0       31      25      33      31  33      23
Process [3] 2569 processing 18 lines...
Process [4] 2570 processing 18 lines...
31      36      21      0       33      21      37      28      37
28      0       28      23      30      17      32  20      0
Process [5] 2571 processing 18 lines...
37      24      34      21      30      29      0       36      25
33      23      31      31      0       35      25  26      20
Process [6] 2572 processing 18 lines...
34      22      0       35      22      35      22      37      24
0       31      23      30      22      33      27  036
Process [7] 2573 processing 18 lines...
27      36      29      30      32      0       34      22      33
26      31      26      0       32      27      33  26      34
0       35      23      34      22      33      24      0       32
25      33      24      32      24      0       34  24      45
Process [8] 2574 processing 2 lines...
23      0
%>
```

DEBUGGING AND THE XTERM WINDOW

When running the debugger on a program that uses `fork`, there is a very high chance that an error will occur, due to the failure of the terminal window opened for each forked child program. This happens because the debugger's `fork` support has been explicitly written for an `xterm` and a console running under OS/2 and nothing else. If you start the forked program under the debugger, it may proceed normally at first and lull you into a false sense of security—until the fork call is made. At this point you will see an error message similar to the following:

```
DB<4> ######### Forked, but do not know how to create a new TTY. #########
Since two debuggers fight for the same TTY, input is severely entangled.
I know how to switch the output to a different window in xterms
and OS/2 consoles only.  For a manual switch, put the name of the created TTY
in $DB::fork_TTY, or define a function DB::get_fork_TTY() returning this.
On UNIX-like systems one can get the name of a TTY for the given window
by typing tty, and disconnect the shell from TTY by sleep 1000000.
main::(./forker:37):                  die "$0 cannot fork: $!" unless defined $pid;
{pid=3384}  DB<4>
```

An error message occurs for each `fork` in our program—each time the `fork` succeeds and the window creation fails. It might almost look like the debugger itself has died, but the debugger is still running. It's just that the filehandles are now so hopelessly entangled with each other, that you may as well stop right there. This large and frightening, although actually quite clear, series of messages is usually enough to send most people running from the room screaming. *Before* you do that, read on.

As mentioned previously, when using the `fork` system call, the debugger is expecting to be run from an `xterm` terminal, so we'll need to start the debugger from within an `xterm` window.

xterm **Support**

To start a new `xterm` window using default values, simply call the `xterm` program with

```
%> xterm
```

This command should generate a new `xterm` window, as shown in Figure 10-1.

Figure 10-1. *The initial* xterm *window*

Running the Forker **Program**

Now we are ready to run the debugger on our program, from *within* the xterm window we just created, using walrus as the input file as shown in Figure 10-2.

Figure 10-2. *The debugger stopped at the first line of the executable code.*

First we use the / command, with fork as a pattern, to find the first line of code which uses the fork command. Next we'll use the l command to list the following lines, and select a suitable line for a breakpoint as shown in Figure 10-3.

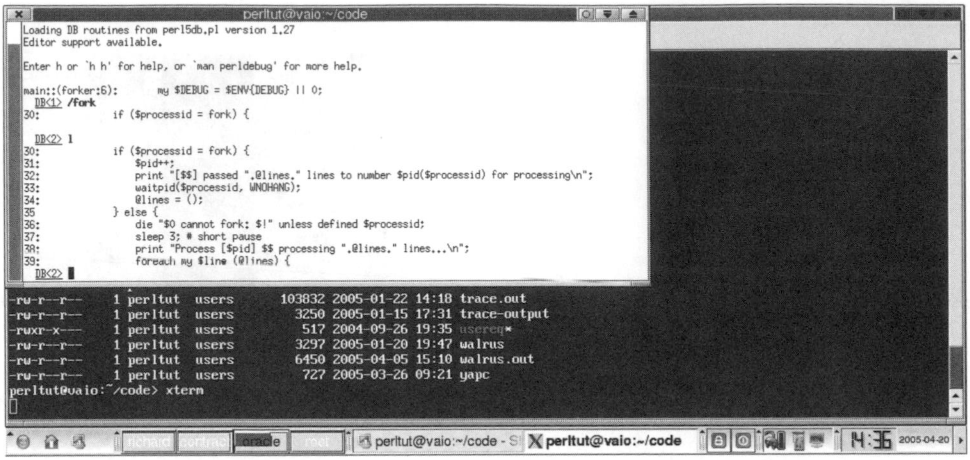

Figure 10-3. *Searching and listing code*

Now set a breakpoint at line 39 (as shown in Figure 10-4), so that when we enter our child processes, we'll have some immediate feedback for where we are via the `print "Process [$pid] $$ processing ".@lines." lines...\n";"` statement on preceding line 38. Follow setting the breakpoint with the common L b command to ensure the breakpoint was set correctly.

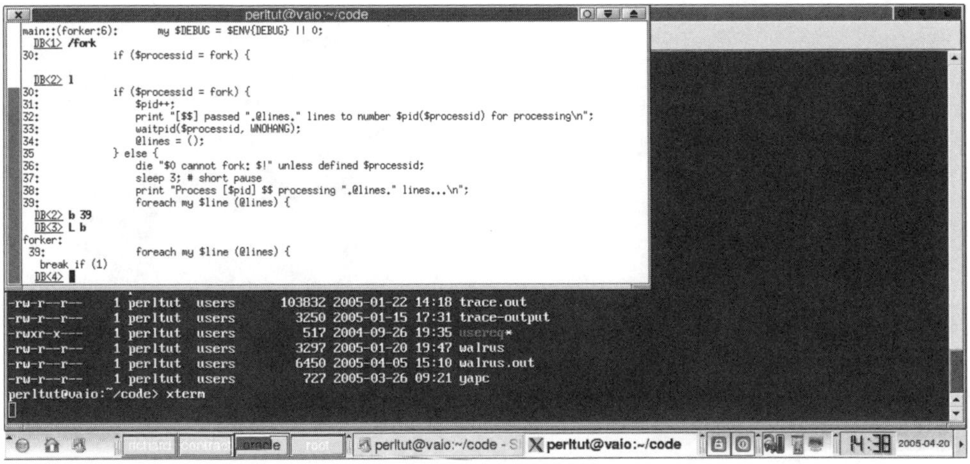

Figure 10-4. *Setting and listing the breakpoint.*

Separation

It's the moment of truth—now we find out if the Perl debugger can really handle a forked program. Enter the c command to continue. As the program opens and works through the file, chunks should be handed off to each of our child processes, and the input file should then close. Because of our sleep commands, the initial xterm screen should look like Figure 10-5 for a couple of seconds.

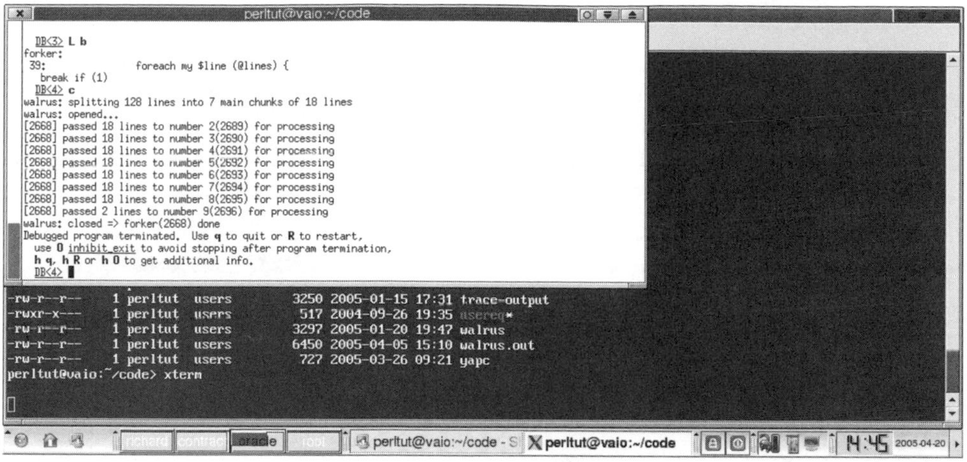

Figure 10-5. *The parent hands control off to each child process*

After the three-second delay, each child process should activate itself, and the screen should be filled with new windows (as shown in Figure 10-6).

Figure 10-6. *Multiple windows are created as the program forks.*

At this point, if all has gone according to plan and your screen looks something like the previous image, we should have a suite of cleanly separated child processes all running in their very own copy of the debugger. In truth, these aren't simply children. They're daughters, which is the name the debugger gives its own children, as you can see from examining the title bars. We can debug each process independently of all the others, for any number of forked processes that your system can handle (as long as you have enough TTYs available).

The Child Debugger Session

Before we look at one of these sessions, it is worth noting that the debugger helpfully attempts to tell you that you are running in a child process by giving the process ID of the *parent* process as part of the title for each new window it creates (as shown in Figure 10-7). In daughter session number 3, we can print the process ID 2696 in our example, and this can be confirmed from the list of data handlers given in the parent process by the 8th process to start.

Figure 10-7. *Feedback to the parent process from the child processes*

Now it's possible to leisurely inspect the data in several of the sessions. First, set the reset display pointer to the current line using the . command to first see where we are, and then dump out a small slice of the @lines array. You can see that each session has completely independent variables and behavior, as you might expect. See Figure 10-8 for more details.

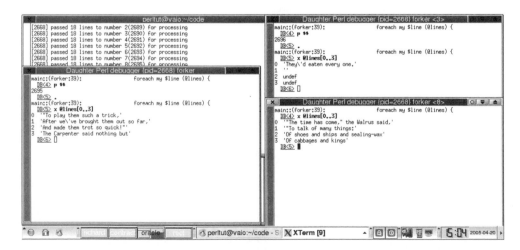

Figure 10-8. *Displaying different contents of the same variable in each forked process*

STDOUT **and** DB::OUT

An interesting thing happens to the output in these sessions. For instance, go to session 8 and use the standard Perl print command (as shown in Figure 10-9) to display the process ID. You'll see that strangely, a blank line appears. The print command prints to the STDOUT filehandle by default, so the output has gone to the original parent xterm window.

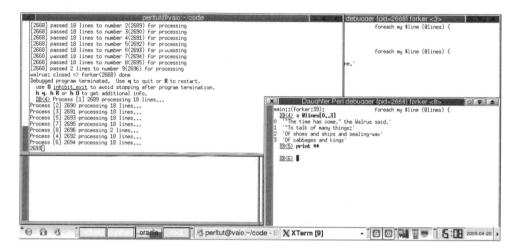

Figure 10-9. *The effect of using the standard print command*

The output of the debugger commands, in contrast, are all going by default to a special file-handle called DB::OUT, and each child has created its own filehandle. We can print the process ID to the DB::OUT filehandle explicitly using the debugger p command (shown in Figure 10-10), in order to see that our output does indeed get printed to the appropriate debugger window.

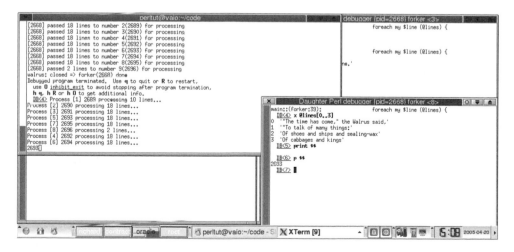

Figure 10-10. *The effect of using the debugger p command*

Finishing Up

Finally, we can choose to return from the current context by running out of the end of the subroutine (shown in Figure 10-11), which will both process the data, and end the session for this daughter debugger. Notice how the results are printed to the original xterm window, in the parent as expected.

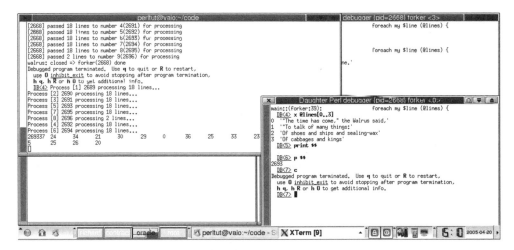

Figure 10-11. *Running off the edge of the program*

Each process can now be worked with independently of the others, and be run to the end of its useful life, but remember that this means you will probably find it necessary to manually exit each debugger session as normal. You could also set the inhibit_exit=0 option to avoid this hanging-around feature in future sessions.

To read more about forking code in Perl, see perlipc and perlfunc/fork.

Using Threads

Having just looked at forked processes, let's have a quick look at threads. Unless you're using a recent version of the Perl debugger, working with threads is a bit like quantum computing, where a variable will take on a different value each time you look at it.

■**Note** Quantum variables may be likened to Schrödinger's Cat. A famous experiment in which Schrödinger suggested that if you put a cat in a box with a bottle of poison, it is not possible to know, until you open the box, whether the cat is dead or alive. In fact, he postulated, until you actually open the box, the cat is in both states at once, and only stabilizes to a single state, either dead or alive, once you open the box and look at the cat.

Let's say you have a threaded Perl program running happily under a Perl installation compiled with threads support, and you wish to run it under the debugger. It's very likely that the program will run all the way through without a hitch—until you wish to interact with it that is. At that point, you are likely to notice some strange behavior, as each variable changes during the course of the program run, without any obvious assignment taking place.

Threads Installation

We are assuming here that you have a working Perl installation with threads enabled. Note that having threads enabled as part of the build is *not* the default. You have to explicitly request it with a command something like:

```
%>./Configure -Dusethreads
```

See the INSTALL documentation for your platform for full details.

The Example Threads Program

For the purposes of our example, we need a simple Perl program that uses threads. The program we chose, aptly titled threads, is shown in Listing 10-2. The threads program takes an input file and divides the content into a number of chunks. Each chunk is then sent to a separate thread, which simply prints the length of the line received.

Listing 10-2. threads

```
01 #!/opt/perlthreads/bin/perl
02
03 use strict;
04 use threads;
05
06 my $DEBUG - $ENV{DEBUG} || 0;
07 my $file  = $ARGV[0] || '';
08 my $count = $ARGV[1] || 10;
09 die("Usage: $0 filename [divisor]")
   unless -r $file && $count =~ /^\d+$/;
10
11 sub process { print length($_[0]).($DEBUG?"\t->@_<-\n":"\t") };
12
13 sub anewthread {
14     my @lines - @_;
15     my $tid = threads->self->tid;
16     print "Thread [$tid] processing ".@lines." lines\n";
17     $DB::single=2 if $tid =~ /[3579]$/;
18     foreach my $line (@lines) {
19         process($line);
20     }
21     print "\n" unless $DEBUG;
22 }
23
24 my ($tot) = grep(/\S+/, split(/\s+/, 'wc $file'));
25 my $num = sprintf('%d', $tot / $count);
```

```
26 print "$file: splitting $tot lines into $count
   main chunks of $num lines\n";
27
28 open(FH, "< $file") or die("$0 unable to open file: $file $!");
29 print "$file: opened...\n";
30
31 my @lines;
32 my $i_cnt;
33
34 while (<FH>) {
35     push(@lines, $_);
36     if ((scalar(@lines) == $num) || eof FH) {
37         chomp(@lines);
38         my $t = threads->create('anewthread', @lines);
39         @lines = ();
40     }
41 }
42
43 close FH && print "$file: closed => $0($$) done\n";
44
45 exit 0;
46
47 __END__
48
49 =head1 NAME
50
51 threads - Perl program using threads
52
53 =head1 SYNOPSIS
54
55     %> perl ./threads inputfilename 3
56
57 =head1 DESCRIPTION
58
59 A program which takes a filename and splits it into
   the optionally given number
60 (or 10) chunks for manipulation via that many threaded process.
61
62 =cut
63
```

Running the Threads Program

To see how the debugger behaves using threads, we can run this program using the walrus input file, and give it an argument of 7 for good luck:

```
%> perl threads walrus 7

Loading DB routines from perl5db.pl version 1.27
```

Editor support available.

Enter h or 'h h' for help, or 'man perldebug' for more help.

```
main::(./threads:6):     my $DEBUG = $ENV{DEBUG} || 0;
 DB<1>
```

The first thing we should do here is to let the program run to its natural end, so we should have some threads which have finished, and some which have been halted by the DB::single=2 variable we set manually in the anewthread subroutine.

Use the c command to tell the debugger to run to the next breakpoint, or off the end of the program:

```
DB<1> c
walrus: splitting 128 lines into 7 main chunks of 18 lines
walrus: opened...
creating new thread
creating new thread
Thread [1] processing 18 lines
46       0       31      27      28      29      32      24      0
29       27      31      22      34      28      0  32      26
Thread [2] processing 18 lines
34       24      29      27      0       28      27      30      24      33
31       0       31      25      33      31  33      23
creating new thread
main::anewthread(./threads:17):     print "Thread [$tid]
processing ".@lines." lines\n";
 DB<1>
```

Looking at the output, we can see that all our threads were started. But, although threads numbered 2, 4, and 6 have all run to the end of their natural lives, threads numbered 3, 5, and 7 are still in a *started* state, because we set $DB::single=2 if $num =~ /[13579]$/ on line 17. Selecting the odd-numbered threads here is a purely arbitrary condition set for the purposes of this example. These threads are still waiting for us in our debugger process though, it is now possible to go and interact with them.

Interacting with Perl Threads Under the Debugger

Now let's use the n command to step over the next statement, which will also print the thread id and show us how many lines we are currently processing:

```
DB<1> n
Thread [3] processing 18 lines
main::anewthread(./threads:18):     foreach my $line (@lines) {
 DB<1>
```

As you can see, our results are so good so far. We appear to be in thread number 3, and the debugger seems to be behaving normally—responding to commands appropriately and so on. So, what about those problems we referred to in the section opening?

Remember early on when we said that we don't like to assume, but prefer to have something proved? We're going to use the p command to simply print the $num variable, which as we've just seen holds the value 3:

```
DB<1> p $tid
5
DB<1>
```

Eh? That's not right! Let's print it again, to double-check what we saw. In fact, we'll print it out three times, for clarity:

```
DB<1> p $tid
7
DB<1> p $tid

DB<1> p $tid
1
DB<1>
```

Aaaaagh! Quantum variables? First it's 7, then it's blank, then 1. What's happening is that the debugger is cycling through the available threads. You can check this by repeating this command *ad infinitum*—but you'll always find that the sequence is simply: *blank, 1, 3, 5, 7.*

As we have seen, each time you look at a variable in a thread, and this includes all the DB:: namespace variables that belong to the debugger too, it is very likely the variable will vary in value. One could even go so far as to say that the value will be stable until you look at it, in which case it may very well adopt a different value, just like Schrödinger's cat! Unfortunately, you'll find that threaded Perl programs using Perl debugger versions older than 5.8.5 are undebuggable.

So, to debug threaded Perl programs you need to use a Perl version that is 5.8.5 or higher and that is enabled for threads support. You'll also need to use the special threaded debugger command line switch -dt, instead of the plain -d. Note that it is *not enough* to simply use a threaded Perl—you need to explicitly enable threaded debugger support with -dt as well. The command will look something like this:

```
%> perl -dt threads walrus 7
Threads support enabled

Loading DB routines from perl5db.pl version 1.28
Editor support available.

Enter h or 'h h' for help, or 'man perldebug' for more help.

main::(./threads:6):    my $DEBUG = $ENV{DEBUG} || 0;
 [0] DB<1>
```

You can see this worked, because the string Threads support enabled appears in the debugger greeting, and there is additional information in the prompt. The prompt now tells you that the thread id is zero (0) because you are in the main process, followed by a standard debugger prompt indicating the number of the command you will enter. Now use the c command to continue to the breakpoint at line 17:

```
[0] DB<1> c
walrus: splitting 128 lines into 7 main chunks of 18 lines
walrus: opened...
creating new thread
creating new thread
```

```
Thread [1] processing 18 lines
46      0       31      27      28      29      32      24      0
29      27      31      22      34      28      0 32      26
Thread [2] processing 18 lines
34      24      29      27      0       28      27      30      24
33      31      0       31      25      33      31 33      23
creating new thread
main::anewthread(./threads:17):    print "Thread [$tid] processing
".@lines." lines\n";
 [3] DB<0>
```

You can see that the debugger has changed the [0] thread id to [3], indicating that we should be in thread number 3. Now use the n command to step over the next statement, which will once again print the thread id and show us the number of lines we are working with at the moment:

```
 [3] DB<0> n
Thread [3] processing 18 lines
main::anewthread(./threads:18):    foreach my $line (@lines) {
 [3] DB<0>
```

This is looking good so far. Now we need to repeat the same commands we used earlier when we saw the $tid variable change each time we inspected its value. Use the p $tid command three times in succession again:

```
 [3] DB<0> p $tid
 3
 [3] DB<1> p $tid
 3
 [3] DB<2> p $tid
 3
 [3]
```

That result is looking altogether different and completely satisfactory. Because we are now more paranoid than is good for us, perhaps we should print out something else too. How about the fourth array element of the data we're working with? Let's also use the !! command to repeat the last command and print it out twice to make sure that the value doesn't change:

```
 [3] DB<3> p $lines[3]
"A pleasant walk, a pleasant talk,
 [3] DB<4> !!
p $lines[3]
"A pleasant walk, a pleasant talk,
 [3] DB<5>
```

If you are going to be working with threads under the Perl debugger, there are a couple of useful thread-specific commands you should know about. A single e will print the current, uniquely generated thread ID, brought to us by the threads library:

```
 [3] DB<5> e
Thread id: 3
 [3] DB<5>
```

The other thread-specific command is a single E. This will print a list of all known threads, and highlight the current one:

```
[3] DB<5> E
Thread ids: 1, 2, <3>
[3] DB<5>
```

Although these commands are not currently very dynamic, it is expected that they could be used in the future for sending debugger commands directly to a particular thread, or to all threads at once. This would be useful for setting a breakpoint in a particular thread for instance, or changing a variable in all threads in one fell stroke. For the impatient amongst you, remember: Rome was not built in a day.

Before we leave the discussion of threads, it is worth pointing out that if you set a breakpoint, for instance, in the main or parent process, it will apply to all threads. This is because this debugger instance is copied into each thread. On the other hand, if you wait until you are inside a running thread before setting a breakpoint, that breakpoint will only be valid for that particular thread, and the other threads won't be impacted. This is a feature of both the implementation and of the threads themselves. After examining this type of restraint, or feature, you can see how the e and E commands may well come in handy for addressing multiple issues when working with threads.

In the current debugging session, the behavior seems quite stable now, and we can probably leave the discussion of threads at this point.

■**Note** To read more about threads in Perl, see `threads` and `perlthrtut`.

Using POE

POE is a multitasking implementation found in Perl. As such, it essentially stands alone, and does not require forking or threading support for its basic functionality.

■**Note** To read more about POE, see the extensive POE documentation, which comes with the module and can also be found online at `http://poe.perl.org`.

A Sample POE Program

First of all, we will need a working POE program. We will use a revised version of the threaded program we used just previously, mixed with a fine example from the first page of the POE documentation. The POE program, found in Listing 10-3, takes a file and splits into the desired number of chunks. Each chunk is then handled by a dedicated POE process, which then simply prints out the length of each line it has received.

Listing 10-3. *A Sample POE Program*

```
01 #!/usr/bin/perl
02
03 use strict;
04 use POE;
05
06 my $DEBUG = $ENV{DEBUG} || 0;
07 my $file  = $ARGV[0] || '';
08 my $count = $ARGV[1] || 10;
09
10 die("Usage: $0 filename [divisor]") unless -r $file
   && $count =~ /^\d+$/;
11
12 sub process { print length($_[0]).($DEBUG?"\t->@_<-\n":"\t") };
13
14 sub _start {
15     my ($kernel, $heap, $session) = @_[KERNEL, HEAP, SESSION];
16     my $sid = $session->ID;
17     my @lines = @_[ARG0..$#_];
18     $kernel->yield('dosession' => @lines);
19 }
20
21 sub anewsession {
22     my ($kernel, $heap, $session) = @_[KERNEL, HEAP, SESSION];
23     my $sid = $session->ID;
24     my @lines = @_[ARG0..$#_];
25     print "Session $sid processing ".@lines." lines\n";
26     # $DB::single=2;
27     foreach my $line (@lines) {
28         process($line);
29     }
30     print "\n" unless $DEBUG;
31 }
32
33 my ($tot) = grep(/\S+/, split(/\s+/, 'wc $file'));
34 my $num - sprintf('%d', $tot / $count);
35 print "$file: splitting $tot lines into $count main
   chunks of $num lines\n";
36
37 open(FH, "< $file") or die("$0 unable to open file: $file $!");
38 print "$file: opened...\n";
39
40 my @lines;
41 my $i_cnt;
42
43 while (<FH>) {
44     push(@lines, $_);
```

```
45    if ((scalar(@lines) == $num) || eof FH) {
46        chomp(@lines);
47         my $session = POE::Session->create(
48             inline_states => {
49                 _start      => \&_start,
50                 dosession   => \&anewsession,
51             },
52             args      => \@lines,
53         );
54         @lines = ();
55    }
56 }
57
58 close FH && print "$file: closed => $0($$) done\n";
59
60 POE::Kernel->run();
61
62 exit 0;
63
64 __END__
65
66 =head1 NAME
67
68 poe - Perl program using POE
69
70 =head1 SYNOPSIS
71
72     %> perl ./poe inputfilename 3
73
74 =head1 DESCRIPTION
75
76 A program which takes a filename and splits it into the
   optionally given number
77 (or 10) chunks for manipulation via that many POE sessions.
78
79 =cut
80
```

Running the POE Program

Unlike the threads example, POE requires no special treatment from the debugger, so we can run this example in the usual manner:

```
%> perl -d poe walrus 7

Loading DB routines from perl5db.pl version 1.27
Editor support available.

Enter h or 'h h' for help, or 'man perldebug' for more help.
```

```
cmain::(poe:6): my $DEBUG = $ENV{DEBUG} || 0;

  DB<1>
```

Now use the c command to run to the first breakpoint:

```
DB<1> c
walrus: splitting 128 lines into 7 main chunks of 18 lines
walrus: opened...
walrus: closed => poe(3066) done
Session 2 processing 18 lines
46      0       31      27      28      29      32      24      0
29      27      31      22      34      28      0  32      26
Session 3 processing 18 lines
main::anewsession(poe:27):              foreach my $line (@lines) {
  DB<1>
```

As you can see from the Session 3 processing 18 lines message, the debugger has stopped the program in the session, using the unique POE generated $session->ID which has a value of 3. Given our previous experience under threads, we know that we would be wise to inspect the value of the $sid variable a few times. We can use the standard debugger p command to print out the value:

```
DB<1> p $sid
 3
DB<2> p $sid
 3
DB<3> p $sid
 3
DB<4>
```

That looks much as we expected, except that it looks as though POE is running through the tasks sequentially, *first 2, followed by 3*, and so on, in a similar manner to the threads example. It isn't apparent whether this is intentional or coincidental behavior, but whatever the case may be, it's one more thing to keep in mind that could help in your debugging efforts.

In closing, a POE program is a Perl module that implements its own multitasking paradigm and offers it to you as both a possible solution (if threads and fork are unavailable to you), and a complete and Perl-only solution of a complex problem domain.

Summary

In this section you have learned how to work with Perl programs that use fork, were introduced to how Perl's threading feature operates,, and gained an appreciation for approaching the debugging of POE programs. When a Perl program forks, remember to use the appropriate xterm, or equivalent environment as required.

The next chapter will cover the debugger's ability to dissect the regular expressions in your Perl program.

## CHAPTER 11

Debugging Regular Expressions

"Can you put your finger on it?"

—Willoughby to Marianne in *Pride and Promiscuity*, by Arielle Eckstut

This chapter shows you how to examine a *regular expression*. If you want to know how to put your finger on the way a regular expression is behaving while Perl is attempting to match a string, this chapter does a great job of walking you through using the debugger to examine what takes place under the hood.

What Is a Regular Expression?

A regular expression is a formal way to describe a pattern that may match a given string. This pattern is built up in almost its own language, using a mixture of plain or literal characters along with the more powerful metacharacters. Metacharacters can consist of \w to describe word characters, \d to describe digits, \s for whitespace and so on. See `perldoc perlre` for a complete description.

Regular expressions can be among the trickiest of subjects for users of Perl to come to grips with. Perl code is renowned for resembling gibberish at times, particularly because of its heavy use of punctuation characters when dealing with regular expressions. Even the phrase regular expression is a bit on the verbose side, and from now on in this chapter we'll use the accepted short form, regex, to describe them.

When your regex doesn't run as expected, the best thing you can do is to take a step back and really look at what you are trying to achieve, and then define exactly what it is that you are trying to match. Many times the answer to a regex problem lies in chopping it up systematically. In this chapter we look at a couple of different ways the debugger can help you to do this.

General Tips

Like any potentially complicated issue, many problems can be dealt with successfully using a combination of traditional approaches in addition to the special tools Perl provides for this purpose. Before moving on however, it's worth discussing one approach that should be applied no matter what the situation: simply make the expression easier on the eyes. There are a number of ways to do this, each of which is discussed in this section.

Leaning Toothpick Syndrome

Many regular expressions fall prey to a phenomenon known as leaning toothpick syndrome (LTS), which occurs when multiple forward slashes (/) found in the expressions must each be escaped by a back slash (\). When these run together this can be very hard on the eye, and can make your work much more error-prone.

Imagine for a moment that we are trying to match a string of the following form, and we wish to extract the elements up to and including the digits in the version number:

```
/usr/local/perl/5.8.5/lib
```

To match this short string, we could simply use a regex full of backslashes, such as

```
/^(\/\w+\/\w+\/\w+\/\d\.\d\.\d)\/\w+$/
```

This is a bit of a mouthful, particularly when you come across more complicated strings. One way of making it easier to see the regex itself, and to not get lost amongst all the slashes, is to surround the regex with different delimiters. Perl allows you to use nearly any character to quote the regex itself, and if we precede it with an m, for example, we could even use the comment character # character:

```
m#^(/\w+/\w+/\w+/\d\.\d\.\d)/\w+$#
```

Framing the regex in characters not used within it, can sometimes make it easier to see the regex's relevant contents. Perhaps the next thing to do with the aim of making this regex simpler to read would be to try to combine the elements where they are repeatable:

```
m#^((\/[a-z]+)+?([\d\.]+))?\/#
```

This has the benefit of using four backslash escapes instead of the 14 we started with, and is much easier on the eyes altogether. Of course there are many ways to match this string, the optimum solution depends on exactly what it is you are trying to do.

Get an Overview

It can be useful to step back and simply ask whether the string in question can in fact be matched by the regex you are using. This can often be accomplished by testing the regular expression on the command line as in the following example.

Note that we use -e '...' to provide the program to Perl directly on the command line instead of using a file to store the source code:

```
%> perl -e 'print ($str =~ /$regex/ ? "yup\n" : "nope\n")'
```

The nice thing about this approach is its simplicity, as well as the ease with which the string and the regex can be modified via experimentation to help you arrive at a successful match.

We could even improve this slightly by looking at what else may have been matched—by including global match capturing parentheses:

```
%> perl -e 'print ($str =~ /($regex)/ ? "yup($1)\n" : "nope\n")'
```

Of course this idea only really helps when you actually match something, so that we can capture it to print it, which is why we don't include the $1 in the negative case.

Divide and Conquer

Another approach which can produce good results is to use the /x modifier, which enables whitespace and comments to mix freely within the regex itself. This can make it a simple matter to discover logic errors or bracketing problems that would otherwise go unnoticed. Let's take a look at a sample regex:

```
$regex = /^\s*(?i:start)([-+]|(plus|minus))(\d+)/x;
```

Now this may not be a particularly complex regex, but compare it to the whitespace indented and commented version:

```
$regex = /^              # start of the string
    \s*                  # which may be followed by whitespace
    (?i:start)           # case insensitive marker (non capturing)
    (                    # looking to capture now -> $1
        [-+]             # a sign
        |                # or
        (plus|minus)     # either the word plus or   minus
    )                    # finishing capture here <-
    (\d+)                # capture some numbers into $2
                         # ignore everything else
/x;
```

Formatting in this manner may take up more space than the condensed version, but it is much clearer for the next person to understand and to modify, and it has no effect on how Perl compiles and executes the regex because the comments are parsed out prior to execution.

So far we have looked at how the regex can be formatted, using a more or less visual exercise to help you remain clear on what you are trying to do. When it comes to really understanding how Perl parses and executes the regex, we need to go deep, and what better way than to use one of the several regex debugging facilities provided by Perl itself.

The use re Pragma

One perfectly respectable solution would be to use the re pragma. We do this by using the -Mre=debug combination. We can see what this would do, by using it on a regex consisting of a minimal character set followed by any character, and compare that to the simple string 'spot':

```
%>perl -Mre=debug -e "'spot' =~/[pso]+./"
Freeing REx: ','
Compiling REx '[pso]+.'
size 12 first at 2
   1: PLUS(11)
   2:   ANYOF[ops](0)
  11: REG_ANY(12)
  12: END(0)
stclass 'ANYOF[ops]' plus minlen 2
Matching REx '[pso]+.' against 'spot'
  Setting an EVAL scope, savestack=3
  0 <> <spot>              |  1:  PLUS
                              ANYOF[ops] can match 3 times out of 32767...
```

```
  Setting an EVAL scope, savestack=3
    3 <spo> <t>              | 11:     REG_ANY
    4 <spot> <>              | 12:     END
Match successful!
Freeing REx: '[pso]+.'
%
```

That may look like a real eyeful, even for such a small regex on an even smaller string, but once you have finished reading this chapter you should be able to dissect and interpret this kind of debugging information without too much difficulty. It will give you a far better understanding of how Perl works through a match or failure, how the regex is parsed and executed inside the regex engine itself, and help you build better regexes in the future.

The re pragma is a very useful tool in debugging regexes and exploring the effects of the taint mechanism in a regex. To find out more about the re pragma see the perldoc re documentation.

Using -Dr to Debug Regexes

The -Dr runtime switch is the command you use to tell Perl that it's going to have to support the debugging of the regex engine. This is a costly exercise in terms of memory and speed, so it is not compiled in by default. Larry wants your Perl to be lean and mean, so this level of debugging support is normally omitted.

Although re pragma produces output very similar to -Dr, as discussed next, the output is subtly different with the -Dr switch because it gives very slightly more information. Another reason for taking a special look at -Dr is that it can be useful to have a Perl built to support all the -D switches. That way we also have access to the opcode parsing (-Dt) and stack trace (-Ds) switches, which we will look at in Chapter 13.

To be able to use the -Dr runtime switch, or any of the other -D switches, your Perl must have been compiled with the -DDEBUGGING switch. You can also use -Doptimize='-g' which includes –DDEBUGGING.

Compile with -DDEBUGGING to Enable -Dr

It is not necessary to bother your poor over-worked system administrator with a request to install a special Perl binary for you. It can be simple to set up a local Perl installation in your home directory for example, and we'll show you how to do exactly that in this section.

To get up and running quickly, you might find a set of commands similar to the following a useful starting point (in this case it's version 5.8.5 of Perl we're compiling). We've downloaded these commands from http://www.perl.org/downloads/perl-stable.

Once you've downloaded the current stable Perl code, you can install it with a short series of commands, using something along these lines:

```
tar -xvzf perl-5.8.5.stable.tar.gz;
cd /usr/local/src/perl-5.8.5/;
sh Configure -Dprefix=/opt/perl/perldb -Uinstallusrbinperl -Doptimize='-g' -de;
perl Makefile.PL && make test && make install PERLNAME=perldb;
```

There are several important things to note about the previous commands:

- To install the binary under /opt/perl, we use –Dprefix.

- We do not wish to overwrite any existing Perl binary (-Uinstallusrbinperl).

- To compile with –DDEBUGGING we use –Doptimize='-g'.

- Except for those changes we specify on the command line, we're going to accept all other installation defaults (-de).

- We want to call the binary using the name: perldb (PERLNAME).

■**Note** You may want to avoid the make test element in the previous command, as the entire test suite may well take some time to run.

Testing Your Configuration

Once the previous commands have been completed and assuming all has gone well, you should now be able to call the new Perl installation to display configuration options. You can do this by using the -V switch to confirm that -DDEBUGGING was enabled. Note the use of perldb in this case and for the rest of this chapter:

```
perldb -V
```

The output should include something similar to the following line:

```
Compile-time options: ... DEBUGGING ...
```

Here's a short example of the sort of output you can expect from exercising this functionality. Here you can see some of the subtle differences from the example given previously:

```
%> perldb -Dr -e '/[^@]+\@(\w+\.)+/'
Compiling REx '[^@]+\@(\w+\.)+'
size 27 Got 220 bytes for offset annotations.
first at 2
rarest char @ at 0
   1: PLUS(13)
   2:   ANYOF[\0-?A-\377{unicode_all}](0)
  13: EXACT <@>(15)
  15: CURLYX[0] {1,32767}(26)
  17:   OPEN1(19)
  19:     PLUS(21)
  20:       ALNUM(0)
  21:     EXACT <.>(23)
  23:   CLOSE1(25)
  25:   WHILEM[1/1](0)
  26: NOTHING(27)
  27: END(0)
floating '@' at 1..2147483647 (checking floating)
     stclass 'ANYOF[\0-?A-\377{unicode_all}]' plus minlen 4
```

```
Offsets: [27]
    5[1] 1[4] 0[0] 0[0] 0[0] 0[0] 0[0] 0[0] 0[0] 0[0] 0[0] 0[0] 6[2] 0[0] 15[1] 0[0]
    8[1] 0[0] 11[1] 9[2] 12[2] 0[0] 14[1] 0[0] 15[0] 15[0] 16[0]
Omitting $` $& $' support.
EXECUTING...
Freeing REx: '"[^@]+\\@(\\w+\\.)+"'
%>
```

Note that using -Dr on a large program, that has many modules, is liable to produce extremely voluminous output, because each and every regex that Perl comes across will be dumped as it is compiled and executed. This means that all the regexes in every module you have been in have (possibly unintentionally) been used. You have been warned.

-Dr Debugging Basics

In this section, we are going to explore the regex debugging mechanism enabled on the command line with the -Dr switch. The general execution format looks like this:

```
%>perldb -Dr program [args]
```

There are two parts to the regex process—the compilation part and the execution part. The compilation part is run on each and every regex in a Perl program, and this is completely independent of whether you use re, -Dr, or neither. The Perl regex engine has an optimizer built into it, so that once the compilation part has run, it can decide not to enter the execution part at all if it decides that the string cannot possibly match, or if it has already matched it. Let's deal with the compilation part first.

The Regex Compilation Phase

Assuming we now have a fully operational Perl installation with -DDEBUGGING enabled, we can now test just the compilation section against a regex given as the Perl program to execute by using -e /regex/ on the command line. This time, we won't even give the engine a string to match against, we'll just enter a regex for it to compile, such as

```
%> perldb -Dr -e '/spot/'
 1: Compiling REx 'spot'
 2: size 3 Got 28 bytes for offset annotations.
 3: first at 1
 4: rarest char p at 1
 5:   1: EXACT <spot>(3)
 6:   3: END(0)
 7: anchored 'spot' at 0 (checking anchored isall) minlen 4
 8: Offsets: [3]
 9:         1[4] 0[0] 5[0]
10: Omitting $` $& $' support.
11:
12: EXECUTING...
13:
14: Freeing REx: '"spot"'
 %>
```

Although the example is fairly simple, the information given is still fairly extensive. Let's be pedantic and go through it one line at a time using the line numbers prefixed to each of the output lines. Remember: these are only there for the purposes of this explanation:

```
1: Compiling REx 'spot'
```

This first line is Perl confirming the regex we are about to compile:

```
2: size 3 Got 28 bytes for offset annotations.
```

The expression generated three offset table entries that took up 28 bytes of space. This is described in more detail following with lines 8 and 9.

```
3: first at 1
```

In this short example we have two nodes: 1 and 3. Line 3 tells us we're going to start the regex at node number 1.

```
4: rarest char p at 1
```

Of the alphanumeric characters of a certain section of the expression, the rarest character found was p at an offset of 1. You may use multiple characters to assist with quickly discarding implausible matches. Running a Boyer-Moore algorithm results in the rarest character comment. If the engine sees that there is no character p at offset 1, it can save a lot of time by stopping the regex from useless backtracking in order to find a match. If there is clearly no point in continuing, the attempt to match can be immediately abandoned:

```
5: 1: EXACT <spot>(3)
```

This (first) node (1:) of our expression is an exact character match against the string spot. From here, the next relevant node at this level is node 3:

```
6: 3: END(0)
```

This (second) node (3:) of our expression happens, in our case, also to be the end of it. Normally there are several (or many) nodes to a regex, some of which may nest down a level or two:

```
7: anchored 'spot' at 0 (checking anchored isall) minlen 4
```

There must be the exact substring spot at an offset of 0 from any part of the string to successfully match. The isall means that because we have all the information required, at least at this point, the optimizer is telling the regex engine that it will not be needed. Finally, the string must be at least 4 characters long:

```
8: Offsets: [3]
```

The offset/length table has three entries (1[4], 0[0] and 5[0]), as described in the following code line:

```
9: 1[4] 0[0] 5[0]
```

Each offset entry describes the nodes (referenced in lines 5 and 6). Node 1 is represented by 1[4], meaning it has an offset of 1 and is 4 characters long. Node 2 is represented by 0[0], meaning it has an offset of 0 and is 0 characters long (in other words, there is no information associated with it). Finally, node 3 is represented by 5[0], meaning it has an offset of 5 and is 0 characters long:

```
10: Omitting $` $& $' support.
```

The special $&, $`, and $' variables are a special case in regex handling. They refer to the string matched by the entire regex ($&), the part of the string to the left of what was matched ($`), and the part to the right ($'). They're referred to as the match, pre-match, and post-match variables, respectively. If a program doesn't use any of these three variables, then the regex engine will not populate them.

This is a *good* thing because including this functionality can unnecessarily slow down *all* regex work in the entire program, as well as every regex contained in all libraries or modules during this Perl instantiation. In this example, then, line 10 is simply notifying us that it is not bothering to populate them:

```
11:
```

This is simply a visual spacer line:

```
12: EXECUTING...
```

This line tells us that the regex engine section is about to be entered.

The EXECUTING section was not actually run because all we did was compile the regex. To actually enter the regex engine we need to supply a string to match *against*. We'll do this in the next section:

```
13:
```

This is another purely visual spacer line:

```
14: Freeing REx: '"spot"'
```

Here we are releasing the memory used by the regex engine, and returning control to the main executing Perl program. At this point we are finished with this example.

The Optimizer

The regex engine has an optimizer, which parses the incoming string and can make certain decisions in advance of actually running the engine. In some cases it can obviate the need to even start the engine itself. The whole point of this optimization stage is to attempt to speed up the total time the match process takes by being able to match, or abandon, the string very early on in the process, perhaps without even going through the extra steps of entering the regex engine itself.

In this next example we provide a simple string (spott), giving Perl a bit more work to do and allowing us to see if the regex engine might actually attempt to execute something:

```
%> perldb -Dr -e '"spott" =~ /spot/'
Compiling REx 'spot'
size 3 Got 28 bytes for offset annotations.
first at 1
rarest char p at 1
   1: EXACT <spot>(3)
   3: END(0)
anchored 'spot' at 0 (checking anchored isall) minlen 4
Offsets: [3]
        1[4] 0[0] 5[0]
Omitting $` $& $' support.
EXECUTING...
```

```
Guessing start of match, REx 'spot' against 'spott'...
Found anchored substr 'spot' at offset 0...
Guessed: match at offset 0
Freeing REx: '"spot"'
```

Now, under the EXECUTING section, we have some more information.

The engine, or rather the optimizer in this case, has found the spot string anchored at an offset of zero. It's found at the beginning of the string, and it is matched instantly with no more work to be done. Finally, the memory set aside for the regex is released again.

The expression was so simple, that the engine was not even entered. The optimizer has already done all of the work of matching the string in question.

Discarding a Match

The optimizer is equally capable of discarding a match as in the following example:

```
%> perldb -Dr -e '"spott" =~ /spot/'
Compiling REx 'spot'
size 3 Got 28 bytes for offset annotations.
first at 1
rarest char p at 1
   1: EXACT <spot>(3)
   3: END(0)
anchored 'spot' at 0 (checking anchored isall) minlen 4
Offsets: [3]
        1[4] 0[0] 5[0]
Omitting $` $& $' support.
EXECUTING...
Guessing start of match, REx 'spot' against 'sxpott'...
Did not find anchored substr 'spot'...
Match rejected by optimizer
Freeing REx: '"spot"'
%>
```

The optimizer has again decided the string is not worth further investigation, as the simple exact match substring just was not found in the target string. The match was rejected before involving the extra overhead of entering the regex engine itself.

The Regex Execution Phase

It's clear that a substring text match is simply not enough to actually enter the regex engine, because the optimizer steps in and avoids the need to call the engine at all.

You can see this if you take the trouble to time the difference between finding a match using a simple substring pattern like /spot/ and finding a match using even a single metacharacter, like the /s\w+tt/ example, discussed later. Neither method takes a great amount of time, but when taken over one million loops (a common number used for testing purposes when using the Benchmark module), it may amount to 4 seconds for the plain substring and 6 seconds for the metacharacter regex version. For hints on using Benchmark and other optimization and performances, see Chapter 13.

Returning to regex execution, to see the regex engine in action, we need to supply a regex that will generate some actual activity. The next example, though still a simple expression, now uses metacharacters, and is just complicated enough to engage the engine itself:

```
%> perldb -Dr -e '"spott" =~ /s\w+tt/'
Compiling REx 's\w+tt'
size 7 Got 60 bytes for offset annotations.
first at 1
rarest char t at 0
rarest char s at 0
   1: EXACT <s>(3)
   3: PLUS(5)
   4:    ALNUM(0)
   5: EXACT <tt>(7)
   7: END(0)
anchored 's' at 0 floating 'tt' at 2..2147483647 (checking floating) minlen 4
Offsets: [7]
        1[1] 0[0] 4[1] 2[2] 5[2] 0[0] 7[0]
Omitting $` $& $' support.
EXECUTING...
Guessing start of match, REx 's\w+tt' against 'spott'...
Found floating substr 'tt' at offset 3...
Found anchored substr 's' at offset 0...
Guessed: match at offset 0
Matching REx 's\w+tt' against 'spott'
  Setting an EVAL scope, savestack=3
   0 <> <spott>            |   1:  EXACT <s>
   1 <s> <pott>            |   3:  PLUS
                                   ALNUM can match 4 times out of 2147483647...
  Setting an EVAL scope, savestack=3
   4 <spot> <t>            |   5:    EXACT <tt>
                                     failed...
   3 <spo> <tt>            |   5:    EXACT <tt>
   5 <spott> <>            |   7:    END
Match successful!
Freeing REx: '"s\\w+tt"'
 %>
```

Here we can see, in the initial section of the regex, that the compiler has defined that we need a single s followed by one or more alphanumeric characters, and then followed by tt. The compiler also defines that the string must be at least four characters long to satisfy this expression.

Viewing this form of a dissected regex and its component parts can be a great aid in deciding whether a particular expression has any chance of working at all. In the execution section, you can see the stages that the engine went through in deciding whether to match this string or not. Looking at these stages can be illuminating and can help you to understand how the string will be dealt with:

```
0 <> <spott>            |   1:  EXACT <s>
```

First we nip the exact s off the front:

```
1 <s> <pott>            |  3:   PLUS
```

Being greedy, we slurp up three alphanumeric characters, leaving one t on the end, to attempt to match that against tt. We know, by looking at t and tt, that these will not match, but remember, the regex engine also has to look, before it can make that same decision—and fail:

```
4 <spot> <t>           |  5:    EXACT <tt>
                           failed...
```

In an attempt to match the tt chunk, we give up a single t character from the end of the string:

```
3 <spo> <tt>           |  5:    EXACT <tt>
```

Notice how the line informs us that node (5) is being used against the target string currently being matched and that the angle-brackets indicate the current position of the regex engine itself. Within the angle-brackets (< and >) you see two chunks of text: the pre-string and the post-string. These surround the precise location of the regex engine within the string at this particular moment. Think of these two bracketed strings as monitoring the string the engine is trying to match against, watching both what is currently matched, and what may match in the next step.

Giving up on the possibility of matching a second t character with the previous one, enables the engine to match the errant tt. Now we can relax—our regex is satisfied and we are done:

```
5 <spott> <>           |  7:    END
  Match successful!
```

Finally, the engine reports the successful match. Great!

Getting the regex engine to report what it is doing at each stage, including inspecting the string, trying a match, failing and backtracking to an earlier position, and so on, can be quite illuminating. This helps you understand the processes within a regex engine and can therefore improve how you setup your regex in the first place.

A Complete -Dr Walkthrough

To better understand exactly happens in a real-world regex, let's walk through a more detailed example that matches an *un*complicated email address. For our example, we'll use this target string:

```
"Spot" <s.p.o.t\@the.dog.net>
```

Note that a backslash is used to escape the @ sign, because otherwise Perl will try and interpolate the nonexistent @.

Here is the regex we will use, which shows negated character classes, non-capturing parentheses, and alternation. It's altogether looking a bit more like a real-world regex than the ones we have seen so far:

```
/([^<@>]+)@((?:\w+\.)+(?:com|net|org)).*/
```

When the regex has finished, we'll print out the name and the domain field we hope to match for reference, followed by a newline for completeness:

```
print "->$1($2)<-\n"'
```

The Command

Putting all of this together, this is our final command line for this example:

```
%> perldb -Dr -e '
             "\"Spot\" \<s.p.o.t\@the.dog.net\>"
                          =~ /([^<@>]+)@((?:\w+\.)+(?:com|net|org)).*/;
   print "->$1($2)<-\n"
   '
```

These four lines are one single command. The actual command for Perl is within the single quotes, but we have spread it over several lines for convenience when printing and reading.

Because of its length, it may be better off placed into a file called regex.pl (example shown in Listing 11-1). In the case where we use Listing 11-1, instead of running this directly from the command line with -e, we can dispense with the backslashed double quotes and the @ character, by using single quotes.

Listing 11-1. regex.pl—*The Regex as a Perl Program*

```
'"Spot" <s.p.o.t@the.dog.net>' =~ /([^<@>]+)@((?:\w+\.)+(?:com|net|org)).*/;
print "->$1($2)<-\n";
```

To run it use this command:

```
%> perldb -Dr regex.pl
```

You can use whichever form you prefer, the output we describe next should be essentially identical.

The Output

Here is the fairly voluminous output we get from running the previous command:

```
Compiling REx '([^<@>]+)@((?:\w+\.)+(?:com|net|org)).*'
size 43 Got 348 bytes for offset annotations.
first at 4
rarest char @ at 0
   1: OPEN1(3)
   3:    PLUS(15)
   4:      ANYOF[\0-;=?A-\377{unicode_all}](0)
  15: CLOSE1(17)
  17: EXACT <@>(19)
  19: OPEN2(21)
  21:    CURLYX[1] {1,32767}(28)
  23:      PLUS(25)
  24:        ALNUM(0)
  25:      EXACT <.>(27)
  27:      WHILEM[1/1](0)
  28:    NOTHING(29)
  29:    BRANCH(32)
  30:      EXACT <com>(39)
  32:    BRANCH(35)
```

```
  33:     EXACT <net>(39)
  35:   BRANCH(38)
  36:     EXACT <org>(39)
  38:   TAIL(39)
  39: CLOSE2(41)
  41: STAR(43)
  42:   REG_ANY(0)
  43: END(0)
floating '@' at 1..2147483647 (checking floating)
 stclass 'ANYOF[\0-;=?A-\377{unicode_all}]' plus minlen 7
Offsets: [43]
 1[1] 0[0] 8[1] 2[6] 0[0] 0[0] 0[0] 0[0] 0[0] 0[0] 0[0] 0[0] 0[0] 0[0] 9[1] 0[0]
 10[1] 0[0] 11[1] 0[0] 21[1] 15[2] 17[1] 15[2] 18[2] 0[0] 21[0] 21[0] 24[1] 25[3]
 0[0] 28[1] 29[3] 0[0] 32[1] 33[3] 0[0] 35[0] 37[1] 0[0] 39[1] 38[1] 40[0]
Omitting $` $& $' support.
EXECUTING...
Guessing start of match, REx '([^<@>]+)@((?:\w+\.)+(?:com|net|org)).*'
 against '"Spot" <s.p.o.t@the.dog.net>'...
Found floating substr '@' at offset 15...
Does not contradict STCLASS...
Guessed: match at offset 0
Matching REx '([^<@>]+)@((?:\w+\.)+(?:com|net|org)).*'
 against '"Spot" <s.p.o.t@the.dog.net>'
Matching stclass 'ANYOF[\0-;=?A-\377{unicode_all}]'
 against '"Spot" <s.p.o.t@the.do'
  Setting an EVAL scope, savestack=3
   0 <> <"Spot" <s.p.>    |  1:  OPEN1
   0 <> <"Spot" <s.p.>    |  3:  PLUS
   ANYOF[\0-;=?A-\377{unicode_all}] can match 7 times out of 2147483647...
  Setting an EVAL scope, savestack=3
 failed...
  Setting an EVAL scope, savestack=3
   8 <ot" <> <s.p.o.t>    |  1:  OPEN1
   8 <ot" <> <s.p.o.t>    |  3:  PLUS
   ANYOF[\0-;=?A-\377{unicode_all}] can match 7 times out of 2147483647...
  Setting an EVAL scope, savestack=3
  15 <p.o.t> <@the.do>    | 15:    CLOSE1
  15 <p.o.t> <@the.do>    | 17:    EXACT <@>
  16 <.o.t@> <the.dog>    | 19:    OPEN2
  16 <.o.t@> <the.dog>    | 21:    CURLYX[1] {1,32767}
  16 <.o.t@> <the.dog>    | 27:      WHILEM[1/1]
 0 out of 1..32767  cc=bfffeb30
  16 <.o.t@> <the.dog>    | 23:        PLUS
    ALNUM can match 3 times out of 2147483647...
  Setting an EVAL scope, savestack=3
  19 <t@the> <.dog.ne>    | 25:        EXACT <.>
  20 <@the.> <dog.net>    | 27:        WHILEM[1/1]
```

```
1 out of 1..32767   cc=bfffeb30
 Setting an EVAL scope, savestack=13
 20 <@the.> <dog.net>     | 23:                PLUS
   ALNUM can match 3 times out of 2147483647...
 Setting an EVAL scope, savestack=13
 23 <the.dog> <.net>>     | 25:                EXACT <.>
 24 <the.dog.> <net>>     | 27:                WHILEM[1/1]
2 out of 1..32767   cc=bfffeb30
 Setting an EVAL scope, savestack=23
 24 <the.dog.> <net>>     | 23:                PLUS
   ALNUM can match 3 times out of 2147483647...
 Setting an EVAL scope, savestack=23
  failed...
 restoring \2 to -1(16)..-1(no)
 restoring \2..\2 to undef
failed, try continuation...
 24 <the.dog.> <net>>     | 28:                NOTHING
 24 <the.dog.> <net>>     | 29:                BRANCH
 Setting an EVAL scope, savestack=23
 24 <the.dog.> <net>>     | 30:                EXACT <com>
failed...
 24 <the.dog.> <net>>     | 33:                EXACT <net>
 27 <the.dog.net> <>>     | 39:                CLOSE2
 27 <the.dog.net> <>>     | 41:                STAR
   REG_ANY can match 1 times out of 2147483647...
 Setting an EVAL scope, savestack=23
 28 <the.dog.net>> <>     | 43:                END
Match successful!
->s.p.o.t(the.dog.net)<-
Freeing REx: '"([^<@>]+)@((?:\\w+\\.)+(?:com|net|org)).*"'
perltut@vaio:~/code>
```

Now that is a real mouthful of regex feedback. However, it's really not as bad as it looks, and we should be able to appreciate that after we've gone through it once, line by line.

The Walkthrough

In this section we'll walk through each line of the generated output. Although we've seen some of this before, it's nonetheless worth explaining each line individually in order to provide you with a complete summation of the mechanism's events. For starters, Perl informs us of the regex it's been given:

```
Compiling REx '([^<@>]+)@((?:\w+\.)+(?:com|net|org)).*'
```

Then it informs us about the offset information it has formed from the regex:

```
size 43 Got 348 bytes for offset annotations.
```

In the next several lines, we are told that we're about to start considering the regex from node number 4:

```
first at 4
rarest char @ at 0
   1: OPEN1(3)
   3:   PLUS(15)
   4:     ANYOF[\0-;=?A-\377{unicode_all}](0)
```

This tells us several things:

- We're opening a capturing parentheses (from node 1:).

- We're looking for anything which does *not* look like @ or or.

- We can have one or more of characters (up to infinity or 2147483647—whichever comes first).

Then, at node 15, we close our capturing parentheses, because this is where the data will be stored from the first match. From here we will continue from node 17:

```
15: CLOSE1(17)
```

At node 17 we discover that the next thing we are looking for is an exact @:

```
17: EXACT <@>(19)
```

Directed from here to go to node 19, we open our second capturing parentheses and hop to node 21:

```
19: OPEN2(21)
```

Now the section between nodes 21and 28 must be considered as a group. Firstly we're looking for one or more alphanumeric characters, followed by a period. This grouping must appear at least once, and no more than 32,767 times, to match. The number 32,767 is effectively an arbitrary very large number that for most normal purposes means "as many as you want." Finally, head off to node 28:

```
21:   CURLYX[1] {1,32767}(28)
23:     PLUS(25)
24:       ALNUM(0)
25:     EXACT <.>(27)
27:     WHILEM[1/1](0)
```

The expression found at node 29 is supposed to match nothing (the empty string). This is *not* the same as not searching for a match. We're matching, but what we're matching is an empty string:

```
28:   NOTHING(29)
```

Now, starting at node 29 and finishing via nodes 32, 35 and 38, we have an alternation consisting of the exact sequences: com, net and org. If any one, or none, of these match, we finish at node 39:

```
29:   BRANCH(32)
30:     EXACT <com>(39)
32:   BRANCH(35)
33:     EXACT <net>(39)
35:   BRANCH(38)
36:     EXACT <org>(39)
38:   TAIL(39)
```

Node 39 is the command to close our second capturing parentheses, and to continue from node 41:

```
39: CLOSE2(41)
```

To finish off, the next two lines indicate that we can have any (including zero) number of characters that we want. Next, we continue to node 43 for our next instruction:

```
41: STAR(43)
42:   REG_ANY(0)
```

Finally, at node 43, we're finished:

```
43: END(0)
```

Note that the trailing .* is redundant. As there are no capturing parentheses and as we want zero or more of anything (in other words potentially nothing), we could just as easily leave the .* off the regex altogether. It's really only there to make it explicitly clear that this is where the rest of the string will end up, in the case of a greedy pattern match.

The next line from the optimizer tells us that at the very least, we require an explicit @ in a character string of at least seven characters, and that this @ could appear anywhere from the first position to any other position we are capable of handling. This floating ' ' element is one of the first things the regex engine is going to search for:

```
floating '@' at 1..2147483647 (checking floating)
 stclass 'ANYOF[\0-;=?A-\377{unicode_all}]' plus minlen 7
```

Next follow a whole bundle of offset annotations. Note that there are many with no relevant information at all, such as 0[0]. This is much like an array that has been automatically generated to hold multiple disparate values:

```
Offsets: [43]
1[1] 0[0] 8[1] 2[6] 0[0] 0[0] 0[0] 0[0] 0[0] 0[0] 0[0] 0[0] 0[0] 0[0] 9[1] 0[0]
10[1] 0[0] 11[1] 0[0] 21[1] 15[2] 17[1] 15[2] 18[2] 0[0] 21[0] 21[0] 24[1] 25[3]
0[0] 28[1] 29[3] 0[0] 32[1] 33[3] 0[0] 35[0] 37[1] 0[0] 39[1] 38[1] 40[0]
```

Finally we are told that we are not required to support the pre-match ($`), match ($&), and post-match ($') variables we discussed earlier:

```
Omitting $` $& $' support.
```

Having analyzed the regex, now we turn our attention to the actual work of matching it against the given string:

```
EXECUTING...
Guessing start of match, REx '([^<@>]+)@((?:\w+\.)+(?:com|net|org)).*'
against '"Spot" <s.p.o.t@the.dog.net>'...
```

The next line tells us that the engine has already found the explicit substring @, which was earlier defined as being a prerequisite for continued work, somewhere in the string. It also tells us at what offset it was found at in the target string:

```
Found floating substr '@' at offset 15...
```

Next we find that the class of characters which are required from node 4 (^\<@\>) at the start of our regex, appear to be satisfied, so we can continue and enter the regex engine itself:

```
Does not contradict STCLASS...
```

This line tells us that so far at the start of the string, our regex looks as though it may indeed match. Therefore it is worth having a deeper look at it, and so we don't reject it at this early stage:

```
Guessed: match at offset 0
```

Now that the optimizer has decided that we may be able to match this string, we can get down to the real work. First we get a confirmation message that we are going to match this regex against that string:

```
Matching REx '([^<@>]+)@((?:\w+\.)+(?:com|net|org)).*'
 against '"Spot" <s.p.o.t@the.dog.net>'
```

Here we are going to open with our defined class of characters to search for:

```
Matching stclass 'ANYOF[\0-;=?A-\377{unicode_all}]'
 against '"Spot" <s.p.o.t@the.do'
```

The first thing we should do is save our position, so that we can return should we fail to succeed on the first try:

```
Setting an EVAL scope, savestack=3
```

We can now open a capture parentheses and try, from an offset of 0, to match the nothing at the start of the string:

```
0 <> <"Spot" <s.p.>    |  1:  OPEN1
```

Note the angle brackets. The first set of angle brackets indicate the string just before our anchor position, and the second pair are the string just after. This will make more sense later on.

Now we try to add some characters from the right-hand side:

```
0 <> <"Spot" <s.p.>    |  3:  PLUS
```

We are now informed that our chunk of string can match up to seven times, before we hit another type of character (such as the first angle bracket: <):

```
ANYOF[\0-;=?A-\377{unicode_all}] can match 7 times out of 2147483647...
```

We should save our position again so that we can come back here if we fail to find a successful match:

```
Setting an EVAL scope, savestack=3
```

Because this does not satisfy our regex (there isn't an ampersand on our right hand side), we fail and bail out:

```
failed...
```

Again, we may be able to guess that this was going to fail just by looking at the string, but don't forget that the regex engine has to look too. Be patient—it has to do this chunk by sweet chunk.

Now that we have bailed out we can go back to a previous state, in this case our initial state, and try again. We know we can't match from anywhere within this chunk, because there is no @ on our right-hand side, so we pickup the next chunk along the string.

You can now see the window of angle bracket pairs positioned so that you can see both the end of the string to our left, which we have not matched, and the piece of string we are now looking at on our right:

```
Setting an EVAL scope, savestack=3
 8 <ot" <> <s.p.o.t>    |  1:  OPEN1
```

This time we start with the s from s.p.o.t just past the first angle bracket, as the start of our next potential match. We reopen our initial capturing parentheses with OPEN1 and then we start trying to gobble up as much of the right-hand side as possible. The engine then tells us we can match up to seven times (again) given our regex:

```
 8 <ot" <> <s.p.o.t>    |  3:  PLUS
    ANYOF[\0-;=?A-\377{unicode_all}] can match 7 times out of 2147483647...
      Setting an EVAL scope, savestack=3
      15 <p.o.t> <@the.do>   | 15:   CLOSE1
```

At this point we have successfully matched (with the close1) the first parentheses, and have the text s.p.o.t in $1. Now we are going to look for the exact character @:

```
15 <p.o.t> <@the.do>   | 17:   EXACT <@>
```

We found the character, but because we're not capturing it this time, it just gets slipped across to the left hand side of our window. Now we'll open a second parentheses, to try to catch the \w+\. in our regex:

```
16 <.o.t@> <the.dog>   | 19:   OPEN2
```

The next several lines specify start trying to match \w+ into $2:

```
16 <.o.t@> <the.dog>   | 21:   CURLYX[1] {1,32767}
16 <.o.t@> <the.dog>   | 27:    WHILEM[1/1]
                             0 out of 1..32767  cc=bfffe7f0
16 <.o.t@> <the.dog>   | 23:     PLUS
```

We get feedback to the effect that we have found three appropriate alphanumeric characters. Note that we cannot have more than 2,147,483,647 characters—which is a Perl defined limit:

```
ALNUM can match 3 times out of 2147483647...
```

Next we save this part of the string, the, in a scratch area again.

```
Setting an EVAL scope, savestack=3
```

And now we try to find \. directly afterwards (on the right-hand side):

```
19 <t@the> <.dog.ne>   | 25:        EXACT <.>
```

Got it! This is looking good. Shuffle that across to the left-hand side as a valid state:

```
20 <@the.> <dog.net>   | 27:        WHILEM[1/1]
```

The engine has found the first group the., and tells us with the message that it matched: 1 out of 1..32767. This means that it matched once, and that it had 32767 places to store additional matches that weren't used. In other words, you can't have more than this many matches in a regex. This is a hard limit:

```
1 out of 1..32767  cc=bfffe7f0
```

We'll now try to find some additional alphanumerics. First, save the current state (again):

```
Setting an EVAL scope, savestack=13
```

Also again, start looking for more alphanumerics:

```
20 <@the.> <dog.net>    | 23:              PLUS
      ALNUM can match 3 times out of 2147483647...
```

We save to a scratch area, and slurp three more characters (as indicated earlier):

```
Setting an EVAL scope, savestack=13
23 <the.dog> <.net>>    | 25:                EXACT <.>
```

Now we find the next period that matched with the backslashed period in the regex, and we have another complete snippet, 2 chunks (of 32767 possibilities), so far:

```
24 <the.dog.> <net>>    | 27:              WHILEM[1/1]
                                  2 out of 1..32767  cc=bfffe7f0
```

Save it away for later and try again for alphanumerics:

```
Setting an EVAL scope, savestack=23
```

Now, this might seem a bit repetitive to you as you are reading this, but this is exactly what we have asked the regex engine to do, and it's good to take some time to watch it doing what we wanted.

Here come the alphanumerics—three again this time:

```
24 <the.dog.> <net>>    | 23:          PLUS ALNUM can match 3 times
out of 2147483647...
```

Still looking good. Remember to keep it handy for the next check (the \.):

```
Setting an EVAL scope, savestack=23
   failed...
```

Because we failed to find that final \., we need to restore the last saved state:

```
restoring \2 to -1(16)..-1(no)
restoring \2..\2 to undef
```

We get feedback on the failure, and notification that we are going to try to continue from our last saved state:

```
failed, try continuation...
```

From here we find we are at a position with nothing between the.dog. and net:

```
24 <the.dog.> <net>>    | 28:              NOTHING
```

Now we can check to see if any of our alternating yet *exact* pattern, com|net|org, matches against the next piece of string on the right-hand side, by branching:

```
24 <the.dog.> <net>>    | 29:              BRANCH
Setting an EVAL scope, savestack=23
24 <the.dog.> <net>>    | 30:                EXACT <com>
                                    failed...
```

Evidently the pattern net does not match the string com, so we go to our next branch and try to match net against net instead:

```
24 <the.dog.> <net>>    | 33:              EXACT <net>
```

This is looking very good, so we find our string, slip it over to the left-hand side and close our second parentheses, storing the value in $2:

```
27 <the.dog.net> <>>     | 39:                    CLOSE2
```

You can now see, in these examples, how this windowing effect of the angle brackets is making it quite easy to see what the regex engine is actually looking at, and where we currently are in the string.

Finally we need to exercise the last piece of our regex, the .*, which is looking for any single character any number of times. Because any number of times (the asterisk in the regex) includes zero times, this matches the rest of the string immediately:

```
27 <the.dog.net> <>>     | 41:                     STAR
           REG_ANY can match 1 times out of 2147483647...
Setting an EVAL scope, savestack=23
```

Seems like we have nothing, so the engine reports that it can match once, which was apparently what we were looking for, and we have arrived at the *end* of the regex:

```
28 <the.dog.net>> <>     | 43:                    END
```

We receive a final report status.

```
Match successful!
```

Last but not least, we get the final reference print of $1($2). This has nothing to do with the debugger or Perl internals here, remember this was part of the code from our original command line.

```
->s.p.o.t(the.dog.net)<-
```

Free the memory from the regex engine, and return to the command prompt:

```
Freeing REx: '"([^<@>]+)@((?:\\w+\\.)+(?:com|net|org)).*"'
 %>
```

Summary

This section has shown you how to use the regex debugging facilities built into Perl and the Perl debugger. You've learned how to view the usually voluminous output and how to interpret the data provided. There is a great deal of support here (usually overlooked by the average programmer) that we hope this chapter has clued you into.

For further ideas on debugging regexes in Perl check out the following perldoc references:

- perldebguts: Explains how the debugger can help to dissect your regexes.

- perlre: The re pragma (particularly use re 'debug'), will also help in a number of cases and a study of the manpage will be time well spent in any case.

- perlretut: The standard regex tutorial.

The next chapter offers an introduction to the customizing of the debugger, either by using the available commands and options, or by replacing the entire library itself.

■■■

## CHAPTER 12

Debugger Customization

Cinderella heard the thuds of bouncing heads.

—Roald Dahl, *Revolting Rhymes*, 1982

You don't have to go as far as the rogue prince in Roald Dahl's interesting retelling of the famous fairy tale, who chops the heads off the ugly sisters to modify their behavior (and existence). In anticipation of all sorts of strange and wonderful requests and commands, the debugger helpfully provides numerous ways to modify the way it operates, in a truly Perl TMTOWTDI (There's More Than One Way To Do It) fashion. It does this so you can have an interesting and productive debugging experience, tailored to your particular requirements without the need for drastic head surgery.

There are two main ways to customize the Perl debugger. The first method involves using the internal methods, enabling you to take advantage of the commands and options that the debugger has provided for you. Most of the time these are ample, and include using the `alias` command, as well as the ability to work with arrow keys, the `.perldbrc` file, and multiple debugger options. The second method involves using the external methods, which Perl provides to the debugger. Although not commonplace, it is also possible to redefine the `DB::DB` routine that provides the core of the debugger functionality, or use a completely new library file to create your own debugger entirely.

Internal Debugger Customization

Using the internal commands and options is the most straightforward approach. You don't need to write any particularly complicated code—you can simply change the way the debugger responds to your commands, map one command to another, save commands for later execution and so on.

Let's begin with the `alias` command.

alias

The `alias` command affords you the convenience of specifying alternative names for commands. The Perl debugger uses the = symbol to set up an alias. The syntax is

```
= [alias value]
```

Why would you want to do this? Well, perhaps you don't like the way the debugger uses the same exclamation mark character (!), for both the recall history command and the shell command. Usually this means that to get a shell command you need to enter two exclamation marks followed by a system command, instead of one, because this is how the debugger differentiates between the defaults. It gets more confusing, because entering two exclamation points followed by no command will cause the debugger to repeat the last history command.

The alias command lets us define our own commands, like sys for a shell command, and his for history. You can use any combination of characters you like, but be careful not to inadvertently interfere with another command.

Here's an example that would work using the history and system call commands. Start the debugger in a clean shell with -e 0 as the arguments:

```
%> perl -d -e 0
Loading DB routines from perl5db.pl version 1.27
Editor support available.
Enter 'h or h h' for help, or 'man perldebug' for more help.
main::(-e:1):   0
  DB<1>
```

We need a couple of commands in the history list to refer to. First, we'll print out the process ID using p $$:

```
  DB<1> p $$
2907
  DB<2>
```

Now try executing a system command with the ! command:

```
  DB<2> !pwd
No such command!
  DB<2>
```

This is an error, because we must use *double* ! characters:

```
  DB<2> !!pwd
/home/perltut/code
  DB<3>
```

That worked fine. Now use H to look at the history listing and to see the numbers of each command and the way to refer to them:

```
  DB<3> H
2: !!pwd
1: p $$
  DB<3>
```

The number in front of the colon is the history command number. You can recall a history command by appending a number to the ! character. Try it with the first command:

```
  DB<3> !1
p $$
2907
  DB<4>
```

Similarly, there is a handy shortcut for using double ! characters to redo the most recent command executed:

```
  DB<4> !!
p $$
2907
  DB<5>
```

Note that although executing double ! characters involves the same syntax as executing a system command, there was no command given, so it was taken to be the redo-last command instead. We'll show you a way of getting around this in a moment.

Now use the alias command (=) to assign the history command ! to the new keyword his, and then assign !! to sys:

```
  DB<5> = his !
his    = !
  DB<6> = sys !!
sys    - !!
  DB<7>
```

The commands are displayed for confirmation as they are assigned and accepted for use. Now it is possible to use his 1 to recall the first history command:

```
  DB<7> his 1
p $$
2907
  DB<8>
```

Equally, the system command may be called using sys commandexpression:

```
  DB<8> sys pwd
/home/perltut/code
  DB<9>
```

Note that this has not affected the original commands. They still exist and will work as before. You can check this by using !1 to recall the first history command again:

```
  DB<9> !1
p $$
2907
  DB<10>
```

If you always want to use this mapping, you can put an entry into the .perldbrc file described next. An alternative to using an alias to do this might be to change the character that calls the command altogether. You can see how to do this in the following options section.

Note that you need to be a bit careful when setting up aliases, in terms of how you set up one command to relate to another. It would be quite easy to inadvertently set the p command to q for example, and then quit the debugger while trying print the value of an expression.

pre- and post-prompt **Commands**

The pre- and post-prompt facilities let you repeat a command each time the debugger waits for input. This means it is possible to automatically execute debugger commands before the prompt is printed. You can also set up a similar situation for one or more Perl commands, both before and after the prompt is displayed.

The syntax for working with a pre-prompt Perl command follows:

```
< (?|[<] expr|*)
```

If you don't give any argument, or you just supply a question mark, you'll get a list of the currently set pre-prompt commands. If you supply an asterisk (*), you delete all of the commands. You can set a new command by giving a valid expression, and you can append to the existing commands by using the command doubled-up, as in << expr.

Let's use the pre- and post-prompt commands as a rudimentary timer for some slow code. Consider this case, where we want to see how long certain function calls take, because we suspect that longer parameters take longer. Here's the code we're concerned with:

```
for my $word ( qw( dog Rumplestiltskin cat gargantuan) ) {
    calculate( $word );
}
```

We could modify the code to print the start and stop time before and after the call to calculate, but let's use the debugger instead. First, we'll start the program in the debugger:

```
%> perl -d slow
Loading DB routines from perl5db.pl version 1.27
Editor support available.
Enter h or 'h h' for help, or 'man perldebug' for more help.
main::(slow:3): for my $word ( qw( dog Rumplestiltksin cat gargantuan) ) {
```

Then, we'll disable Perl's output buffering, so we can see output from our prompts as they happen:

```
DB<1> $|++
```

Now, we'll set the pre-prompt. This is the command that will get printed before each prompt, so it is also the time that the previous line has stopped executing:

```
DB<2> < print "Stop: ", scalar localtime(), "\n";
```

Calling localtime() in a scalar context prints a recognizable date. Now, let's have the time print after the debugger command has been entered, but before the next line in the program executes:

```
DB<3> > print "Start: ", scalar localtime(), "\n";
```

Finally, we'll have another post-prompt display that shows the word we're working on:

```
DB<4> >> print "Word=$word\n" if $word;
```

You'll note that we used >> to append this command to the list. Otherwise, we would have deleted the previous print.

Now let's step through the code, but let's step over the call to calculate with the n command, rather than stepping into it:

```
  DB<5> n
Start: Wed Apr 13 21:42:55 2005
main::(slow:4):     calculate( $word );
Stop: Wed Apr 13 21:42:55 2005
  DB<5>
```

We're into our for loop, and the next n will call calculate:

```
  DB<5> n
Start: Wed Apr 13 21:42:57 2005
Word=dog
main::(slow:4):     calculate( $word );
Stop: Wed Apr 13 21:42:58 2005
  DB<5> n
```

Only took about a second to run with our word as dog. Let's try the next one:

```
  DB<5> n
Start: Wed Apr 13 21:43:01 2005
Word=Rumplestiltskin
main::(slow:4):     calculate( $word );
Stop: Wed Apr 13 21:43:08 2005
  DB<5>
```

Aha! It still takes seconds, even when we call it with Rumplestiltskin. Our theory looks like it could be true.

This example has just scraped the surface of the possibilities for these commands. Here we simply displayed some diagnostics, but the pre- and post-prompt commands can be any Perl code, and could even modify your program's data directly. For a full listing of all the syntax possibilities, for the pre- and post-prompt Perl commands and the pre-prompt debugger command, see Chapter 15.

Options

The debugger supports many modifiable options that allow you to customize your session. There are options to alter the way data is presented, from simple indenting options on hashes to depth control of complex structures. There are options to modify the amount of information given when tracing, an option to define whether to print the return value from a subroutine when using the r command. There are options to control remote debugging and hints to the debugger as to whether you are currently debugging a Tk application, or an application which itself uses ReadLine.

The list is not *quite* endless but you can see if you use h o to get a help options menu listing, the options supported are fairly extensive:

```
DB<3> h o
o [opt] ...    Set boolean option to true
o [opt?]    Query options
o [opt=val] [opt="val"] ...
        Set options.  Use quotes in spaces in value.
   recallCommand, ShellBang    chars used to recall command or spawn shell;
```

```
    pager              program for output of "|cmd";
    tkRunning              run Tk while prompting (with ReadLine);
    signalLevel warnLevel dieLevel    level of verbosity;
    inhibit_exit        Allows stepping off the end of the script.
    ImmediateStop        Debugger should stop as early as possible.
    RemotePort              Remote hostname:port for remote debugging
  The following options affect what happens with V, X, and x commands:
    arrayDepth, hashDepth    print only first N elements ('' for all);
    compactDump, veryCompact    change style of array and hash dump;
    globPrint              whether to print contents of globs;
    DumpDBFiles        dump arrays holding debugged files;
    DumpPackages        dump symbol tables of packages;
    DumpReused              dump contents of "reused" addresses;
    quote, HighBit, undefPrint    change style of string dump;
    bareStringify        Do not print the overload-stringified value;
  Other options include:
    PrintRet        affects printing of return value after r command,
    frame        affects printing messages on subroutine entry/exit.
    AutoTrace    affects printing messages on possible breaking points.
    maxTraceLen    gives max length of evals/args listed in stack trace.
    ornaments    affects screen appearance of the command line.
    CreateTTY      bits control attempts to create a new TTY on events:
            1: on fork()    2: debugger is started inside debugger
            4: on startup
  During startup options are initialized from $ENV{PERLDB_OPTS}.
  You can put additional initialization options TTY, noTTY,
  ReadLine, NonStop, and RemotePort there (or use
  'R' after you set them).
  DB<4>
```

Let's take a look at another interesting option: DumpReused.

Whenever you use any of the V, X, or x commands to dump a structure, by default the DumpReused option is not set. This means that a typical dump will have the string REUSED_ADDRESS as the value of any reference which has been seen before. To make this clearer, let's have a look at a specific example of this.

First of all, you need to set up a data structure of some sort. In this case it's a simple hash with a key=value pair, an array reference, and a hash reference. Although we could have specified this all on one line, it's much easier to read if we enter a multi-line command. Note how the debugger supports the entering of multiple lines of code by backslashing the newline at the end of each line:

```
DB<4> %hash = (\
cont:    this => 'that',\
cont:    arrayref => [qw(some array vars)],\
cont:    hashref  => {\
cont:      key => val,\
cont:    }\
cont: );
DB<5>
```

Now use the x command to dump a reference to the %hash structure, so we can see what we are dealing with:

```
  DB<5> x \%hash
0   HASH(0x8529bc4)
     'arrayref' => ARRAY(0x854d134)
         0   'some'
         1   'array'
         2   'vars'
     'hashref' => HASH(0x84f85f0)
     'key' => 'val'
     'this' => 'that'
  DB<6>
```

Now assign a reference to the arrayref reference to the circle key of the %hash:

```
  DB<6> $hash{circle} = $hash{arrayref}
  DB<7>
```

Now dump a reference to the %hash structure out once more:

```
DB<7> x \%hash
    0   HASH(0x8529bc4)
       'circle' => ARRAY(0x854d134)
           0   'some'
           1   'array'
           2   'vars'
       'arrayref' => ARRAY(0x854d134)
           -> REUSED_ADDRESS
       'hashref' => HASH(0x84f85f0)
           'key' => 'val'
       'this' => 'that'
      DB<8>
```

You can see that the assigned circle reference has the value of the array reference from the arrayref from the original %hash. (Since this is a hash, your keys may be in a different order.) The arrayref reference, on the other hand, now displays the REUSED_ADDRESS value. This is the dumper telling us that it knows about the data at this position and it has already dumped out this value. In order to reduce the likelihood of issues with recursive data structures, and to save us space, it has replaced the position for the purposes of the display with a simple marker.

What if we really wanted to see what was down there, under that marker? The debugger provides an option called DumpReused, which is normally set by default to a boolean value of zero. This ensures the standard behavior described previously. You can check the current value of this option with the o commandname ? command:

```
  DB<8> o DumpReused?
DumpReused = '0'
  DB<9>
```

Set this option to true, by calling the option command with the name of the option as an argument. For boolean options this minimal command is enough:

```
  DB<9> o DumpReused
DumpReused = '1'
  DB<10>
```

Now use the x command to dump a reference to the %hash once more:

```
DB<10> x \%hash
   0   HASH(0x8529bc4)
      'aref' => ARRAY(0x854d134)
         0   'some'
         1   'array'
         2   'vars'
      'arrayref' => ARRAY(0x854d134)
         0   'some'
         1   'array'
         2   'vars'
      'hashref' => HASH(0x84f85f0)
         'key' => 'val'
      'this' => 'that'
   DB<11>
```

Now you can see that the value at the arrayref location is indeed exactly the same as the value at the aref location. Perl knew this, and it is safe to assume it from the REUSED_ADDRESS marker given previously, but sometimes you just need to look at the data yourself.

Beware: the debugger will go into an infinite loop if you switch the DumpReused option on and the data structure contains a self-referential element.

For a comprehensive listing of all available options, and a short description of what they all do, see Chapter 15.

.perldb Initialization File

The debugger supports a *run command* file, like many other utilities that have a Unix heritage. The commands in this file are run as the debugger starts up. The filename is .perldb, and the debugger looks for it first in the current directory, and then in the user's home directory.

You can put nearly any valid Perl code you like in the .perldb file. This Perl code will be executed within the DB:: namespace at startup, when the .perldb file is *require*d by the Perl debugger. The .perldb file is executed using do, just after the greeting has been constructed and just before the debugger is informed about how to create a new TTY (should it need to fork for instance). Once this file has been required the afterinit subroutine is run, if there is one.

afterinit()

There is a special subroutine called afterinit(), which will be called, if it exists, after debugger initialization has completed. The .perldb file is the typical location for the definition of this subroutine.

@DB::typeahead

This is a special debugger array, which can be used to set up debugger commands to be run on start up. It is an unsupported interface and is likely to change in the future, but it's quite useful for the time being. Any commands you enter as elements of this array will be executed as if you entered them from the command line, before the debugger prints the first prompt. This is useful for common functions that you may want to do repeatedly, such as setting up lists of breakpoints.

Putting these together, you could come up with an initialization file, which looked something like Listing 12-1.

Listing 12-1. *The* `.perldb` *File*

```
$DB::trace=1;
sub afterinit {
    push(@DB::typeahead,
        'b 12',
        'b 24',
        '< print "$_\n"',
        '= his !',
        '= sys !!',
        'L',
        '<?',
    );
}
```

When running the debugger, these commands will all be run before execution begins. Note how, in the following example, tracing has been turned on before the code has begun to be loaded or executed. Hence, even the use module commands are traced and the debugger prints the resulting verbose output:

```
%> perl -d charcount
Loading DB routines from perl5db.pl version 1.27
Editor support available.
Enter h or 'h h' for help, or 'man perldebug' for more help.
main::CODE(0x81809e0)(charcount:3):
3:      use strict;
main::CODE(0x81809e0)(charcount:3):
3:      use strict;
main::CODE(0x81809e0)(charcount:3):
3:      use strict;
strict::import(/opt/perl/lib/5.8.5/strict.pm:28):
28:        shift;
strict::import(/opt/perl/lib/5.8.5/strict.pm:29):

<...multiple snipped lines...>

Exporter::Heavy::heavy_export(/opt/perl/lib/5.8.5/Exporter/Heavy.pm:195):
195:           (*{"${callpkg}::$sym"} = \&{"${pkg}::$sym"}, next)
196:               unless $sym =~ s/^(\W)//;
main::(charcount:6):   my $file = $ARGV[0] || '';
```

Finally, the debugger returns to the execution of the code in the main program. But, before the prompt is displayed, it runs the code in the @DB::typeahead array, one after the other. Notice how the auto(-n) prompt informs you of its progress:

```
auto(-7)  DB<1> b 12
auto(-6)  DB<2> b 24
auto(-5)  DB<3> < print "$_\n"
auto(-4)  DB<4> = his !
his      = !
auto(-3)  DB<5> = sys !!
sys      = !!
auto(-2)  DB<6> L
charcount:
 12:     my $FH = FileHandle->new("< $file")
         or die("unable to open file($file): $!");
   break if (1
 24:        $i_vows += my $vows = &parse($line, '[aeiou]');
   break if (1)
auto(-1)  DB<6> <?
pre-perl commands:
        < -- print "$_\n"
  DB<7>
```

The run ends with the two commands (L and <?), which display the currently set breakpoints and pre-prompt commands for confirmation of the setup.

The @DB::typeahead command can be particularly useful when you are returning to debug the same piece of code in repetitive situations, and you need to set up complex debugger commands. Like many of the commands available with Perl, it simply makes the hard things easy and the impossible things doable.

PERLDB_OPTS

The debugger also looks for the PERLDB_OPTS environment variable. The options in this variable are parsed after the .perldb file has been executed and can set several options that must be defined at startup time.

Although you can set most options from within the debugger session itself, some of these options must be set before the debugger is running, in order to have an effect on the current session. A typical PERLDB_OPTS, and the canonical version which is in the standard documentation, might look like this:

```
"NonStop=1 LineInfo=db.out AutoTrace"
```

This would have the effect of telling the debugger to run non-interactively while tracing, and to put all the trace information in the db.out file for later perusal. Note that these options are not case-sensitive and that they only need to be uniquely identified. Also, remember that the boolean options may be toggled on and off by simply referencing them. So an equivalent setting would be

```
"non auto lin=db.out"
```

The options that must be set before the debugger is running are the following:

- NonStop: When enabled, the debugger will go into non-interactive mode until it's interrupted.

- noTTY: When enabled, it forces non-interactive mode, with no connection to an input device.

- ReadLine: When disabled, it will disable debugger readline support.

- RemotePort: Specifies the host and port to connect for remote debugging.

- TTY: When enabled, it specifies the input device to use when debugging I/O.

Even though it's most common to have these options set in PERL5OPTS, you have another way to do it. Set an option in the current session and then restart the session, using the R command, if you want the options to take effect without being reinitialized.

All other options may be set from within the debugger session itself and take effect immediately.

Arrow Keys

One of the most common questions concerning using the command line debugger and customizing its interface involves using the arrow keys in the debugger. The answer is to use the Term::ReadLine::Perl module. It contains the support for the ReadLine functionality that the debugger terminal interface lacks. Simply use the module from the command line:

```
DB<3> use Term::ReadLine::Perl
DB<4>
```

Now your arrow keys should be fully functional, with basic command editing support. If entering this each time you start up the debugger is annoying, you could include this in your .perldb file.

External Debugger Customization

If you decide that the Perl debugger isn't enough, you can write your own. When Perl is started with the -d switch, it calls the code that is defined in the PERL5DB environment variable. This is normally equivalent to

```
BEGIN { require "perl5db.pl" }
```

This file is included in the standard Perl distribution and contains the source code for the Perl debugger. If you want to replace any of the behavior of the Perl debugger, all you have to do is to write a replacement library, and set this variable to point to it.

To build your own debugger you need to know about the available hooks, in particular, you need to know about the DB::DB subroutine. Although the Perl debugger is a labyrinthine piece of complex code, essentially it does most of its work using the hooks provided for it by Perl itself. The main hook is the DB::DB subroutine, which is called by Perl for every statement run during the execution of your program.

Let's define the DB::DB subroutine ourselves directly into the code in the PERL5DB variable and run the debugger on the charcount program again. In this example, we take advantage of the insider information that the debugger provides, in this case, the %::_*filename* array as a reference to a list of the lines of code of the given filename. We can then print out each line as it is executed, in a similar but customized manner, to the tracing with the debugger. The code looks worse than it is:

```
%> PERL5DB='BEGIN { sub DB::DB { my ($p, $f, $l) = caller; \
        print "file($f) line($l): \n\t".(@{"::_<$f"}->[$l])."\n"; \
    } }' perl -d charcount

file(charcount) line(6):
        my $file = $ARGV[0] || '';

file(charcount) line(7):
        my $verbose = $ARGV[1] || 0;

file(charcount) line(9):
        unless (-f $file) {

file(charcount) line(10):
            die("Usage: $0 filename [-v]");

Usage: charcount filename [-v] at charcount line 10.

%>
```

Because we neglected to supply charcount with an input file, it (correctly) dies at line 10. If it didn't, we would find ourselves wading through reams of tracing data. That example wasn't really very smart, because there wasn't any interactivity, and no chance to stop and set a breakpoint or change a variable, etc. In fact, when it comes to rewriting the entire debugger functionality, you might be surprised at quite how much it can do, and how well it does it on your behalf.

Let's do another version that enables you to interactively control the debugger yourself. The code in the following file debugger.pl (shown in Listing 12-2) will stop at the first line of executable code in your program, and will accept a very rudimentary set of commands. You can see which commands it will accept by entering h for help. This mini-debugger will allow you to step to the next line of code with n, print the current line of code, with l, and finally quit with q. Other than that it is extremely unsophisticated and will simply send any other input from you directly to Perl for evaluation.

Listing 12-2. *The* debugger.pl *Script*

```
package DB;

use 5.008000;
use Term::ReadKey;
use strict;

my $i;
```

```perl
sub DB::DB {
    no strict qw(refs);
    my ($p,$f,$l) = caller;
    my $line = @{"::_<$f"}[$l] || shift;
    print "$f [$l]: $line\n";
    ReadMode(0);
    while (1) {
        $i++;
        print "dbgr <$i> : ";
        chomp(my $input = ReadLine(0));
        if ($input eq 'h') { print "h(help) l(print line)
                                    n(go to next line) q(quit)" };
        if ($input eq 'l') { print "$f [$1]: $line" };
        if ($input eq 'n') { last };
        if ($input eq 'q') { print "exiting\n"; exit };
        my @res = eval "package $p; $input;\n";
        print "\n";
    }
}

1;

=head1 Name

debugger - an extremely rudimentary alternative

=head1 Usage

=over 4

=item PERL5DB="BEGIN {require 'debugger.pl'}" perl -d program args

...

=head1 AUTHOR

Richard Foley, E<lt>debugger.example@rfi.net<gt>

=cut
```

To make sure that Perl will call the new debugger library, alter the PERL5DB environment variable to point to the new library:

```
%> export PERL5DB="BEGIN {require 'debugger.pl'}"
```

Start Perl using the new debugger, and call the ubiquitous charcount program with the walrus file for input once more:

```
%> perl -d charcount walrus
charcount [6]: my $file = $ARGV[0] || '';
dbgr <1> :
```

The debugger stops at the first executable line. You can see it is the one created from the debugger.pl file because of the completely new interface and prompt. The first thing to do is to find out how to use the new debugger with the h command:

```
charcount <1> : h
h(help) l(print line) n(go to next line) q(quit)
dbgr <2> :
```

Not much, but enough to get on with. Now use the n command to step to the next executable statement:

```
dbgr <2> : n
charcount [7]: my $verbose = $ARGV[1] || 0;
dbgr <3> :
```

In a similar way to the standard debugger, the line that is about to be executed is displayed. Now that the $file variable has been defined, print out the value:

```
dbgr <3> : print $file
walrus
dbgr <4> :
```

This seems to work fine. Now, step over another line of code to see the line number tracking and to ensure that the correct line of code is displayed above the prompt:

```
dbgr <4> : n
charcount [9]: unless (-f $file) {
dbgr <5> :
```

Finally we can exit the current debugger session using the q command:

```
dbgr <5> : q
exiting
%>
```

The purpose here is not to rewrite the debugger, but to show you all the possibilities. The hooks are there to use and Perl is happy to run either the code it already knows about, or the code you supply to it as a replacement. There's no reason your debugger needs to be interactive. For example, the standard Perl profiler analyzes the use of the code by going through the DB hooks.

Alternative Modules

In addition to writing your own debugger, you can also use someone else's. The examples earlier in this chapter have shown you how to do this. But, for further alternatives, you could look into one or more of the following modules:

- `Devel::TestEmbed`: A module which uses `Test::More` to extend the standard Perl debugger functionality.

- `Devel::eBug`: Provides a drop-in replacement for the standard Perl debugger, and includes walkthrough support for debugging regexes.

- `DB`: The original OO replacement for the standard debugger, development of which is currently more or less in a state of suspended animation.

For further information on these interesting modules, and the many others available online from the CPAN, see the extensive documentation which comes with each module when you download the latest version.

Summary

In this chapter you have learned how to customize the Perl debugger, from using the `alias` command to changing the depth of a hash dump using `HashDepth`. You also learned to modify the `DB::DB` subroutine and replace the entire `PERL5DB` debugger library itself.

In the next chapter, you will learn various approaches for optimizing your Perl program. You will read about several performance hints and tips, which could be useful to make your Perl program go faster.

■ ■ ■

## CHAPTER 13

Optimization and Performance Hints and Tips

"What . . . the speed of light is not a constant?"

—Einstein's biographer Hoffmann, quoted in *Faster Than the Speed of Light*
by Joao Magueijo

Perhaps if we write enough lines of code, our program will become so heavy that the speed of light will change, making your program go faster—but it's doubtful. Instead, we will probably have to use more mundane methods to help make the program run faster, but fortunately there are a number of techniques we can use to improve performance of your code.

This chapter offers Perl optimization and performance hints, accompanied by several examples of both development-oriented modules available via the CPAN, and modules from the standard distribution.

Benchmarking and Optimizing Code

Bear in mind that we're not talking about absolute execution speed here. Optimizing your Perl code can certainly mean improving application response time, but it can also mean cleaning it up or refactoring your program for generic reusage, or preparing it for an improved API.

In this section, we'll introduce the following techniques and strategies, and show you how each can one can help you improve your Perl code:

- **Measuring Execution Time**: In this section, you'll learn how to use the time system call to accurately measure execution time.

- **Benchmarking Code**: In this section, you'll learn how to compare two different functions with the Benchmark module to see which is faster.

- **Code Profiling**: In this section, we'll introduce useful techniques for finding the slow parts of your code automatically.

- **Code Coverage**: In this section, we introduce using Devel::Cover for ensuring that your test suite is complete.

- **Perl's** -D DEBUGGING **Flags**: This section discusses the additional debugging capabilities available to you when Perl is compiled with the -DDEBUGGING flag.

- **The Perl Compiler O (frontend) and B (backend)**: This section shows you how to better understand how Perl is parsing and processing your code.

Using Time

Perhaps one of the very first things to do concerning program speed, is to actually measure it. Sounds obvious, but without employing some sort of mechanism other than our own inherently flawed perception, we won't know whether it is actually faster, or by how much. To find out how much time a particular program is taking to do something, we can use the system call time. This will tell us how long a program took to run.

For this example we will measure the execution time of the Perl program named charcount, which we first introduced in Chapter 3:

```
%> time perl charcount tmon.out.sample
<... program output omitted ... >
real    0m0.857s
user    0m0.824s
sys     0m0.033s
```

The relevant output from time is found in the last three lines of output, labeled real, user, and sys. We'll discuss exactly what this output implies next.

Interpreting the Output from the time Command

The real indicator is the overall time taken to execute the script, while user is the CPU time used by this specific user for the process, and sys is the CPU time actually required to get the work done. This in itself is very useful, and tells us that at a basic level this particular program is going to take nearly a full second to run, at least in the user's perception. While it's only an overview of what is going on internally, the real indicator still reports useful information on response time. Programmers, in our experience, don't do even this minimum amount of measurement nearly often enough.

Naturally this type of measurement must be repeated a number of times, with the average amount taken, for it to be meaningful.

■**Note** See man time for more information about the time command.

Benchmarking Code to Compare Running Time

As you make changes to your code in an attempt to speed it up, you need a way to accurately tell if one version of the function is faster than the other. The Benchmark module times chunks of code by running them for a given number of iterations, before reporting how long each chunk took. In this section we'll take a look at this module.

A Refactoring Example

Consider the following piece of code:

```
sub myfunc {
    my $this = $o_ref->{this};
    my $that = $o_ref->{that};
    my $x = $this + $that;
    # ...
}
```

Although this is a fairly minimal piece of code, it would still be reasonable to wonder whether it might be possible to speed it up, by rewriting it in a more efficient fashion, also known as *refactoring* it.

Perhaps we could de-reference the variables in place, rather than copying their values into a new variable. We might come up with another version, which could look something like this:

```
sub myfunc {
    my $x = $o_ref->{this} + $o_ref->{that};
    # ...
}
```

Rather than simply assume the change is an improvement, we should measure how long each version takes and compare them, using the Benchmark module. This will tell us which technique is likely to be faster.

A Benchmark Program

Benchmarking is when we run two similar sets of code in the same way, so we can see how long each one takes to run compared to the other. First, we need to create a short program to hold the code we want to benchmark. In this example (Listing 13-1), there are two subroutines: direct(), which accesses the argument variables directly, and dereference(), which de-references the same variables to lexical variables before using them. The timethese() subroutine is a Benchmark function which takes as an argument the number of times to run the code (which defaults to 1,000,000 if no argument is given), as well as references to the chunks of code to check.

Listing 13-1. *The* direct_or_reference *Script*

```perl
#!/usr/bin/perl
use Benchmark;
my $o_ref = {
    'this'  => 2,
    'that'  => 3,
};
timethese($ARGV[0] || 1000000, {
    'direct'       => "&direct()",
    'dereference'  => "&dereference()",
});
sub direct {
    my $x = $o_ref->{this} + $o_ref->{that};
}
```

```
sub dereference {
    my $this = $o_ref->{'this'};
    my $that = $o_ref->{'that'};
    my $x = $this + $that;
}
```

Now we can run Listing 13-1 and the Benchmark module will tell us how long each piece of code took, for example:

```
%> ./direct_or_dereference
Benchmark: timing 1000000 iterations of dereference, direct...
  dereference: 7 wallclock secs (6.54 usr +  0.00 sys =  6.54 CPU)
  @ 152905.20/s (n=1000000)
       direct: 4 wallclock secs (4.79 usr + 0.01 sys = 4.78 CPU)
  @ 209205.02/s (n=1000000)
%>
```

Of course, your timings may be different, depending on the speed of your machine. However, the speed difference should be about the same, with dereference's timing taking about 50% longer than direct's.

Interpreting the Output of the Benchmark Module

From the output of the program, which is all generated from the Benchmark module, you can see that when running each subroutine one million times (n=1000000), the dereference() subroutine took about seven seconds, while the direct() subroutine took only about four seconds. No other code was run, just these two chunks of code, called one million times.

It may seem obvious that there is some small overhead involved in de-referencing a variable, but most of us don't bother to consider it in the greater scheme of things. However, it can be worth doing so. In the example we just used we saw that the effect of assigning just two variables to lexicals on a million line file would increase the execution time of this particular subroutine by about half. Of course, few subroutines are this simple, but it illustrates the dramatic difference that a change in specific coding style can make in execution time.

Speed is also relative to the time of the entire program. Shaving off a few seconds of a twenty-minute program is probably not worth the effort, but cutting that twenty-minute time in half by not declaring lexicals may well be.

As in all cases where measurements and statistics are concerned, it is possible to frame the numbers in any manner you please. Even so, instead of drifting along with guesswork, actually having this information available can make a huge difference when deciding to take one approach over another.

■**Note** For more information about the Benchmark module, see the Benchmark documentation.

Profiling Code to Find Where It Spends Its Time

Luckily for us, we can *profile* our code. Code profiling helps us determine the overall time a program took, including both how long a subroutine call requires, and how much execution time each subroutine requires.

Hotspots

Using a code profiler can help to pinpoint the points in the program that consume the most execution time, also known as *hotspots*.

Of course you have to be careful how you interpret the output. It's possible to identify the subroutine that is taking the longest time, but that's not surprising if it is called several million times in a short program. On the other hand, if your targeted subroutine can be sped up even a little, the effect on the overall running time may be substantial indeed.

While the DProf module is the standard Perl code-profiling tool that ships with Perl program, there are also several other modules that can help with profiling your Perl code:

- Devel::DProf: The standard Perl code profiler.

- Devel::Profile: Another Perl code profiler written to address certain issues with Devel::DProf.

- Devel::SmallProf: A Perl code profiler with a smaller footprint than Devel::DProf and designed to be less temperamental.

Using DProf

We will use the DProf module as an example of code profiling. It is called from Perl with the -d:modulename syntax and will produce an output file containing all the information it accumulates while the program is running. If you do not specify an output filename, the name of the output file will be tmon.out.

Once the program has finished execution, the tmon.out file can be read with the dprofpp tool that comes with the DProf distribution. This can produce differing priority listings for which subroutine took the longest, with or without their child subroutines, exclusive and cumulative times, and so on.

Let's reuse the charcount program from earlier, again using the tmon.out.sample file for input:

```
%> perl -d:DProf charcount tmon.out.sample
    0:  hard.......8  soft.......9  spec......10
    1:  hard.......6  soft.......3  spec.......2
    2:  hard.......8  soft.......9  spec......10
    3:  hard.......6  soft.......3  spec.......2
    4:  hard.......8  soft.......9  spec......10
    5:  hard.......6  soft.......3  spec.......2
    6:  hard......23  soft.......7  spec......14
    7:  hard.......4  soft.......1  spec.......2
    8:  hard......23  soft.......7  spec......14
    9:  hard......11  soft.......5  spec......16
   10:  hard......10  soft.......8  spec......10
   11:  hard......10  soft.......6  spec.......4
   12:  hard......13  soft.......6  spec.......9
  <...snip...>
  352:  hard......41  soft......20  spec......27
  353:  hard......21  soft.......6  spec......13
  354:  hard......26  soft......16  spec......26
  355:  hard......21  soft.......6  spec......10
```

```
 356:   hard......21   soft.......7   spec......10
 357:   hard......28   soft......11   spec......18
 358:   hard......17   soft.......4   spec.......9
 359:   hard......19   soft.......9   spec......13
 360:   hard......24   soft.......8   spec......29
 361:   hard......24   soft.......8   spec......29
 362:   hard......21   soft.......6   spec......17
 363:   hard......14   soft......10   spec......17
 364:   hard.......7   soft.......7   spec.......9
total:   hard     7133  soft    2919   spec    4842
%>
```

If we used the time program to measure the runtime duration, it would be clear that the runtime of the program is certainly increased by all the extra work that is being done to record execution times (although there should be no other effect).

Using dprofpp

At this point we can run dprofpp on the output. The default input file for dprofpp is tmon.out, so it is not necessary to specify it as an argument, though for the sake of the example, we will do so explicitly:

```
%> dprofpp tmon.out
Exporter::Heavy::heavy_export has 2 unstacked calls in outer
Exporter::export has -2 unstacked calls in outer
Total Elapsed Time = 0.845582 Seconds
  User+System Time = 0.505582 Seconds
Exclusive Times
%Time ExclSec CumulS #Calls sec/call Csec/c  Name 59.9    0.303
 0.303   1095    0.0003 0.0003  main::parse
 7.91   0.040  0.109      7    0.0057 0.0156  IO::File::BEGIN
 5.93   0.030  0.060      5    0.0060 0.0119  IO::Seekable::BEGIN
 5.93   0.030  0.169      2    0.0149 0.0844  main::BEGIN
 3.96   0.020  0.020      2    0.0100 0.0100  Exporter::as_heavy
 3.96   0.020  0.020      4    0.0050 0.0050  IO::BEGIN
 1.98   0.010  0.020      2    0.0050 0.0100  Exporter::export
 1.98   0.010  0.010      2    0.0050 0.0049  File::Spec::BEGIN
 1.98   0.010  0.010      2    0.0050 0.0049  XSLoader::load
 0.00   0.000  0.000      2    0.0000 0.0000  Exporter::Heavy::heavy_export
 0.00      - -0.000      1      -      -      Symbol::gensym
 0.00      - -0.000      1      -      -      Symbol::BEGIN
 0.00      - -0.000      1      -      -      warnings::BEGIN
 0.00      - -0.000      1      -      -      warnings::import
 0.00      - -0.000      1      -      -      IO::bootstrap
%>
```

The output is sorted by the amount of time spent in each subroutine. You can also sort by the number of times a subroutine was called or by how long each individual call took. There are over a dozen different options for analyzing the profiling data. Check the perldoc dprofpp for all the details.

Inspecting the Output

Perhaps the most relevant line in the previous example is the one referring to the `main::parse` subroutine:

```
59.9   0.303  0.303   1095   0.0003 0.0003  main::parse
```

Here it is clear that the `main::parse` subroutine is using nearly 60% of the available execution time, so that would be the first place to start looking to make optimizations, even though over a thousand calls took less than a third of a second.

Before you modify the code, be sure to save a copy of your results so that you can compare the changes you've made to the original. If you're using a version control system, such as CVS or Subversion, this is taken care of automatically when you check your code in—you are using a version control system, aren't you?

When we have found satisfactory, alternative code to try, it could be run again with another `dprofpp` run, and the speeds objectively compared.

Optimizing Already-Optimized Code

It's worth mentioning that some people believe that there is always more to be done regarding code optimization. An example of this is when one of the authors of this book was asked to optimize some existing legacy code and successfully brought the runtime down from ninety minutes to forty minutes. Some months later this new code was presented by management for optimization again, with the expectation of being able to make it run in 20 minutes, by optimizing it again—or perhaps by magic.

Despite the attempts to improve execution time, remember that there ultimately is some practical limit to our efforts. It's entirely reasonable that our `charcount` program might need to take 0.0003 of a second per call for the `main::parse` subroutine. We need to be able to make a decision on whether this is the case by looking at the code, the data it has to work, and the environment it is running.

■**Note** For more information on code profiling with `DProf`, see the `DProf` and `dprofpp` manpages.

Coverage

In addition to the code profiling tools, there are also modules that you can use to find out which parts of your code are actually run, and from where. These modules can help you identify areas of code that aren't touched by testing, or areas of code that are never executed (the latter being a prime target for removal). The data produced are called coverage reports, and may be generated using the following Perl modules:

- `Devel::Coverage`: This code coverage analysis tool's ouput may be reported on using the `coverperl` tool.

- `Devel::Cover`: This code coverage metrics analysis tool uses `cover` to produce reports from the data collected.

For this example, the we will use a command similar to ones used in previous examples, but this time we'll let `Devel::Cover` run against the code:

```
%> perl -d:Cover charcount tmon.out.sample
Devel::Cover 0.31:
Collecting coverage data for branch, condition, statement, subroutine and time.
Pod coverage is unavailable.  Please install Pod::Coverage from CPAN.
Selecting packages matching:
Ignoring packages matching:
Ignoring packages in:
 .
 /opt/perl/lib/5.8.4
 /opt/perl/lib/5.8.4/i686-linux
 /opt/perl/lib/site_perl
 /opt/perl/lib/site_perl/5.8.4
 /opt/perl/lib/site_perl/5.8.4/i686-linux
  0:  hard.......4  soft.......0  spec.......1
  1:  hard.......2  soft.......0  spec.......3
  2:  hard.......2  soft.......1  spec.......7
  3:  hard......10  soft.......8  spec.......1
  4:  hard......14  soft......13  spec......12
       <...snip...>
 2577:  hard.......0  soft.......1  spec.......1
 2578:  hard.......0  soft.......1  spec.......1
 2579:  hard.......4  soft.......2  spec.......3
 2580:  hard.......1  soft.......0  spec.......1
 2581:  hard.......1  soft.......0  spec.......1
 2582:  hard.......1  soft.......0  spec.......1
 2583:  hard.......1  soft.......0  spec.......1
 2584:  hard.......7  soft.......5  spec.......6
 2585:  hard.......0  soft.......0  spec.......1
 2586:  hard.......7  soft.......5  spec.......6
 total:  hard     422  soft    2443  spec    2680
Devel::Cover: Writing coverage database to /home/perltut/code/cover_db
---------------------------------- ------ ------ ------ ------ ------ ------
File                               stmt  branch  cond   sub    time   total
---------------------------------- ------ ------ ------ ------ ------ ------
charcount                          95.65  33.33  50.00 100.00 100.00  79.41
Total                              95.65  33.33  50.00 100.00 100.00  79.41
---------------------------------- ------ ------ ------ ------ ------ ------
```

As you can see, the program ran normally, and at the end, `Devel::Cover` printed a short report on the code paths that it tracked.

Interpreting the Output

You can see from the report shown previously the following information about the executed code:

- 96% of the statements in the code were executed at least once.

- 33% of possible branch statements were executed.

- 50% of possible conditions or expressions were executed.

- 100% of available subroutines were executed.

Note For more information on interpreting the output, and the options this module supports, see the `Devel::Cover` documentation.

Overhead

There is no such thing as a free lunch. Measuring or tracking the runtime of a program will affect its execution, because the measuring tool has to get inside the program.

To indicate the amount of work these kind of helper libraries have to do, you can time the run of the program on its own, with no outside monitoring, and then time the run with the profiling or coverage tools attached and compare the difference. The results can be quite interesting. In these two examples, note that we use > /dev/null, which discards any program output, because we're only interested in the runtime, and not the content or results.

First we'll time the program's execution without affecting the runtime by collecting any statistics:

```
%> time perl charcount tmon.out.sample > /dev/null
real    0m0.999s
user    0m0.929s
sys     0m0.020s
perltut@vaio:~/code>
```

Next we'll run the same program under the control of Devel::Cover, to see if there is any difference in runtime:

```
%>  time perl -d:Cover charcount tmon.out.sample > /dev/null
real    0m6.343s
user    0m5.875s
sys     0m0.133s
```

There's quite a difference, as you can see. This level of slowdown is not uncommon when using profiling tools.

Perl's -D DEBUGGING Flags

Perl itself supports a number of debugging flags that can be given on the command line at runtime and that tend to give voluminous output. These particular debugging flags are defined by supplying the –D flag with one or more specific arguments, and all require your Perl interpreter to have been compiled with -DDEBUGGING. The installation procedure is discussed in Chapter 11.

We'll look at a couple of examples in a moment. First let's see the complete set of options which Perl makes available to us. In the debugging flags listing shown next, note that –D1 and –Dp are equivalent, as would be –D32 and –Dc, for example.

A list of debugging flags follows:

```
      1  p  Tokenizing and parsing
      2  s  Stack snapshots
            with v, displays all stacks
      4  l  Context (loop) stack processing
      8  t  Trace execution
     16  o  Method and overloading resolution
     32  c  String/numeric conversions
     64  P  Print profiling info, preprocessor command for -
            P, source file input state
    128  m  Memory allocation
    256  f  Format processing
    512  r  Regular expression parsing and execution
   1024  x  Syntax tree dump
   2048  u  Tainting checks
   4096     (Obsolete, previously used for LEAKTEST)
   8192  H  Hash dump -- usurps values()
  16384  X  Scratchpad allocation
  32768  D  Cleaning up
  65536  S  Thread synchronization
 131072  T  Tokenising
 262144  R  Include reference counts of dumped variables (eg when using -Ds)
 524288  J  Do not s,t,P-debug (Jump over) opcodes within package DB
1048576  v  Verbose: use in conjunction with other flags
2097152  C  Copy On Write
```

Bytecode, Opcodes, and the Stack

The bytecodes make up the intermediate layer that your program has been compiled into just before Perl executes it. The bytecodes produced by the Perl compiler at runtime are composed mainly of opcodes and the stack. This is analogous to the bytecode Java source code is compiled into before the Java Virtual Machine executes it.

The Opcode Tree

Let's look at the opcode tree, which will show us the opcodes that Perl is going use to execute our program, using the -Dt flag:

```
%> perl -Dt -e 'print join("=", $$, $0, "this", "$^O\n")'

EXECUTING...

(-e:0)    enter
(-e:0)    nextstate
(-e:1)    pushmark
```

```
(-e:1)     pushmark
(-e:1)     const(PV("="\0))
(-e:1)     gvsv(main::$)
(-e:1)     gvsv(main::0)
(-e:1)     const(PV("this"\0))
(-e:1)     gvsv(main:: )
(-e:1)     const(PV("\n"\0))
(-e:1)     concat
(-e:1)     join
(-e:1)     print
(-e:1)     leave
2457=-e=this=linuxThe Stack
```

Next, before we explain all of this, let's see what the stack looks like for exactly the same code, using the -Ds flag this time:

```
%> perl -Ds -e 'print join("=", $$, $0, "this", "$^O\n")'

EXECUTING...

                =>
                =>
                =>
                =>   *
                =>   **
                =>   **   PV("="\0)
                =>   **   PV("="\0)   IV(2458)
                =>   **   PV("="\0)   IV(2458)   PVMG("-e"\0)
                =>   **   PV("="\0)   IV(2458)   PVMG("-e"\0)
                         PV("this"\0)
                =>   **   PV("="\0)   IV(2458)   PVMG("-e"\0)
                         PV("this"\0)   PVMG()
                =>   **   PV("="\0)   IV(2458)   PVMG("-e"\0)
                         PV("this"\0)   PVMG()
         PV("\n"\0)
                =>   **   PV("="\0)   IV(2458)   PVMG("-e"\0)
                         PV("this"\0)
         PV("linux\n"\0)
                =>   *  PV("2458=-e=this=linux\n"\0)
                =>   SV_YES
2458=-e=this=linux
```

Putting the Opcodes and the Stack Together

Though interesting, on their own opcodes and the stack never really explain what's going on. These two switches are better off combined (-Dts), so the output produced will look something like this (line numbers added for ease of reference):

```
%> perl -Dts -e 'print join("=", $$, $0, "this", "$^O\n")'
1
2            EXECUTING...
3
4                =>
5         (-e:0)     enter
6                =>
7         (-e:0)       nextstate
8                =>
9         (-e:1)       pushmark
10                => .*
11        (-e:1)   pushmark
12                => **
13        (-e:1)   const(PV("="\0))
14               => ** PV("="\0)
15        (-e:1)   gvsv(main::$)
16               => ** PV("="\0)  IV(2364)
17        (-e:1)   gvsv(main::0)
18               => ** PV("="\0)  IV(2364)  PVMG("-e"\0)
19        (-e:1)   const(PV("this"\0))
20               => ** PV("="\0)  IV(2364)
                        PVMG("-e"\0)  PV("this"\0)
21        (-e:1)   gvsv(main:: )
22               => ** PV("="\0)  IV(2364)
                        PVMG("-e"\0)  PV("this"\0)
            PVMG()
23        (-e:1)   const(PV("\n"\0))
24               => ** PV("="\0)  IV(2364)
                        PVMG("-e"\0)  PV("this"\0)
            PVMG()  PV("\n"\0)
25        (-e:1)   concat
26               => ** PV("="\0)  IV(2364)
                        PVMG("-e"\0)  PV("this"\0)
            PV("linux\n"\0)
27        (-e:1)   join
28               => * PV("2364=-e=this=linux\n"\0)
29        (-e:1)   print
30               => SV_YES
31        (-e:1)   leave
32            2364=-e=this=linux
```

Interpreting the Output

To make sense of all of this, let's walk through each line of the output:

```
%> perl -Dts -e 'print join("=", $$, $0, "this", "$^O\n")'
1
2            EXECUTING...
3
```

To begin, lines 1 and 3 are simply formatting space, and line 2 is Perl telling us it is now executing the code it has compiled:

```
4                    =>
```

Line 4 is the first line where you can see what is on the stack, currently nothing:

```
5          (-e:0)     enter
```

Line 5 is our first opcode: `enter`. This is always the first opcode in every Perl program, just as the last one is always `leave`:

```
6              =>
```

Again, there is nothing on the stack:

```
7          (-e:0)     nextstate
```

Go to the next statement, which is the first statement in the code:

```
8              =>
```

There still isn't anything on the stack:

```
9          (-e:1)     pushmark
```

This is the first time that the program actually interacts with the stack in any meaningful way. To make a note of this position and to keep track of what arguments are stored on the stack, Perl pushes a mark onto it:

```
10             =>   *
```

Now when the stack is displayed, you can see the mark (an asterisk):

```
11         (-e:1)     pushmark
```

Because the next statement is a `join()` opcode, Perl pushes another mark onto the stack. It does this to track the arguments it will receive, that the `join()` opcode will need to work on later.

Next, the two marks (asterisks) stored on the stack:

```
12             =>   **
```

Next the constant value "=" with an end of string marker is pushed onto the stack:

```
13         (-e:1)     const(PV("="\0))
```

The stack now holds two asterisks and the constant value "="\0:

```
14             =>   **  PV("="\0)
```

Next Perl pushes the `$main::$` variable (`$$`) onto the stack:

```
15         (-e:1)     gvsv(main::$)
```

The $$ variable is the process number of the running program. Your value will probably not be 2364. The next line is

```
16             =>   **  PV("="\0)  IV(2364)
```

Next comes the $main::0 ($0) variable, which evaluates to the name of the program: "-e", with the end of string marker:

```
17          (-e:1)      gvsv(main::0)
```

The "-e"\0 is at the end of the stack:

```
18                  =>  **  PV("="\0)  IV(2364)  PVMG("-e"\0)
```

Now the constant value "this" with the end of string marker gets pushed on to the stack:

```
19          (-e:1)      const(PV("this"\0))
```

The "this"\0 is shown at the end of the stack:

```
20                  =>  **  PV("="\0)  IV(2364)  PVMG("-e"\0)  PV("this"\0)
```

Then comes the $main::^0 ($^0), which is the name of the operating system and will be returned by the PVMG() macro:

```
21          (-e:1)      gvsv(main::  )
```

At the end of name of the operating system, there needs to be a newline, as per the instructions in the code ("$^0\n"):

```
22                  =>  **  PV("="\0)  IV(2364)  PVMG("-e"\0)PV  ("this"\0) PVMG()
```

There is the newline followed by the end of string marker:

```
23          (-e:1)      const(PV("\n"\0))
```

The last two values on the stack need to be brought together in a single string:

```
24                  =>  **  PV("="\0)  IV(2364)  PVMG("-e"\0)  PV("this"\0)  PV("\n"\0)
```

This is where the concat opcode brings the output of the PVMG() macro and the newline together to build a new string:

```
25          (-e:1)      concat
```

which you can see at the end of the stack:

```
26                  =>  **  PV("="\0)  IV(2364)  PVMG("-e"\0)  PV("this"\0)  PV("linux\n"\0)
```

Now the join opcode takes the first argument from the stack, the "="\0, and uses it to join all the other arguments on the stack. The result is stored on the stack:

```
27          (-e:1)      join
```

The stack now shows that the second asterisk has been removed, because the join() opcode has been executed:

```
28                  =>  *  PV("2364=-e=this=linux\n"\0)
```

The next opcode is print(), which prints everything on the stack and consequently removes the remaining asterisk. Finally, it returns a true value and pushes that onto the stack:

```
29          (-e:1)      print
```

The SV_YES now on the stack is the true value returned from the print() opcode:

```
30                  => SV_YES
```

The last opcode, as in every Perl program, is leave:

```
31        (-e:1)     leave
```

Finally, the data, which is the result of the join and print statements is seen on STDOUT:

```
32        2364=-e=this=linux
```

For further information on the opcodes, you can also look up the short description of an opcode with a short one-liner command. For example, if you want to find out what sassign does, you might use a command such as

```
%> perl -MOpcode -le 'print Opcode::opdesc("sassign")'scalar assignment
```

Reading through both opcode.pl in the source distribution and perldoc Opcode will explain most of the intricacies of opcodes, which Perl builds each time it compiles your code into the bytecodes it executes.

The Perl Compiler

The O module (that's a capital letter oh, not a zero), is a frontend to the Perl compiler. The B module is the backend, and it supplies all the access to Perl internals that a programmer might wish to use via the O interface.

There are various backends that can be given as arguments for inspecting or debugging what's going on in your Perl program. While these may seem a bit esoteric, they can be just what you need to get a different perspective on your application. For instance, you may be interested in reviewing where all the variables in your program are defined, or learning more about how Perl actually parses your code.

These are cases where the backend B and frontend O modules can help. By frontend, the programmer API (Application Programming Interface) is intended, and by backend, we're referring to the actual modules that do the work, but are not supposed to be used without going through the API.

Documentation for the B and O Modules

To use these modules you'll need to go through the appropriate interface, using the frontend O module, to get at the documentation you need to go through the backend B. Even though the frontend modules are called O modules, they're still in the B:: namespace. This means that if you want to look at the Lint module that's called like this:

```
%> perl -MO=Lint
```

you need to remember that the module name is B::Lint, and look up its documentation like this:

```
%> perldoc B::Lint
```

Let's take a brief look at a several B modules that you can use with the O interface, such as the following:

- Lint: Checks Perl programs for less-than-ideal programming constructs.

- Xref: Generates a cross-reference listing of all variables.

- Deparse: Exposes how Perl will parse your code.

- Concise: Shows the opcode tree.

■**Note** Read the O and B manpages for more information on these and other modules which offer access to Perl internals.

Lint

The B::Lint module was inspired by the lint program used for checking C programs. It enables a form of *extended* warnings, covering more than -w, and can expose dubious programming practices that even strict and warnings would allow.

Let's run this against charcount to see how it works:

```
%> perldb -MO=Lint charcount
Implicit scalar context for array in shift at charcount line 44
Implicit scalar context for array in shift at charcount line 45
charcount syntax OK
%>
```

As you can see, although our charcount program runs fine under -w, B::Lint still picks up on what it considers to be unorthodox practice. This is not to say we should clean up everything that B::Lint exposes, but when we want to put our program through a fine toothed comb, this is a great tool to use. Who knows? Maybe next time it will tell us about something that is important enough to change.

■**Note** To find out more about using O::Lint, see the B::Lint documentation. (Remember, even though it's an O:: module, it's in the B:: namespace.)

Xref

The B::Xref module generates a cross-referenced listing of variables, subroutines, and objects in your program, as well as all the modules or libraries which it uses, whether directly or indirectly. We can execute it against our charcount program like this:

```
%> perldb -MO=Xref charcount
File /opt/perl/lib/5.8.2/Carp.pm
  Subroutine Carp::carp
    Package Carp
      &shortmess        &193
    Package main
```

```
      @_                    193
  Subroutine Carp::confess
    Package Carp
      &longmess            &192
    Package main
      @_                    192
  Subroutine Carp::croak
    Package Carp
      &shortmess           &191
    Package main
      @_                    191
File /opt/perl/lib/5.8.2/Exporter.pm
  Subroutine (definitions)
    Package Fcntl
      &O_ACCMODE            s60
<...snip...>
File /opt/perl/lib/5.8.2/i686-linux/IO/Seekable.pm
  Subroutine (definitions)
    Package IO::Seekable
      &seek                s116
      &sysseek             s121
      &tell                s126
  Subroutine IO::Seekable::seek
    Package ?
      *??                   115
    Package IO::Seekable
      &croak               &114
    Package main
      @_                    114
  Subroutine IO::Seekable::sysseek
    Package ?
      *??                   120
    Package IO::Seekable
      &croak               &119
    Package main
<...snip...>
    Package UNIVERSAL
      &VERSION             s0
      &can                 s0
      &isa                 s0
    Package main
      &parse               s26
  Subroutine (main)
    Package (lexical)
      $FH                  i16, 34
      $cons                i26, 29, 29
      $file                i10, &16, 13, 16, 16
```

```
    $i_cnt           i18, 29, 34
    $i_cons          i19, 26, 37, 37
    $i_spec          i21, 28, 37, 37
    $i_vows          i20, 27, 37, 37
    $line            i25, 26, 27, 28, 33
    $spec            i28, 29, 29
    $verbose         i11, 33
    $vows            i27, 29, 29
  Package main
    $!               16
    $0               14
    $_               25, 34
    &parse           &26, &27, &28
  Subroutine parse
   Package (lexical)
    $cnt             i46, 47
    $reg             i45, 46
    $str             i44, 46
    @cnt             i46
   Package main
    @_               44, 45
%>
```

You can see that it goes through each referenced library and each subroutine it finds in the program, printing out all the places a variable is referenced, and noting the line numbers where it is used.

Interpreting the Output

Note that the letter that sometimes prefixes the line numbers may indicate certain features for the variable:

- i: First or *initial* use

- s: Subroutine definitions

- &: Subroutine and method calls

For our purposes, the most interesting entries may be the ones toward the end, under parse and main, as these contain the code we created.

This information is useful for determining when a variable is only ever referenced once. This is important because it leads one to wonder if the variable is even required, or whether it is even the correct variable. Let's say we have a program that's failing mysteriously with errors pointing to a missing file or directory. If we used O::Xref to take a look for variables with names like: filename, filnam, xfile_name, filname, it might point to inappropriate usage of the filehandle, perhaps.

■Note To learn more about using O::Xref, see the B::Xref documentation.

Deparse

The Deparse module will parse the code so you can see how Perl will interpret it. This is where you find out that even when *you* don't use parentheses, Perl does (thank goodness). Deparse will also show you how a foreach loop is translated internally into a while loop. The point is, sometimes it doesn't matter how your code is written—during Perl's pre-runtime optimization phase your code will be rewritten by Perl itself, or rather Perl's optimizer. In this example, the module is given -p as an argument, which instructs Deparse to display parentheses in its output. This calling syntax, with commas separating arguments, allows us to add parameters when calling the module:

```
%> perldb -MO=Deparse,-p charcount
use FileHandle;
use strict 'refs';
(my $file = ($ARGV[0] || ''));
(my $verbose = ($ARGV[1] || 0));
unless (-f($file)) {
    die("Usage: $0 filename [-v]");
}
((my $FH = 'FileHandle'->new("< $file"))
    or die("unable to open file($file): $!"));
(my $i_cnt = 0);
(my $i_cons = 0);
(my $i_vows = 0);
(my $i_spec = 0);
while (defined(($_ = <$FH>))) {
    (my $line = $_);
    ($i_cons += (my $cons = &parse($line, '[bcdfghjklmnpqrstvwxyz]')));
    ($i_vows += (my $vows = &parse($line, '[aeiou]')));
    ($i_spec += (my $spec = &parse($line, '[^a-z0-9\\s]')));
    print((((((((((((sprintf('%6d', $i_cnt) . ':') . ' hard') .
 ('.' x (8 - length($cons)))) . $cons) . ' soft') .
 ('.' x (8 - length($vows)))) . $vows) . ' spec') .
 ('.' x (8 - length($spec)))) . $spec)
 );
    print(($verbose ? " $line" : "\n"));
    (++$i_cnt);
}
print((((((((((((' total: hard' . (' ' x (8 - length($i_cons)))) .
$i_cons) . ' soft') .
 (' ' x (8 - length($i_vows)))) . $i_vows) . ' spec') .
 (' ' x (8 - length($i_spec)))) . $i_spec) . "\n")
 );
sub parse {
    (my $str = shift(@_));
    (my $reg = shift(@_));
    (my $cnt = (my(@cnt) = ($str =~ /($reg)/gi)));
    return($cnt);
}
```

```
exit(0);
charcount syntax OK
%>
```

■Note To find out more about using Deparse and the other useful options it supports, see the Deparse documentation.

Summary

In this chapter you have learned various methods for finding out what exactly your code is doing, where it's dragging its feet, and how to improve it's response time.

You have learned how to benchmark and profile your code, and how to optimize and refactor it to improve the runtime. Finally, you learned how to inspect your code for strange or non-optimal programming constructs, using the frontend O and backend B modules, which provide access to the Perl internals.

The next chapter offers a complete reference listing of all commands, options, and variables available within the Perl debugger, including both environment and internal debugger variables.

## CHAPTER 14

Command Line and GUI Debuggers

"A picture is worth a thousand words."

—Fred R. Barnard, *Printers Ink*, 1927

Many people believe that this famous quotation is centuries old. It turns out that an advertising agent used it in an article in 1927 as a slogan to demonstrate how appropriate graphics could be used to sell a product more effectively than plain text. He thought people would catch on to the idea and believe it more intensely if the phrase was framed as if it came from an ancient Chinese proverb.

On the other hand, there is no doubt that there's always been truth to the statement, even if the explicit phrase itself is moderately recent. An observable fact related to Perl use is that many people are more comfortable using a Graphical User Interface, or GUI, than the command line when dealing with computers, even those erstwhile command line protagonists—programmers.

Variety Is the Spice of Life

Although the Perl debugger has a long and venerated history as a command line program, various incarnations of GUI overlays or replacements have existed for a long time. There is an extraordinarily large number of GUI debuggers to choose from, with every system type, shape, and color you can think of. There are those you have to pay for, those that are free, and every variation in between. While we can't discuss every available debugger, we will introduce the major features of the most commonly used variants, and discuss the features every typical GUI should possess. The intent is to provide you with enough information to make an informed decision as to which GUI debugger might be the right one to use in your particular environment.

GUI Features

Almost every GUI debugger will share certain features; once you've worked with one then the interface, output and general behavior of others will be relatively familiar.

Beyond these fairly standard facilities, each GUI debugger will tend to go its own way in terms of presenting greater control or more features, depending on what it believes is the greatest priority or the most useful command. At the end of the day, remember that all debuggers, GUI or not, will be reliant on the support of the underlying operating system. The debugger won't support fork and threads if the underlying OS doesn't.

Operating System Variations

The defining criterion for choosing a GUI will be your operating system. If it works with one of the Unix variants, it will probably work with all of them. This chapter covers the options available for Linux/Unix, Mac OS X, and Windows. If you're running Plan9, you're on your own.

Next, we'll describe this information in greater detail and give you URIs with further information, free or trial downloads, and sometimes even the ability to purchase.

Dedicated GUI Debugger or Embedded IDE Debugger?

Although almost every Perl debugger you will ever use, whether command line or GUI, will have similar behavior, you should know the difference between wrapper GUI debuggers, standalone GUI debuggers, and GUI debuggers which are part of an IDE (Integrated Development Environment).

Wrappers

Wrapper debuggers work with the standard debugger, providing a GUI interface for the programmer to work with. These debuggers, partly because they don't introduce as much new code, will emulate the underlying debugger and all its features nearly perfectly. Ptkdb and DDD, designed to run on Linux and Unix variants as well as Windows, are examples of wrapper debuggers.

Standalone GUI

Standalone debuggers have been written from the ground up to work with a particular operating system, such as the Affrus debugger that was designed for the Mac OS X. The entire internal workings of the debugger need to be faithfully reproduced or improved upon because this is all new code. The standalone debugger will be using precisely the same hooks Perl provides for the command line debugger.

Remember that Perl provides these hooks for any debugger to use, not just its own, and therefore the functionality may be reduced, identical, or even improved, depending on how the standalone version has been implemented.

IDE

The IDE debugger is a GUI debugger written as part of a greater application, like Komodo for Windows. In most cases, these are complete rewrites, much like the standalone debugger. The features are likely to be similar or identical to the standard command line debugger with the addition of the convenience of being able to use a mouse to point to variables.

The feature set may be identical in all GUIs or all IDEs, although you can certainly expect some of the later features that work with the command line debugger to be missing in a number of the GUI versions. Some features that might be missing are support and the stepping backwards feature.

Perl GUI Debuggers

Here is a list of URIs for the currently known Perl GUI debuggers, whether they are embedded or standalone. In several cases, we have included a representative image so that you can see how the GUI may appear on your screen. The selection is moderately arbitrary and should not be taken to imply favoritism or any particular preference.

ActivePerl Pro Studio

ActiveState (http://www.activestate.com/Products/ActivePerlProStudio) provides a complete Perl IDE in ActivePerl Pro Studio (as shown in Figure 14-1). It includes Komodo as an IDE for working with dynamic languages, PDK (Perl Developers Kit) Pro Pack, and Visual Perl.

Komodo provides a built-in GUI Perl debugger to APS running on most Linux/Unix and Windows systems. In fact, Komodo provides an IDE for working with several dynamic languages, including Perl, PHP, Python, Tcl, and XSLT with "comprehensive debugging support."

In addition to providing the definitive Perl for Win32 systems, ActiveState provides several Perl products that can help with building applications and debugging, as well as offering the capability of turning Perl applications into standalone executables on both Windows and Linux/Unix platforms.

Komodo supports multiple languages and integrates with source code control software like Subversion, CVS, and Perforce. It also includes web support (CGI, XML, and XSLT), as well as a regular expression toolkit.

ActivePerl Pro Studio and Komodo run on Linux, Solaris, and Windows 9x/NT/2000/XP. They are not free, though you may download a trial version from their web site.

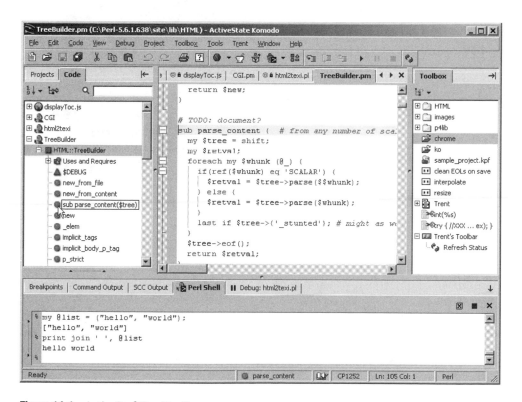

Figure 14-1. *ActivePerl Pro Studio*

DDD

Written by Andreas Zellar and Andrew Gaylard, DDD (http://www.gnu.org/software/ddd/) is a GUI front-end for many different debuggers running on Linux and Unix variants. In addition to the Perl debugger, DDD supports gdb, dbx, jdb, the bash, python debuggers and many more.

You need to tell DDD to use the Perl debugger when you start it up on your program, by passing the --perl command line switch to DDD. Using the charcount program, the command line would look something like this:

```
%> ddd --perl charcount walrus 3
```

DDD (shown in Figure 14-2) runs only on Linux and other Unix variants. It's free and can be downloaded from the GNU web site.

Figure 14-2. *The DDD GUI front-end*

Perl Builder

Written by SolutionSoft, Perl Builder (http://www.solutionsoft.com/perl.htm) is a complete IDE and provides a built-in GUI Perl debugger running on Linux and Windows. SolutionSoft provides both a standard and professional version. Perl Builder incorporates a CGI Wizard that can help you to build web-aware applications and an integrated editor.

Perl Builder (shown in Figure 14-3) runs on Windows 9x/NT/2000/XP, and the professional version includes a pre-release version running on Linux. Perl Builder is not free though you may download a trial version from the company web site.

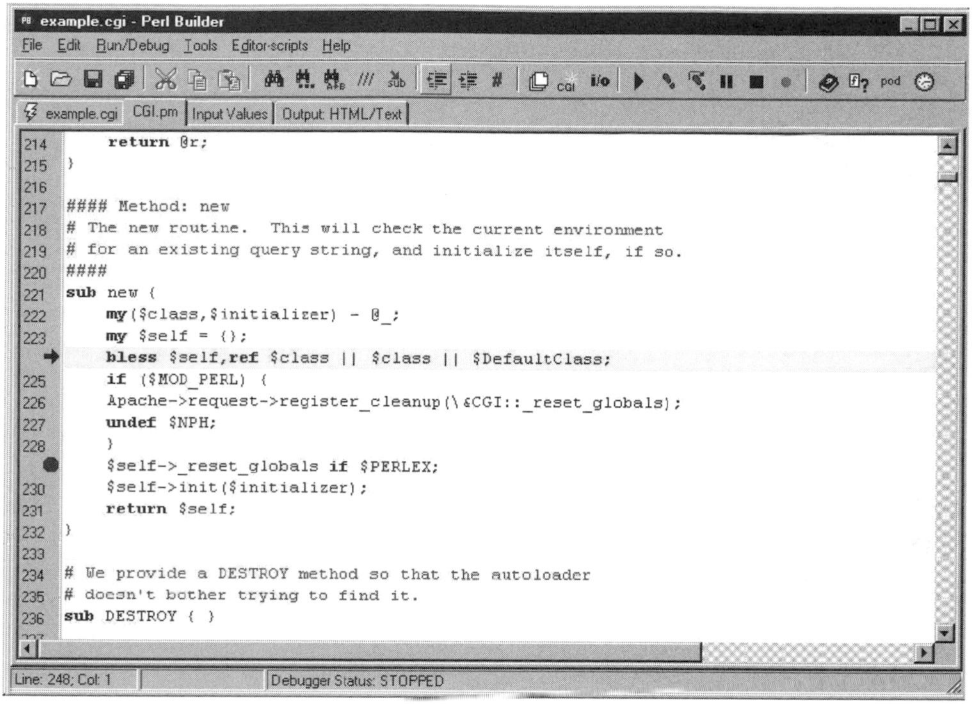

Figure 14-3. *The PerlBuilder debugger*

perldbgui

Written by Curt McKelvey, and using Perl/Tk, perldbgui (http://members.tripod.com/ ~CurtMcKelvey/perldbgui) is a wrapper for the standard command line debugger, much like Ptkdb.

perldbgui runs on all known Linux/Unix systems, and is freely available from the previously listed web site. See Figures 14-4 and 14-5 to see an example of the perldbgui Source and Debugger windows.

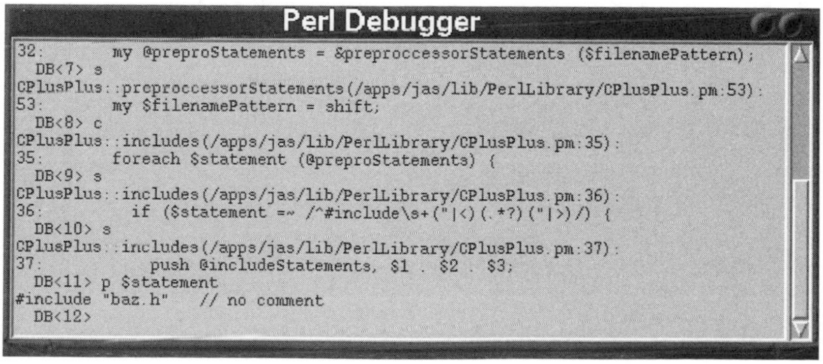

Figure 14-4. *The perldbgui Source window*

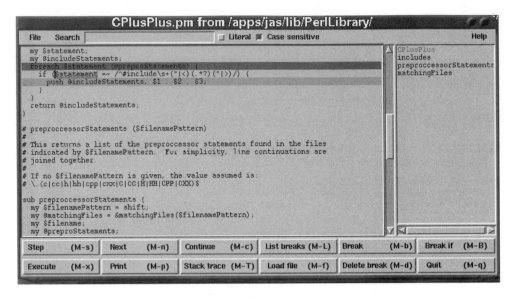

Figure 14-5. *The perldbgui Debugger window*

Ptkdb

Ptkdb (http://world.std.com/~aep/ptkdb) was written by Andrew E. Page, who used the Perl Tk library to provide a convenient and generic GUI wrapper for standard command line debuggers running on Linux, Unix, and Windows.

Ptkdb (shown in Figure 14-6) requires Perl 5.004 on Unix/Linux, and Perl 5.6.0 on Win32. It is freely available from the creator's web site.

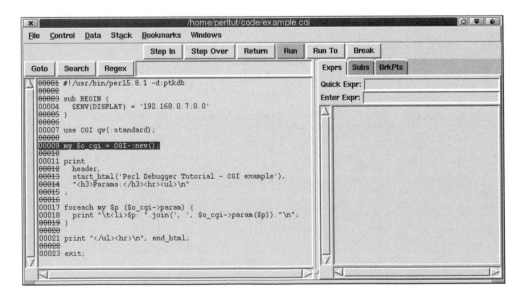

Figure 14-6. *The Ptkdb debugger*

vdb

vdb (http://www.qub.com/group/our/vdb.htm) is a wrapper for the standard command line debugger. It's written in Wish, which you must install yourself. You must also install a patch to the Perl debugger to disable the console.

vdb (as shown in Figure 14-7) is available for Linux/Unix as well as Windows. It's freely available from the aforementioned web site.

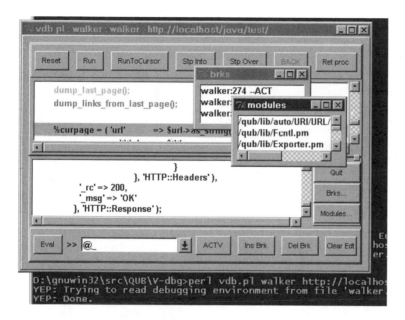

Figure 14-7. *The vdb debugger wrapper*

Summary

In this chapter you have been presented with the wide variety of options available to you if you wish to use either a GUI debugger or IDE with an embedded debugger, instead of the standard command line debugger interface. There are many possibilities, and the one you should choose depends on the operating system you are running, your personal preferences for Tk solutions over Windows solutions, and how much money or time you wish to spend.

The next chapter offers a complete command reference for all commands, variables, and options supported by the debugger.

■■■

Comprehensive Command Reference

". . . And, like other modes of speech, little is said, but much is intended."

—Merlin to Wart from *The Sword in the Stone*, by T. H. White

In the same way that Merlin explains to the young Arthur that the minimal speech of animals and birds is still full of meaning, the Perl debugger also uses short, but very useful, commands for most of its instructions. This section is a comprehensive reference for all the available debugger commands, variables, and options, and there are quite a few.

The debugger has evolved over the years, so only commands that were introduced after Perl 5 first came out will be noted.

Tip Keep in mind that when using the debugger, h will bring up a short mini-help window, and that h cmd will display the help for a specific command.

Movement Control

Movement commands control the execution of the debugger and how it steps through your program's code, whether you tell it to run on until told to stop, run to a particular line number, cross over a function call, or step into a subroutine.

Continue (c)

The c command (detailed in Table 15-1) tells Perl to continue execution until the debugger reaches a preset variable, breakpoint, or some other instruction.

Table 15-1. c *Commands and Definitions*

Command	Definition
c	Continues program execution until hitting a breakpoint or a command, which tells the debugger to stop (like a watch variable for instance).
c lineno	Continues program execution to the line number given is reached.
c subname	Continues execution until the first line of subroutine name given is reached, effectively placing a one-time only breakpoint there. Introduced in Perl v5.5.

Next (n)

Step to the next statement, stepping over subroutine or method calls (shown in Table 15-2). When next-stepping, the variable $DB::single is set to 2.

Table 15-2. n *Commands and Definitions*

Command	Definition
n	Step to the next statement, unless stopped by a debugger command or breakpoint.
n expr	Step to the next statement, unless expr contains subroutine calls, in which case stop before each one (as if you were typing n continuously). Introduced in Perl v5.5. See also $DB::single under $DB::Variables later in this chapter to learn how to do this programmatically.

Return (r)

This command returns you from your current subroutine as shown in Table 15-3.

Table 15-3. r *Commands and Definitions*

Command	Definition
r	Run to the end of the current subroutine and return to the calling context. The return value is printed if the PrintRet option is set. Note that until Perl v5.5 this was the f command, which stood for finish subroutine.

Step Into (s)

Step to the next executable statement—if there is a function call, step into it (shown in Table 15-4). When single stepping, the variable $DB::single is set to 1.

Table 15-4. s *Commands and Definitions*

Command	Definition
s	Step into each subroutine, stop and await a command.
s expr	Step into and through the expression given, including any subroutines which may be called during execution of the expression. See also $DB::single under $DB::variables to set this programmatically.

Repeat (<CR>)

Repeats last c, n, or s command, as defined in Table 15-5. The <CR> is a carriage return. This is effectively an empty command line.

Table 15-5. *Carriage Return Command*

Command	Definition
<CR>	Repeat the last motion (c, n, or s) command.

Tracing (t, T)

Tracing, shown in Table 15-6 displays the call stack for the program at the current position. When tracing, $DB::trace is set to 1.

Table 15-6. t *or* T *Commands*

Command	Definition
t	Toggles the trace mechanism on and off, until either a $DB::trace variable is set to 0, or tracing is toggled directly once more.
t expr	Toggles the trace mechanism on and off for the given expression. Introduced in Perl v5.5.
T	Displays the current stack trace, once only. See also $DB::trace and AutoTrace in the Options section later in the chapter.

Controlling Execution

These commands control the execution of your code. They automate the checking of conditions in your code as it runs, allowing you to perform repetitive tasks during your debugging session, and keep an eye open for things you want to watch for.

Actions (a)

An action is a Perl command to execute at a particular line of a program, before the line is executed. The following commands (shown in Table 15-7) will allow you to create, delete, and list actions.

Table 15-7. *Creating, Deleting, and Listing Action Commands*

Command	Definition
a expr	Create an action to execute the given Perl expression on the current line. The expression will be evaluated the next time the current line is about to be executed.
a lineno expr	Create an action to run the supplied perl expression each time the code on the given line number is about to be executed.
A lineno	Delete the action for the given line number. Introduced in Perl v5.8.
A *	Delete all actions. Introduced in Perl v5.8. Beware that prior to Perl 5.8, a simple A would delete all actions in the session.
L a	List all of the actions that are currently set in the current session. Introduced in Perl v5.8.

Breakpoints (b)

A breakpoint tells the debugger to stop the running program at that point during its execution. You can only set a breakpoint on a line where you have valid Perl code, so you cannot set a breakpoint on a blank line, for instance. Just like with actions, you can create, delete, and list breakpoints, as shown in Table 15-8.

Table 15-8. *Creating, Deleting, and Listing Breakpoints*

Command	Definition
b	Creates a breakpoint on the current line, stopping the debugger each time the current line of code is executed.
b condition	Creates a conditional breakpoint on the current line, and stops if the given condition is true at the next time the current line of code is executed.
b lineno	Creates a breakpoint on the given line number where the debugger will stop each time the code on this line is executed.
b lineno condition	Creates a conditional breakpoint on the given line number and stops the debugger if the given condition is true at the time the code on this line is executed.
b postpone subname	Creates a breakpoint at the first line of the given subroutine name, and stops there the next time the subroutine is compiled. Introduced in Perl v5.5.
b postpone subname condition	Creates a breakpoint at the first line of the given subroutine name, so that the next time the subroutine is compiled it stops the debugger if the given condition is true at that time. Introduced in Perl v5.5.
b load filename	Creates a breakpoint at the first line of the given filename, and stops the debugger at that line the next time the file is loaded, after a restart, for instance. Introduced in Perl v5.5.
b subname	Creates a breakpoint at the first line of the subroutine name given, and stops the debugger the next time this subroutine is entered.
b subname condition	Creates a conditional breakpoint at the first line of the subroutine name given, and stops the debugger if the given condition is true at the time the subroutine is entered.
b $var	Creates a breakpoint at the subroutine referenced by $var. Introduced in Perl v5.6.
b compile subname	Creates a breakpoint at the first line of the given subroutine the next time the subroutine is compiled, but before it is executed. Introduced in Perl v5.5.
B lineno	Deletes the breakpoint on the given line number. Note that prior to Perl v5.8 this command was d lineno.
B *	Deletes all breakpoints. Note that prior before Perl 5.8, this command was D.
L b	Displays a list of all breakpoints currently set. Introduced in Perl v5.8.

Watch Expressions (w)

A watch expression tells the debugger to stop when a particular expression's value is modified. You can think of it as a one-time breakpoint that resets itself each time it is activated. You can see all the commands for creating, deleting, and listing watchpoints in Table 15-9.

Table 15-9. w *Commands and Definitions*

Command	Definition
w expr	Creates a watch expression that stops the debugger each time the expression changes. Typically you might set this to the name of a variable, so that the debugger would stop each time the variable was modified. Introduced in Perl v5.5. Note that prior to Perl v5.8 this command was W expr, and that w was used to view a window of code—just like v does now.
W expr	Deletes the watch expression. Introduced in Perl v5.8. Beware that prior to Perl v5.8 this command would set the expression.
W *	Deletes all watch expressions. Introduced in Perl v5.6. Beware that prior to Perl v5.8 a simple W would delete all watch expression without warning.
L w	Lists all watch expressions. Introduced in Perl v5.8.

Listing All Actions, Breakpoints, and Watch Variables (L)

Although you can list the contents of each of the previous commands separately, there is one command with which to view all actions, breakpoints and watch variables simultaneously, one command to bind them all . . . and it's the L command.

Pre- and Post-Prompts

You can set up both a Perl command and a debugger command to be executed before the debugger prompt is printed. You can also set up a Perl command to be executed after the debugger prompt is printed. Setting a debugger command to execute after the prompt is deemed redundant as it is already awaiting input from you at that point.

Pre-Prompt Perl Commands (<)

These commands manipulate the Perl commands to be executed before the debugger prompt is displayed (see Table 15-10).

Table 15-10. *Pre-Prompt Perl Commands (<)*

Command	Definition
< expr	Creates a pre-prompt Perl command to execute before each prompt. Note that this will overwrite any existing commands.
<< expr	Appends a pre-prompt Perl command to the existing list of commands. Introduced in Perl v5.5.
< ?	Lists all pre-prompt Perl commands. Introduced in Perl v5.8.
< *	Deletes all pre-prompt Perl commands. Introduced in Perl v5.8.

Pre-Prompt Debugger Commands ({)

These commands (shown in Table 15-11) manipulate the debugger commands to be executed before the debugger prompt is displayed.

Table 15-11. *Pre-Prompt Debugger Commands ({)*

Command	Definition
{ expr	Creates a pre-prompt debugger command to execute before the prompt. Note that this will overwrite any existing commands. Introduced in Perl v5.5.
{{ expr	Appends a pre-prompt debugger command to the existing list. Introduced in Perl v5.6.
{ ?	Lists all pre-prompt debugger commands. Introduced in Perl v5.8.
{ *	Deletes all pre-prompt debugger commands. Introduced in Perl v5.8.

Post-Prompt Perl Commands (>)

These commands (shown in Table 15-12) manipulate the Perl commands to be executed after the debugger prompt is displayed.

Table 15-12. *Post-Prompt Perl Commands (>)*

Command	Definition
> expr	Creates a post-prompt Perl command to execute after the prompt. Note that this will overwrite any existing commands.
>> expr	Appends a post-prompt Perl command to the existing list. Introduced in Perl v5.5.
> ?	Lists all post-prompt Perl commands. Introduced in Perl v5.8.
> *	Deletes all post-prompt Perl commands. Introduced in Perl v5.8.

Listing and Examining Code (f, l)

These commands (as shown in Table 15-13) list the code in the current file at the current position, or from any particular line number or subroutine. If you have used the f command referred to previously, the new file becomes the current file. You can also switch to viewing any file currently loaded.

Table 15-13. *Listing and Examining Code (f, l)*

Command	Definition
f filename	Starts to view the code in the given filename, from the first line. The filename is a regex matched against the contents of the %INC hash. Introduced in Perl v5.5.
l	Lists code from the current display pointer position onward. The number of lines of code to list is defined by the windowSize option, described later.
l lineno	Lists code from the given line number onward, using the windowSize option again.
l min+incr	Lists code from line number min plus incr lines.
l min-max	Lists code from line number min to line number max.
l subname	Lists code from the first line of the given subroutine name, using the windowSize option to determine how many lines of code to display.
l $var	Lists code for the given subroutine name referenced by $var, using the windowSize option. Introduced in Perl v5.6.

Viewing a Window of Code (v)

The v command, as shown in Table 15-14, is a simple historical convenience mechanism for viewing windowSize chunks of code, and is internally mapped to the l [lineno] commands.

Table 15-14. *Viewing a Window of Code (v)*

Command	Definition
v	Views windowSize number of lines of code around the current display pointer position.
v lineno	Views windowSize number of lines of code from the given line number onward. Note that prior to Perl 5.8, this command was w.

Listing Code Backwards (-)

Where l and v display code listings in a down or forwards direction, from the position of the display pointer. The - command lists code in an up or backwards direction. See Table 15-15 for more details.

Table 15-15. *Listing Code Backwards (-)*

Command	Definition
-	List windowSize number of lines of code backwards from (or previous to) the current display pointer.

Reset the Display Pointer (.)

This command, as mentioned in Table 15-16, returns the display to the line which the debugger is going to execute next: aka the current position.

Table 15-16. *Reset the Display Pointer (.)*

Command	Definition
.	Reposition the display pointer to the line the debugger is about to execute.

Searching Code (/, ?)

Several commands are available for searching code in the currently open file. The file being viewed can be changed using the f command we went over previously. Table 15-17 shows you the commands you'll need for searching both forwards and backwards in your code.

Table 15-17. *Searching Forward (/) and Searching Backwards (?) in Code*

Command	Definition
/regex/	Search forward (down), through all the code from the current position to the end of the current file, for the first case of the given pattern. Note that the trailing slash is optional. Introduced in Perl v5.5.
/	Repeat the most recent forward search. Introduced in Perl v5.5.
?regex?	Search backwards (up) for the given pattern. The search will stop when the top of the file is reached. Note that the trailing question-mark is optional. Introduced in Perl v5.5.
?	Repeat the most recent backward search.

Examining Data (p, x)

These commands handle displaying data during your debugging session. They're similar to the functionality of Data::Dumper, but have their own unique quirks. Data in a program may be printed to the DB::OUT filehandle using the p command, which simply wraps Perl's own print command.

The x command, on the other hand, should not be confused with Data::Dumper, although they behave in a very similar manner and, for our purposes, do essentially the same thing. It is better to supply a reference to a data structure, as it will then be pretty-printed in a much nicer fashion with sensible indenting. For more details, see Table 15-18.

Table 15-18. *Printing (p) and Examining (x) Data*

Command	Definition
p expr	Prints the given expression to DB::OUT.
x expr	Dumps the given expression to DB::OUT. Introduced in Perl v5.5.
x maxdepth expr	Dumps the expression to the given maximum depth. Note that if the expression includes a number, this might be interpreted as a maximum depth instruction, so it may be wise to explicitly bracket the expression. Introduced in Perl v5.8. See also arrayDepth, compactDump, dumpDepth, DumpDBFiles, DumpPackages, DumpReused, veryCompact under the following options.

Informational Commands (e, E, m, M, i, S)

These commands offer information as to which commands and subroutines may be called on a given expression, are classified as class or object instance, and which modules are currently loaded. Take a look at Table 15-19 for a list of commands for threads, methods, modules, inheritance trees, and subroutines.

Table 15-19. *Threads (e, E), Methods (m), Modules (M), Inheritance Trees (i), and Subroutines (S)*

Command	Definition
e	Displays the current thread id. Introduced in Perl v5.8.
E	Displays a list of all known thread ids, and highlights the current thread. Introduced in Perl v5.8
m expr	Displays methods callable against the first result returned from the given expression. The expression may be a subroutine call, an object reference, or any executable Perl expression. Introduced in Perl v5.5.
m class	Displays a list of the methods callable against the given class. Introduced in Perl v5.5.
M	Displays the list of currently loaded modules in %INC. Note that prior to Perl 5.8, this command was v.
i class	Displays the inheritance tree for the given class or object reference. Introduced in Perl v5.8.5
S	Displays the list of all known subroutine names.
S pattern	Displays the list of all known subroutine names, constrained to match the given pattern. Introduced in Perl v5.5.
S !pattern	Displays the list of all known subroutine names that do not match the given pattern. Introduced in Perl v5.5.

Variables (V, X, y)

These commands will print out the name and content of all the variables in a program or class.
V and X use the dumpDepth option to define how deep to dump nested structures. Take a look at
Table 15-20 to examine commands for variables in a package (V) and variables in the current
package (X), which essentially maps to the V current_package ... command.

Table 15-20. *Commands for Variables (V, X)*

Command	Definition
V	Displays all known variables and their values including nested structures.
V pkg	Displays all known variables and their values, in the given package.
V pkg regex	Displays all known variables and their values based on the regex, in the given package.
V pkg !regex	Displays all known variables in the given package which do *not* match the given regex, along with their values.
X	Displays all variables and their values, in the current package.
X regex	Displays all variables and their values in the current package that match the given regex.
X !regex	Displays all variables in the current package that do *not* match the given regex, along with their values.

Lexical Variables (y)

This command, shown in Table 15-21, displays lexical or my variables. Note that this command
relies on the PadWalker module, which must be installed for this to work. You must also be in
a subroutine to provide scope for this to be effective.

Table 15-21. *Commands for Lexical Variables (y)*

Command	Definition
y	Lists lexical variables in the current scope. Introduced in Perl v5.8.
y level	Lists lexical variables in the scope level levels up. Introduced in Perl v5.8.
y level regex	Lists lexical variables in the scope level levels up that match the given regex. Introduced in Perl v5.8
y level !regex	Lists lexical variables in the scope level levels up, that do not match the given regex. Introduced in Perl v5.8.

Perl Command (...)

Any expression not understood as a debugger command will be handed off to Perl for evaluation directly and executed. See Table 15-22 for more details.

Table 15-22. *Command for Perl Command (...)*

Command	Definition
expr	If an expression *might* be considered a debugger command, and you wish to make sure Perl will get to it first, supply a leading semicolon.

Command History and Aliases (H, !, =)

Debugging can be tedious and error-prone, and the debugger's command history helps by making debugging easier and less likely to run afoul of typos. Take a look at Table 15-23 for commands involving History and Aliases.

■**Note** For history listings (H), the debugger maintains a history of the commands entered so they can be referred to and perhaps used later; see History Redo (!). Remember that any commands that are only one character in length are ignored for the purpose of history listings and recall.

Table 15-23. *Commands for History and Aliases (H, !, =)*

Command	Definition
H	Displays complete history listing of all commands executed in the current session.
H -n	Displays last-number history listing.
H *	Deletes complete history listing (not undoable). Introduced in Perl v5.8.
!	Redoes the last command executed.
! number	Redoes history command referred to by number.
! -number	Redoes the *number*th-to-last history command.
! pattern	Redoes the last command that matches the given pattern. Note that the match has an implicit ^ placed in front of it to bind it to the beginning of the command.
=	Lists all the currently set aliases.
= alias value	Defines a debugger command alias to the given value.

Restarting a Debugger Session (R)

There are several ways of restarting a debugger session. It is possible to start again from the beginning of the current session. You can also go *backwards*, or at least that's what it looks like, alternatively you can choose to go to a particular command history number. Examine these commands in Table 15-24.

Table 15-24. *Restarting a Session (R)*

Command	Definition
R	Restarts the current debugger session, with as much of the current environment and the original command line as is possible to maintain. This will bring you back to the start of the session, but will maintain breakpoints, actions and watch variables from the current session. Introduced in Perl v5.5.

Moving Backwards (rerun)

This command, shown in Table 15-25, emulates moving backwards by replaying your current session to the current or given position, internally using the Restart command described previously.

Table 15-25. *Commands for Moving Backwards (*rerun*)*

Command	Definition
rerun	Restart and run this session again to return to the current position. Introduced in Perl v5.8.5.
rerun number	Restart and run the session to the given command history number. Note that this is the command history number and not the line number! Introduced in Perl v5.8.5.
rerun -number	Restart and run the session to the given *number*th-to-last command. Introduced in Perl v5.8.5.

Save and Source Commands (save, source)

You can save to, and run debugger commands from, an external file. See Table 15-26 for details.

Table 15-26. *Commands for* Save *and* Source

Command	Definition
save filename	Saves debugger commands from the current session in the given filename. This command uses the actual history of commands entered, not the reduced listing you see with the H command. Introduced in Perl v5.8.
source filename	Runs all of the debugger commands in the given filename as if they were entered one after the other manually. Introduced in Perl v5.8.

External and Paging Commands (!!, |)

These commands communicate directly with the shell, or system (see Table 15-27).

Table 15-27. *Commands for External (!!) and Paging (|)*

Command	Definition
!! command	Run the given shell *command* from the debugger session. Introduced in Perl v5.6.
	dbcmd	Run the given command through the system pager. Very useful for *any* output likely to overshoot the window size. Introduced in Perl v5.6.

Documentation (h, h h, man, doc, |)

The debugger comes with multiple help facilities. You can call the internal help menu, as well as the external or system help documentation. Help commands refer to the debugger's own help pages, while man refers to all of the installed manpages and perldocs available through both the man command, as well as the doc and perldoc commands. See Table 15-28 for more details.

Table 15-28. *Commands for Documentation* (h, h h, man, doc, |)

Command	Definition
h	Prints a small help window with most commands squeezed into as small a space as possible for convenience. Note that prior to Perl v5.8.0 the h and h h commands were reversed.
h h	Prints an extended help menu, with all available commands and most options. Usually you'll want to use this with the pager command: | h h. Introduced in Perl v5.5.
h cmd	Displays the available help for the given command. Introduced in Perl v5.6.
man perlpage	Displays the manual page for the given Perl manpage, via the pager. Introduced in Perl v5.6.
perldoc pagepage	Displays the perldoc documentation for the given page, via the pager. Note that perldoc perldebug, man debug, and doc debug are all synonymous. Introduced in Perl v5.6.

Quitting the Debugger Session (q, ^D)

Leave the debugger and return to the system using the commands in Table 15-29.

Table 15-29. *Commands for Quitting the Debugger System*

Command	Definition
q	Quits the current session, and returns to the system prompt.
^D	Control-D is a synonym for q.

Environment and $DB:: Variables

There are a number of variables which affect debugger behavior (see Table 15-30). Some of these are important to set before the debugger starts to run, like the environment variables and certain options, others may be set during the program's runtime execution.

Table 15-30. *Commands for Environment and $DB:: Variables*

Command	Definition
PERL5DB	A string that defines the debugger code to use at startup. Introduced in Perl v5.5 e.g.: "BEGIN {require 'perl5db.pl'}"
PERLDB_OPTS	A string that contains debugger options (see the following) to be used at startup. Introduced in Perl v5.5. e.g.: "Auto NonStop=1 LineInfo=db.out"
PERL_DEBUG_MSTATS	When set, tells the debugger to attempt to get memory statistics and display them after program execution. If set to an integer greater than one, tells Perl to dump memory stats after compilation. Note that Perl must be compiled with its own malloc() for this to work. Introduced in Perl v5.5.
PERLDB_THREADED	Boolean value that defines whether the debugger will cooperate with threads. This value is set via the perl -dt ... command line switch. Introduced in Perl v5.8.6.

Command	Definition
$DB:: Variables	In the DB:: namespace there are several dedicated debugger variables which may be set either directly from the command line, included in environment variables, modified from within your code, or are set as a side effect of another command.
$DB::fork_TTY	A string that defines the tty to use for forked processes. Introduced in Perl v5.5. e.g.: "/dev/pts/3"
$DB::signal	Boolean value to tell the debugger to stop execution if true. This can be set in your program as a signal to the debugger.
$DB::single	An integer value that tells the debugger to stop execution if true. If the value is 1, step into subroutines. If the value is 2, step over subroutines.
$DB::trace	Boolean value to tell the debugger to display a stack trace. This is set by the trace commands: T, t and the AutoTrace option. The default value is false.
$DB::doccmd	A string to identify the pager to use for man, perldoc and | commands. Introduced in Perl v5.6.
@DB::typeahead	An array of debugger commands, which you may set in the afterinit() subroutine, to execute before the debugger starts. Introduced in Perl v5.5. e.g.: push(@DB::typeahead, 'b 14', 'b subname', 'b 370', 'L b')

Options (o)

The debugger has a number of options which affect its behavior at runtime. You can set these in PERLD_BOPTS (see previous), or set them within the debugger session itself.

Setting and Displaying Options (o)

Note that prior to Perl v5.8 the options command was an uppercase O, which meant you had to use the shift key in combination. In the list following, the optname placeholder is replaced by the option name explained in the next section. The syntax is usually: o optname..., as follows in Table 15-31.

Table 15-31. *Commands for Setting and Displaying Options (o)*

Command	Definition
o?	Displays the value of all options.
o optname?	Displays the value for a specific option. Beware of a space between the option and the question mark, this will have the effect of setting a boolean option (see following), and then returning an invalid option error for the ?.
o optname	Toggles a boolean option. Beware of using this method unless you are certain it is what you want to do.
o optname=val	Sets an option to a specific value. You can set boolean options this way too, by using o opt=1 or o opt=0. Not using quotes is acceptable where the value is a single word or number.
o optname="val"	Sets an option to a specific value by surrounding it with quotes. Using quotes is essential when the option has blanks in the value, and is in any case advisable where there is any doubt. The majority of options were introduced in Perl v5.005_3.

■Note In *most* versions of the debugger, all options may be given shortened to a unique value, and in a case-insensitive manner. For example, the following queries o dumpde, o DumpDepth?, and o dumpDep? should all be considered equivalent.

Options List

Of the following options, those with an asterisk(*) may only be set at startup, via PERLDB_OPTS (discussed previously). See Table 15-32 for more details.

Table 15-32. *Commands for Various Options*

Command	Definition
arrayDepth	An integer that defines the depth of the printing of an array with the x command. Default value = undefined. Introduced in Perl v5.5.
AutoTrace	A Boolean value that toggles tracing on or off. Introduced in Perl v5.5. Default = 0.
bareStringify	Prints the overloaded stringify value (1) or not (0). Introduced in Perl v5.5. Default value is false.
compactDump	A Boolean that defines the style of dumping hashes and arrays with the x command. If set to true, arrays and hashes print using a minimum of space, even fitting on one line if possible. Introduced in Perl v5.5. Default value is false.
dieLevel	An integer that modifies the way die subroutines are handled. Introduced in Perl v5.5. Default value is 1.
DumpDBFiles	A Boolean that indicates a request to dump the contents of file references along with other program variables when using X and V. Introduced in Perl v5.5. Default is false.
dumpDepth	An integer that defines the depth to which hashes are dumped using the x command. Introduced in Perl v5.8.
DumpPackages	A Boolean that defines whether to dump the symbol tables of packages with x, V and X. Introduced in Perl v5.5.
DumpReused	A Boolean that defines whether to dump reused memory addresses, when using x. Beware: enabling this option can cause infinite recursion. Introduced in Perl v5.5.
frame	The frame option is an integer to define the amount of information to display during a stack trace. The integers may be added together to give tight control over exactly what information is required. Values 1 & 2 were introduced in Perl v5.5, with the rest in Perl v5.6. The default value is 0. Possible frame values can vary. frame=0 prints a plain stack trace. frame=1 shows enter and exit subs. frame=2 prints arguments and context. frame=4 displays tied and referenced vars. frame=8 prints the return value from subs.
globPrint	A Boolean that defines whether to print globs or contents of globs. Default is false. Introduced in Perl v5.5.
highbit	A Boolean that defines whether to quote octal characters (1) or not (0). Default is false. Introduced in Perl v5.5.
ImmediateStop	Stops the debugger as soon as is possible (1) or not (0). Introduced in Perl v5.5.
inhibit_exit	Boolean to define whether to fall off the end of the program (1) or not (0). The default behavior is to stop so you can continue to work. Introduced in Perl v5.5.

Command	Definition
LineInfo	A string that identifies the file or pipe to send the debugger STDOUT to. Defaults to /dev/tty. Introduced in Perl v5.5. This option may be placed in PERLDB_OPTS and will be registered at startup.
maxTraceLen	An integer that sets the maximum length of subroutine arguments when frame=4. Default is 100. Introduced in Perl v5.5.
NonStop	A Boolean that defines whether to wait for human interaction (1) or to continue autonomously (0). This option may be placed in PERLDB_OPTS and will be registered at startup. Introduced in Perl v5.5.
noTTY	A Boolean that defines whether to attach to a TTY (1) or not (0). This option may be placed in PERLDB_OPTS and will be registered at startup. Introduced in Perl v5.5.
ornaments	A string that defines the Termcap codes to describe the command line. The default value is us,ue,md,me. Introduced in Perl v5.5.
pager	A string that defines which pager to use for piped man and perldoc commands. Introduced in Perl v5.5.
PrintRet	A Boolean that decides whether to print the return values (1) from subroutines or not (0). Introduced in Perl v5.5.
quote	A string that defines how to quote printed strings. Introduced in Perl v5.5.
ReadLine	A Boolean value that defines whether Term::ReadLine is being used (1) or not (0). Default value is 1. Introduced in Perl v5.5. This option may be placed in PERLDB_OPTS and will be registered at startup.
recallCommand	A string that defines the character to be used for history command usage. Default value is !. Introduced in Perl v5.5.
RemotePort	A string that defines which remote debugger *host* and *port* to attach to. There is no default value. Introduced in Perl v5.6.
shellBang	A string that defines the character used to invoke a shell. Default is !. Introduced in Perl v5.5.
signalLevel	An integer that alters the way signal subroutines are handled. Default is 1. Introduced in Perl v5.5.
tkRunning	A string that defines whether (and if so which) TTY to use for Devel::ptkdb. Introduced in Perl v5.5.
TTY	A string that defines TTY for use in debugger input. This option may be placed in PERLDB_OPTS and will be registered at startup. Default value is /dev/tty. Introduced in Perl v5.5.
undefPrint	A Boolean that defines whether to print undefined values as undef or ''. Default is false. Introduced in Perl v5.5.
UsageOnly	A Boolean that defines whether to print memory usage statistics with V or X commands (1) or not (0). Default is false. Introduced in Perl v5.5.
veryCompact	A Boolean that defines whether to tightly format the data (1) when dumping hashes, using the x command, or not (0). Default is false. Introduced in Perl v5.5.
warnLevel	An integer that modifies the way warn subroutines are handled (1) or not (0). Default is 1. Introduced in Perl v5.5.
windowSize	An integer that defines the number of lines to display when listing code. Default is 10. Introduced in Perl v5.8.

Calling Conventions

For the history buffs, we've included some previous calling conventions. The debugger used to be called with

```
%> perldb program args
```

This was changed a long time ago when the galaxy was still young (Perl v4.0). These days we use the familiar -d switch:

```
%> perl -d program args
```

To use a Devel:: module instead of the debugger, give the appropriate module name as an argument, after a colon, at runtime:

```
%> perl -d:ptkdb program args
```

and

```
%> perl -d:Trace program args
```

To enable threading support under the debugger, use the -dt runtime switch, which will only work for Perl v5.8.6 and above:

```
%> perl -dt threadedprogram args
```

Summary

This reference chapter has described every command, option and public DB:: variable provided by the Perl debugger. You will be able to use any of these tools to control your program's execution, study its behavior, and inspect or change any data during the runtime of the program. Finally, you learned how to call the debugger in several different cases, depending on the context required.

■ ■ ■

## CHAPTER 16

Book References and URLs

"Marilyn had been able to find 17 bugs in only 13 statements."

—Gerald Weinberg, *The Psychology Of Computer Programming,* 1971

As you can see from this chapter's quote, there is still nothing new under the sun, even as we head into the next millennium.

This chapter consists of a list of useful book and URL references, and provides more information, not just on the Perl debugger, but also on the more generalized topic of debugging itself.

Perldocs

The documentation that comes with the Perl program is a particularly good source of information relevant to the Perl debugger. You call `perldoc` from the shell using a command of the form:

`perldoc docname`

There are several useful options, help for which you can see with the `perldoc -h` command:

- `perldebug`: The essential Perl debugger reference, all information regarding debugger usage should be found.

- `perldebguts`: The guts of the debugger are explained here in some detail (for those daring souls who wish to get their feet wet).

- `perldebtut`: The lightweight debugger tutorial. A starting point for anyone not familiar with the Perl debugger.

- `perldiag`: A manpage of all the Perl error messages used by the interpreter. If you want to know what "Glob not terminated" means, you can look it up in here.

- `ptkdb`: If you wish to use the Perl/Tk GUI debugger, and have it already installed, the manpage can be read with `perldoc Devel::ptkdb`.

- `perl5db.pl`: Worthy of particular note is the debugger internals pod, which explains its purpose. You can obtain this by running `perldoc` directly on the debugger by calling `perldocperl5db.pl`, or by looking it up online at `http://ibiblio.org/mcmahon/perl5db.html`.

- `perlbug`: If you think you've found a bug in Perl , or would like to read about all the ones that have been fixed, trundle along to `http://bugs.perl.org`.

There's a wealth of information out there, a lot of which comes with Perl as part of the standard distribution. Do yourself a favor and take some time to browse it.

References

There are many sites on the web that have debugger-related information, and a search on Google or Jeeves will bring up a host of alternatives. In Table 16-1 we list several sites specific to the debugger, or which have a particular relevance to it.

Table 16-1. *URLs with Debugger-Related Information*

Web Site	What You Need to Know
The Perl Debugger Web Site	The central online site for discussion regarding the Perl debugger: `http://debugger.perl.org`.
The Perl Debugger Mailing List	To subscribe, send an email to `debugger subscribe@perl.org`. You can also look up the archives at `http://www.mail archive.com/debugger@perl.org`.
Dr. Dobb's Journal	Brian D. Foy wrote articles on using the Perl debugger, and how to create your own, for Dr Dobb's Journal. `http://www.ddj.com/documents/s=1498/ddj0103bpl/` `http://www.ddj.com/documents/s=1498/ddj0108pl/`
GDB	What debugging book would be complete without mentioning gdb, the C-level debugger that can crack nuts between its fingers? `http://www.gnu.org/software/gdb/gdb.html`

Books

The following books are particularly recommended for further and related reading on the subject of the Perl debugger. We've separated them into categories, including books that are Perl-centric, debugging or testing specific, or purely interesting to anyone interested in programming. See Tables 16-2, 16-3, and 16-4 for more information.

Table 16-2. *Perl-centric Books*

Book	Description
The Perl Debugger Pocket Reference Richard Foley O'Reilly & Associates, 2003 ISBN 0-596-00503-2 `http://www.oreilly.com/books/debugpr`	*The* reference book(let) for the Perl debugger.
Perl Debugged Peter Scott and Ed Wright Addison-Wesley, 2001 ISBN 0-201-70054-9	A wide treatment of debugging applications and bug prevention measures using Perl, with many invaluable hints and tips for using the correct technique in a particular situation.
Writing mod_perl with Perl and C Doug MacEachern and Lincoln Stein O'Reilly & Associates, 2002 ISBN 1-565592-567-X	An illuminating read describing one of the most useful glue-programs of all time (besides Perl). This book also mentions the very useful `Apache::DB` debugger for `mod_perl`.

Book	Description
Effective Perl Programming Joseph Hall Addison-Wesley, 1998 ISBN 0-201-41975-0	This book concentrates on improving your existing Perl programming skills, including some interesting work with references. It includes a section that discusses the debugger.
Mastering Regular Expressions Jeffrey E. F. Friedl O'Reilly & Associates, 1997, 1998, 2002 ISBN 0-596-00289-0	The reference for everything you ever wanted to know about regular expressions (but were afraid to ask). An absolute gem.
Object Oriented Perl Programming Damian Conway Manning Publications Co., 1999 ISBN 1-884777-79-1	The essential guide to Object Oriented programming with Perl, thoroughly exploring the paradigm. Reams of interesting information here.

Table 16-3. *Debugging or Testing Related Books*

Book	Description
The Art of Software Testing Glenford J. Myers Wiley-Interscience, 1979 ISBN 0-471-04328-1	A sound text on testing software, this book has many pointers for solving generic software problems and preventing them (via testing) from becoming bugs in the first place. Note the date: your problem is not new!
Debugging David J. Agans Amacom, 2002 ISBN 0-8144-7168-4	An engineer's approach to solving mostly hardware based problems, with a list of nine (reduced from ten) indispensable rules for debugging to hang on your wall. An extremely entertaining read, that helps you to realize how many problems develop because people keep assuming certain cases instead of getting out the tools and taking a proper look for themselves.
Writing Solid Code Steve Maguire Microsoft Press, 1993 ISBN 1-55615-551-4	An insight into how Microsoft manages to produce so much code with comparatively few bugs. As Steve says: "I wish I knew a way to persuade programmers to step through their code. . . ."
Code Complete, Second Edition Steve McConnell Microsoft Press, 2004 ISBN 0-73561-967-0	This classic covers software construction from requirements through coding and testing. Chapter 23 covers debugging specifically, but the rest of the chapters explain how to keep bugs out.

Table 16-4. *Other Interesting Books*

Book	Description
Extreme Programming Explained Kent Beck Addison-Wesley, 1999 ISBN 0-201-61641-6	A marvelous treatise on Extreme Programming. Although pair programming has come under some attack, and rightfully so, the main thrust of this book concerns testing and frequent releases. An essential modern developer's handbook.

Continued

Table 16-4. *Continued*

Book	Description
The Psychology of Computer Programming Gerald M. Weinberg Dorset House, 1971, 1998 ISBN 0-932633-42-0	An interesting read that explores the ways that programmers think about and implement their given tasks. It's extraordinary how often the same problems or misunderstandings occur between a group of people who design and implement a particular specification, again and again. And again.
Object Oriented Modeling and Programming Joseph Rumbagh et al. Prentice-Hall Inc., 1991 ISBN 0-136-29841-9	The canonical language-neutral treatment of Object Oriented programming, with many diagrams to help explain the setup of, and interaction between, disparate objects. This book makes clear the demarcation between what something is and what it can do, helping you to build objects which know their limitations.

Summary

There are many other references available, though some online ones are more transient than others. If we haven't included them here, it's because we haven't come across them ourselves yet, or felt that the books we mentioned in this chapter covered the ground sufficiently.

We would of course like to hear of any particularly good books, or permanent URLs, that we may have inadvertently overlooked. Please contact the authors or use the Perl debugger web site or mailing list.

Index

forums.apress.com

JOIN THE APRESS FORUMS AND BE PART OF OUR COMMUNITY. You'll find discussions that cover topics of interest to IT professionals, programmers, and enthusiasts just like you. If you post a query to one of our forums, you can expect that some of the best minds in the business—especially Apress authors, who all write with *The Expert's Voice*™—will chime in to help you. Why not aim to become one of our most valuable participants (MVPs) and win cool stuff? Here's a sampling of what you'll find:

DATABASES
Data drives everything.

Share information, exchange ideas, and discuss any database programming or administration issues.

INTERNET TECHNOLOGIES AND NETWORKING
Try living without plumbing (and eventually IPv6).

Talk about networking topics including protocols, design, administration, wireless, wired, storage, backup, certifications, trends, and new technologies.

JAVA
We've come a long way from the old Oak tree.

Hang out and discuss Java in whatever flavor you choose: J2SE, J2EE, J2ME, Jakarta, and so on.

MAC OS X
All about the Zen of OS X.

OS X is both the present and the future for Mac apps. Make suggestions, offer up ideas, or boast about your new hardware.

OPEN SOURCE
Source code is good; understanding (open) source is better.

Discuss open source technologies and related topics such as PHP, MySQL, Linux, Perl, Apache, Python, and more.

PROGRAMMING/BUSINESS
Unfortunately, it is.

Talk about the Apress line of books that cover software methodology, best practices, and how programmers interact with the "suits."

WEB DEVELOPMENT/DESIGN
Ugly doesn't cut it anymore, and CGI is absurd.

Help is in sight for your site. Find design solutions for your projects and get ideas for building an interactive Web site.

SECURITY
Lots of bad guys out there—the good guys need help.

Discuss computer and network security issues here. Just don't let anyone else know the answers!

TECHNOLOGY IN ACTION
Cool things. Fun things.

It's after hours. It's time to play. Whether you're into LEGO® MINDSTORMS™ or turning an old PC into a DVR, this is where technology turns into fun.

WINDOWS
No defenestration here.

Ask questions about all aspects of Windows programming, get help on Microsoft technologies covered in Apress books, or provide feedback on any Apress Windows book.

HOW TO PARTICIPATE:
Go to the Apress Forums site at **http://forums.apress.com/**.
Click the New User link.